D1050939

About Island Press

Island Press is the only nonprofit organization in the United States whose principal purpose is the publication of books on environmental issues and natural resource management. We provide solutions-oriented information to professionals, public officials, business and community leaders, and concerned citizens who are shaping responses to environmental problems.

In 2001, Island Press celebrates its seventeenth anniversary as the leading provider of timely and practical books that take a multidisciplinary approach to critical environmental concerns. Our growing list of titles reflects our commitment to bringing the best of an expanding body of literature to the environmental community throughout North America and the world.

Support for Island Press is provided by The Jenifer Altman Foundation, The Bullitt Foundation, The Mary Flagler Cary Charitable Trust, The Nathan Cummings Foundation, The Geraldine R. Dodge Foundation, The Charles Engelhard Foundation, The Ford Foundation, The German Marshall Fund of the United States, The George Gund Foundation, The Vira I. Heinz Endowment, The William and Flora Hewlett Foundation, The W. Alton Jones Foundation, The John D. and Catherine T. MacArthur Foundation, The Andrew W. Mellon Foundation, The Charles Stewart Mott Foundation, The Curtis and Edith Munson Foundation, The National Fish and Wildlife Foundation, The New-Land Foundation, The Oak Foundation, The Overbrook Foundation, The David and Lucile Packard Foundation, The Pew Charitable Trusts, The Rockefeller Brothers Fund, Rockefeller Financial Services, The Winslow Foundation, and individual donors.

MODELING IN NATURAL RESOURCE MANAGEMENT

MODELING IN NATURAL RESOURCE MANAGEMENT

DEVELOPMENT, INTERPRETATION, AND APPLICATION

EDITED BY
TANYA M. SHENK AND
ALAN B. FRANKLIN

ISLAND PRESS
Washington • Covelo • London

Library of Congress Cataloging-in-Publication Data
Modeling in natural resource management : development, interpretation, and application / edited by Tanya M. Shenk and Alan B. Franklin.
   p.   cm.
Includes bibliographical references (p.   ).
   ISBN 1–55963–739–0 (cloth : alk. paper) — ISBN 1–55963–740–4 (paper : alk. paper)
   1. Ecology—Statistical methods. 2. Population biology—Statistical methods. 3. Natural resources—Management—Statistical methods. 4. Ecology—Mathematical models. 5. Population biology—Mathematical models. 6. Natural resources—Management—Mathematical models.
I. Shenk, Tanya M.   II. Franklin, Allan B.   III. Title.
   QH541. 15.S72 M64   2001
   333.95'01'5118—dc21   00-012956
                                                                      CIP

British Library Cataloguing-in-Publication Data available.

Printed on recycled, acid-free paper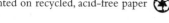

Manufactured in the United States of America
10 9 8 7 6 5 4 3 2 1

We dedicate this book to Bill Gasaway.

Contents

Part III: Applying Models

Foreword

Every day, the men and women engaged in natural resource management use models. Indeed, nearly every decision they make concerning the management of natural resources is based on a model of one kind or another. Some of these models are mental constructs of the system in question. Others may describe statistical relationships in natural resource data. Still other models are simulations of populations or ecological systems. The natural environment is so complex that simplification through an abstraction is necessary to communicate concepts and relationships concerning different components of the ecosystem, to comprehend possible reactions of natural resources to manipulation, and to decide a course of action in conservation.

Though we all use models or abstractions in our everyday lives, learning systematically about theories and types of models can seem a formidable task. Eyes sometimes take on a zombielike glaze when viewing page after page filled with mathematical equations: chloroform in print. These equations, however, may represent the beauty of a process. They may describe how we make decisions about our finances, our social lives, and our leisure time—decisions we often take for granted.

This book presents an overview of the many facets of modeling to help natural resource managers and scientists overcome their fear of models. The book is for the nonmodeler who wants to explore this mysterious thing called modeling as well as the modeler who wants to explore model validation and the use of models in the decision process. Undergraduates just discovering models and their uses will find this book of tremendous benefit. Yet even the seasoned modeler will enjoy exploring many of the ideas. In fact, these veterans may discover in this simplified presentation basic explanations of sophisticated techniques in modeling that will help them express their ideas to others.

The book is based on an all-day symposium titled "How to Practice Safe Modeling: The Interpretation and Application of Models in Resource Management." This title must have caught the attention of many—if the large audience for this symposium in 1997 during the fourth annual conference of The Wildlife Society in Snowmass, Colorado, is any indication. The symposium was sponsored by the Biometrics Working Group of The Wildlife Society. Because one of the working group's primary goals is to communicate and promote sound use of quantitative applications in wildlife management and science, this forum had a fourfold objective: to clarify the differences among model types, to explore their strengths and weaknesses, to examine the role of modeling in making inferences for natural resource management, and to demonstrate how various models further our understanding of processes and applications for natural resource management. As a member of the audience, I learned something new from each of the speakers. I also felt that each of these four objectives was met with outstanding success.

The symposium's organizers and speakers, as well as the entire Biometrics Working Group, wanted to pass on all that we had learned. With that end in mind, everyone concerned with making this book a reality has worked diligently to synthesize the vast body of knowledge concerning models and their use in natural resource management. Each chapter has been edited carefully and reviewed by at least two outside referees. Authors and referees alike have worked to ensure that this information is usable to a broad audience. The reviewers are listed at the back of the book and deserve hearty thanks for a job well done.

The contributors were selected from the many experts in natural resource modeling and wildlife management. They have taken their work for this book seriously. The information you find here is clear and will be easily understood by managers, ecological researchers, and others interested in the application of models. Modeling can appear to be a complex, mystical, highly technical, and challenging task. Each author, however, has attempted to simplify, demystify, and paint a realistic picture of modeling and the use of models in natural resource management and science. This task was not easy, but the fruits of their labor should prove useful for natural resource professionals.

Two people at the forefront of this effort have devoted themselves wholeheartedly to the project. Without their organizational skills, tenacity, and all-around hard work, this book would never have made it into your hands. Tanya Shenk and Alan Franklin had a vision concerning the need for this body of information about modeling. They organized the symposium and edited this book. Although these tasks take only a short paragraph to mention, their efforts represent a great deal of thought and dedication. The Biometrics Working Group, The Wildlife Society, and natural resource professionals everywhere should be proud to have two such dedicated people as part of their membership.

The Biometrics Working Group hopes you will find this book useful. Through efforts like this, we foresee a promising future for the application of models to problems of natural resource management. And ultimately, through this improved application of models to research and management, our natural resources should benefit from better decisions.

STEVEN L. SHERIFF
1997 Chair of the Biometrics Working Group
The Wildlife Society

Acknowledgments

This book was developed from a symposium given at the fourth annual conference of The Wildlife Society. We thank the participants of that symposium for their excellent presentations that stimulated the development of this book. We also thank the officers and members of the Biometrics Working Group of the Wildlife Society, especially Christine Bunck and Steve Sheriff, who actively supported the project from its inception.

Thanks are extended as well to the contributors. We invited these authors to contribute chapters because of their expertise in natural resource modeling. Each chapter, therefore, represents their expert summation of ideas, viewpoints, and supporting evidence for the development, interpretation, and use of models in natural resource management.

We also wish to thank the many reviewers who contributed their time and expertise to this project (see "Reviewers" at the end of this volume). Each chapter was reviewed by two referees and was further enhanced by their comments.

As novices to the process of publishing, we especially thank Barbara Dean of Island Press for her guidance in bringing this book to fruition. Barbara spent many extra hours helping us through each step. We are also grateful to Barbara Youngblood and Cecilia González at Island Press for their careful work in preparing the manuscript for production.

Chapter 1

Models in Natural Resource Management: An Introduction

Tanya M. Shenk and Alan B. Franklin

We began our careers as field biologists who were primarily interested in natural history. Although we still consider ourselves field biologists, at some point in our careers we recognized the importance of modeling—not only for understanding the natural world but also for guiding natural resource management and developing conservation strategies. There are many types of models, modeling approaches, and actual models being used in natural resource management. We found it a challenge to learn the roles of various models in science and management as well as explore the strengths and weaknesses of these models and modeling approaches. Remembering how we ourselves struggled to integrate modeling into our work, we felt the need for an introductory overview of the critical components of modeling—an overview that would explain how models are developed and used appropriately in natural resource management. Recognizing the potential for capturing such a wealth of knowledge in a single printed volume, we pursued the development of a book that would concentrate the best and most current information about modeling.

This book focuses on the fundamental components of development, interpretation, and application of models in natural resource management.

It is not a blueprint for how to develop specific models. Rather, it presents the basic principles for understanding and evaluating models. Above all, we view this book as a primer designed to demystify models. Each chapter emphasizes how models should be constructed and interpreted and highlights how models can be used and misused. For those already familiar with modeling, the book is a refresher course because many of the principles presented here include recent progress in developing and interpreting models—such as model selection and evaluation—and approaches to individual and spatially explicit modeling. We have divided the book into three parts. Part I, "Overview of Models," provides a conceptual framework for the book by defining what models are and how the different classes of models fit into the process of science. Part II, "Developing and Interpreting Models," discusses the key components necessary for addressing the question "Is this model appropriate and useful for the question at hand?" Here we build on the first part of the book by presenting chapters that discuss different modeling paradigms and explain how models can be evaluated. Part III, "Applying Models," shows how models are used in natural resource management and looks ahead to the future use of modeling in both the science and management of natural resources.

When talking about models, it is impossible to avoid the use of mathematics. Thus a number of the chapters include mathematical equations. For many in our profession, mathematical equations cause frustration and disinterest. We hope these readers will focus first on the philosophy and approaches espoused by the various authors and then on the details to become more informed about the mathematics of modeling. As the science of modeling progresses, so too will its application to natural resource management problems. Application of models requires the same understanding we need to develop the model: we have to comprehend models in order to use them appropriately. Most important, managers who are presented with a model that proposes solutions must be able to evaluate whether the model is appropriate for the problem at hand. Decisions based on biological knowledge and caution, for example, may be more appropriate than those that rely on a complex model replete with untested assumptions and based on sparse data. While such a complex model may appear more like "science," it cannot provide reliable knowledge (see Romesburg 1981).

Our primary goal is to communicate to two very different groups of readers: scientists involved with natural resource management and managers who apply models to real-world problems. These groups often speak different "languages," and communication between them is usually less than ideal. In developing each chapter, we asked authors to present their material in a manner that would be clear to the general reader but would also be acceptable to their own peers.

THE ROLE OF MODELS

As natural resource professionals, we meet the term *model* everywhere in the scientific literature and planning documents. And as models are frequently developed to guide management decisions, natural resource professionals must understand what models are and learn their strengths and weaknesses. A common misconception is that a model is a complex, computer-driven set of rules and equations that mysteriously produces a result. Indeed, the term *model* has often become synonymous with models that are computer-intensive, yet there are many types of models that serve different purposes. Models range from the very simple—a simple linear regression equation is a model—to the very complex.

James D. Nichols (Chapter 2) defines three classes of models: theoretical, empirical (statistical), and decision-theoretical. Each class functions at different stages of the scientific method. The management objective determines which class should be developed. Theoretical models, for example, are developed to suggest mechanisms and thus lead to predictions even before data are collected (see Mangel et al. in Chapter 4). Popper (1962) proposed that advances in science come from the rejection of hypotheses. Given the time constraints imposed on natural resource managers, it may be frustrating to see the ever increasing production of theory that appears to impede the process of science in an endless cycle of hypothesis generation. Yet theorists contribute to the scientific method by suggesting new ways of looking at problems—a worthy attribute in scientific investigation. The concept of a suite of alternative hypotheses must always be given a high priority in inductive scientific process (see Franklin et al. in Chapter 5). And it is theoretical models that formulate these alternative hypotheses.

Statistical models, by contrast, are used to make inferences from data (see White in Chapter 3). If estimating a parameter such as survival or recruitment is the objective, for example, a statistical model is the most appropriate approach to meeting it. Statistical models may also be used to test hypotheses. Maurer (1998) suggests that statistical analysis of several complex hypotheses requires the complementary skills of theoreticians and empiricists. Theoreticians must develop models that are empirically testable—models with parameters for which rigorous empirical estimates can be obtained. Field ecologists must know the relevant theory and be prepared to design sophisticated experiments and observational studies that provide data to analyze the models developed by theoreticians. Model selection (see Franklin et al. in Chapter 5) can be used to evaluate the plausibility of each theoretical hypothesis within a suite of hypotheses to explain the data—thus merging the use of theoretical and statistical models.

The third class is decision-theoretical models. Too often we hear that research does not address the concerns of natural resource managers. This complaint is often justified. Researchers and managers must collaborate more effectively in addressing key problems. But natural resource managers must frequently develop management plans before hypotheses are tested or research is complete. Decision-theoretical models can be used to indicate which decisions are likely to meet management objectives in light of uncertainty and dynamic systems. Models based on adaptive management results (see Kendall in Chapter 10) or on optimizing decisions (see Conroy and Moore in Chapter 6) can be used in such situations.

Using models to address specific issues in natural resource management has led to the development of various disciplines. Population viability analysis is one such modeling discipline (see Boyce in Chapter 8); wildlife resource selection is another (see McDonald and Manly in Chapter 9). Investigating the effect of individual heterogeneity on population demography has led to the development of individual-based models (see DeAngelis et al. in Chapter 11). With the proliferation of models has come a parallel concern about their validity. Douglas Johnson (Chapter 7) outlines the problems associated with validating models and suggests approaches to model evaluation. Since the utility of a modeling procedure is hampered when biological input is ignored, a collaboration among managers, field biologists, and modelers is the most efficient means for solving natural resource problems. (See Clark and Schmitz in Chapter 12; Anderson et al. 1999.)

HOW MODELS ARE USED: AN EXAMPLE

Early attempts to predict population growth stemmed from specific concerns about human population growth and economically important species (see Cole 1957). Before the eighteenth century, however, no modeling or formulation of any general concepts other than the balance of nature was inferred from studies on population growth (McIntosh 1985). In his *Essay on the Principle of Population,* Thomas Malthus (1798) recognized that population abundances were constrained within bounds set by the availability of the space and resources required by individuals. The implications of this essay stimulated both Charles Darwin and Alfred Russel Wallace to formulate their concepts of natural selection and the idea that environment limits populations, which then led to the concept of population regulation.

Howard and Fiske (1911) were the first to propose the role of *density* to explain changes in population abundance. In their work on the control of pest insect populations by parasites, they distinguished between "facultative" and "catastrophic" mortality factors. Catastrophic factors, such as storms, were defined as those that destroyed a fixed percentage of a population without regard to population density. Facultative factors, such as predators or parasites, destroy a greater proportion of individuals within a population as the population increases. These facultative factors later became part of the theory of density-dependent population regulation. Replacement of the terms *catastrophic* and *facultative* with *density-independent* and *density-dependent,* respectively, followed the work of Smith (1935).

Parallel to the development of the theory of density-dependent populations, mathematical descriptions—that is, models—of population growth with respect to some equilibrium density were suggested. The most successful attempt, the logistic equation, was proposed by Verhulst in 1838 (Kingsland 1985), but the equation was not widely acknowledged at the time. Later, however, Pearl (1927) developed and successfully promoted the same population growth equation. Several laboratory experiments supported the logistic equation as an accurate model of population growth (Pearl and Parker 1922; Gause 1934). Field data, however, were equivocal in their support of density-dependent population growth. Although Lack (1954) provided evidence of logistic population growth in many bird populations, Andrewartha and Birch (1954) concluded that population growth of Australian thrips was related more to weather than to density. They argued that most populations, insects and small invertebrates in particular, are influenced primarily by density-independent factors.

Strong opposition followed the claims made by Andrewartha and Birch. Nicholson (1954) in particular argued that within a balance-of-nature framework, population densities continually move toward a stable level in relation to fluctuating environmental conditions. He suggested that a regulating mechanism must limit populations by operating with greater severity as population abundances approach stability. Nicholson (1954) proposed that interspecific competition was the density-dependent controlling factor. The Cold Spring Harbor Symposium on Quantitative Biology held in 1957 addressed the controversy over these competing models of population regulation. Eventually, the theoretical model of density-dependent regulation became widely accepted. Interest then turned to the detection of density dependence in natural populations using empirical (statistical) models. This focus on statistical models sparked a minor controversy of its own, however, centered on the form of the statistical model to use and what data were appropriate for testing density dependence in a natural population. (See the review in Shenk et al. 1998.) Given the controversy at the time over the existence of density dependence, a natural resource manager responsible for developing conservation strategies would have benefited from decision-theoretical models designed to predict the outcomes of various management strategies (that is, models that incorporated density dependence and models that did not).

HOW MODELS ARE MISUSED: AN EXAMPLE

Models are misused when invalid inferences are made from their results. Invalid inferences are made when poor data or incorrect estimation procedures are used in the model or when an inappropriate model is used. A 13-year controversy between C. H. T. Townsend, an entomologist, and I. Langmuir, a Nobel Prize–winning physicist, over the flight speed of male deerflies provides an example of invalid inferences stemming from the misuse of models (see Wenner 1989).

Townsend (1926) claimed that male deerflies were capable of flying 818 mph. His velocity calculations were based on poorly estimated times and distances, which he observed traveled by a deerfly. Townsend published his findings, ignoring the inaccuracies of the data used to calculate his estimate and without fully exploring or understanding the implications such a flight speed would have for an insect. In his publication he noted that a flight speed of 818 mph would allow the fly to go around the world in a "daylight day" [sic], a world flight record. After publication, the record, but not the flight speed, was challenged. Townsend took this as support for the flight speed and went on to model the wing structure of the fly that would allow for such speed.

With the publication of the wing structure model, the flight speed was finally challenged by Langmuir (1938) based on the biological infeasibility of a fly attaining such speed. Using a series of established mathematical models relating velocity, resistance, power, and force, he established that a flight speed of 818 mph traveled by an object the size of a deerfly would have resulted in (1) pressure high enough to crush the insect, (2) greater energy requirements than could be met by the fly, (3) a force on impact that would penetrate human flesh, and (4) rendering the fly invisible in flight. Thus, using appropriate theoretical models, Langmuir refuted Townsend's flight speed and proposed his own flight speed of 25 mph. Despite Langmuir's strong evidence against the probability of his published flight speed, Townsend (1939) continued to support his own estimated flight speed of 818 mph and wing structure that would allow it.

This example highlights how models can be misused. First, Townsend used poor data to model flight speed and, secondly, he did not fully explore the implications of his results. Had he worked with someone more familiar with the mathematics of flight, such as Langmuir, he might have avoided making the invalid inference of an impossible flight speed for the deerfly. Ignoring both of these flaws, however, he continued to build on his estimate of flight speed to develop a model of the design of the fly wing to support such speeds, a model that would clearly be wrong. Lastly, despite strong evidence to the contrary, he continued to support his single, pet hypothesis and avoided altogether any notion of competing hypotheses and model selection. Although Langmuir did not misuse models, he never evaluated his own model. He could have contributed more had he worked with a field biologist to collect data on observed flight speeds to evaluate his own proposed flight speed of 25 mph.

In natural resource management, an analogous situation would be the use of poor or sparse data in a model whose results are then incorporated into a management plan that is implemented but never evaluated in terms of its success or failure to meet its objective. Such scenarios could be avoided if all the professionals involved (managers, researchers, model developers) had a better understanding of the development, interpretation, and application of models to ensure that both the biology and the mathematics are sound (see Clark and Schmitz in Chapter 12).

We designed this book to help the reader understand the kinds of models available and how to interpret and evaluate them for use in natural resource management. The book is directed to natural resource managers, who must make decisions based on models, and to researchers who use models to improve their understanding of scientific and management questions. While the scientific literature has addressed specific topics, there is no single source compiling the multitude of issues and viewpoints relevant to the development, interpretation, and application of natural resource models. This book begins to fill the gap.

REFERENCES

Anderson, D. R., K. P. Burnham, A. B. Franklin, R. J. Gutiérrez, E. D. Forsman, R. G. Anthony, G. C. White, and T. M. Shenk. 1999. A protocol for conflict resolution in analyzing empirical data related to natural resource controversies. *Wildlife Society Bulletin* 27:1050–1058.

Andrewartha, H. G., and L. C. Birch. 1954. *The Distribution and Abundance of Animals.* Chicago: University of Chicago Press.

Cole, L. C. 1957. Sketches of general and comparative demography. *Cold Spring Harbor Symposia on Quantitative Biology* 22:1–15.

Gause, G. F. 1934. *The Struggle for Existence.* Baltimore: Williams & Wilkens.

Howard, L. O., and W. F. Fiske. 1911. *The Importation into the United States of the Parasites of the Gipsy Moth and the Brown-tail Moth.* Bureau of Entomology Bulletin 91. Washington, D.C.: U.S. Department of Agriculture.

Kingsland, S. E. 1985. *Modeling Nature.* Chicago: University of Chicago Press.

Lack, D. 1954. *The Natural Regulation of Animal Numbers.* London: Oxford University Press.

Langmuir, I. 1938. The speed of the deer fly. *Science* 87:233–234.

Malthus, T. R. 1798. *An Essay on the Principle of Population.* London: Johnson.

Maurer, B. A. 1998. Ecological science and statistical paradigms: At the threshold. *Science* 279:502–503.

McIntosh, R. P. 1985. *The Background of Ecology: Concept and Theory.* Cambridge: Cambridge University Press.

Nicholson, A. J. 1954. An outline of the dynamics of animal populations. *Australian Journal of Zoology* 2:9–65.

Pearl, R. 1927. The growth of populations. *Quarterly Review of Biology* 2:532–548.

Pearl, R., and S. L. Parker. 1922. On the influence of density of population upon the rate of reproduction in *Drosophila. Proceedings of the National Academy of Sciences* 8:212–218.

Popper, K. R. 1962. *Conjectures and Refutations: The Growth of Scientific Knowledge.* New York: Basic Books.

Romesburg, H. C. 1981. Wildlife science: Gaining reliable knowledge. *Journal of Wildlife Management* 45:293–313.

Shenk, T. M., G. C. White, and K. P. Burnham. 1998. Sampling-variance effects on detecting density dependence from temporal trends in natural populations. *Ecological Monographs* 68:445–463.

Smith, H. S. 1935. The role of biotic factors in the determination of population densities. *Journal of Economic Entomology* 28:873–898.

Townsend, C. H. T. 1926. Around the world in a daylight day: A problem in flight. *Scientific Monthly* 22:309–311.

———. 1939. Speed of *Cephenemyia. Journal of New York Entomological Society.* 47:43–46.

Wenner, A. M. 1989. Concept-centered versus organism-centered biology. *American Zoologist* 29:1177–1197.

PART I

....

Overview of Models

CHAPTER 2

••••••••••••••••••••••

Using Models in the Conduct of Science and Management of Natural Resources

James D. Nichols

Most scientists and managers would agree that models are an important part of the processes by which we learn about and manage natural systems. Nevertheless, there are substantive differences of opinion about their specific roles in science and natural resource management. In this chapter I present some views on the functions served by models. I argue that a model's utility is closely tied to its intended use. This relationship leads to a consideration of three classes of model use: theoretical, empirical, and decision-theoretical. A model's utility can be assessed, as well, in the context of the following dichotomies relevant to model development and construction: simplicity versus complexity, mechanistic versus phenomenological models, and use of more versus less integrated parameters. I suggest that progress in science and management is strongly conditional on a priori hypotheses and their associated models and that the conditional nature of learning should lead to increased emphasis on these constructs.

OPERATIONAL DEFINITIONS

I begin with some definitions that reflect my preconceptions. I think of *hypothesis* as simply a story about how the world, or a subset of it, works. A *theory* is a hypothesis that has survived repeated efforts to falsify it, to the extent that we have some faith in predictions deduced from it. A model, very generally, is an abstraction or simplification of a real-world system. Our focus here will be on models used in evaluating hypotheses and making management decisions.

Much has been written about the conduct of science and the role of models in this process, and this literature provides many definitions. Some authors draw little distinction between theories, hypotheses, and models. Neyman (1957:8), for example, stated that "scientific theories are no more than models of natural phenomena." Hawking (1988:9) wrote that "a theory is just a model of the universe, or a restricted part of it, and a set of rules that relate quantities in the model to observations that we make"—and added that "any physical theory is provisional, in the sense that it is only a hypothesis" (p. 10).

Others view these terms hierarchically. Pease and Bull (1992:295), for example, stated that "hypotheses address much narrower dimensions of nature than the models from which they are derived." Hilborn and Mangel (1997:25) reverse the relative positions of these terms in the hierarchy: "One can think of hypotheses and models in a hierarchic fashion with models simply being a more specific version of a hypothesis."

Thus the scientific literature contains many different definitions of the terms *theory, hypothesis,* and *model.* Some of these definitions are consistent with my preconceptions; others are not. In the absence of universal agreement, then, I will retain my preconceptions as operational definitions.

KINDS OF MODELS

Models can be categorized in a variety of ways. A *conceptual model* refers to a set of ideas about how a particular system works. By translating these ideas into words, we create a *verbal model.* Similarly, translating ideas or words into a set of mathematical equations yields a *mathematical model.* These different types nevertheless correspond to our operational definition of *model* in that they reflect attempts to abstract key features of a system into a simple set of ideas, words, or equations.

Most of this chapter concerns the use of mathematical models. But as noted by Skellam (1972), just as physical phenomena are modeled by mathematical constructions, so can mathematical schemes be modeled by phys-

ical constructions. Skellam (p. 14) went on to state that this "reverse modeling" includes "the most powerful instrument known for advancing empirical knowledge—the designed experiment." Experiments are consistent
with our operational definition of *model,* as they represent attempts to simplify a real-world system for the purpose of focusing on variation associated
with a small number of factors.

The term *empirical model* can be applied to a single experiment or to a
system amenable to experimentation. Probably the most famous empirical
model in animal population ecology is the *Tribolium* model—a laboratory
experimental system developed in the mid-1920s by R. N. Chapman for
studying population growth and regulation using flour beetles (Chapman
1928) and most commonly associated with the later work of T. Park and his
students at the University of Chicago. (See, for example, Park 1948, Neyman et al. 1956, Mertz 1972, and Wade and Goodnight 1991.) Work with
the *Tribolium* model has been characterized by close interaction between
empirical and mathematical modeling and has led to strong inferences
about many important aspects of population dynamics. A recent example
involved prediction of points of transition in parameter values of a nonlinear mathematical model of animal population dynamics (Constantino et al.
1995). Subsequent testing of these predictions by altering adult mortality in
experimental *Tribolium* populations produced, as predicted, shifts from point
equilibria to stable periodic oscillations to aperiodic oscillations (Constantino et al. 1995). The impressive success of investigations using the *Tribolium*
model suggests that animal ecologists and managers should try to develop
similar systems promoting the interactive use of mathematical and empirical models.

Physical models (for example, scale replicas of individual animals) have
been used in physiological ecology to estimate heat exchange with the
environment for the purpose of parameterizing mathematical models
(Porter et al. 1973; Tracy 1976). The *mechanical model* of Pearson (1960) can
be viewed as a kind of physical model and is certainly one of the most
interesting models ever developed for use in animal population ecology.
Pearson's model had the appearance of a large pinball machine with steel
balls (representing individual animals) released onto an inclined board with
holes drilled into it. Balls falling into the holes represented deaths. When a
ball rolled over pairs of bronze strips, an electric circuit was completed and
new balls (reproduction) were released from the top of the board. Pearson
(1960) developed an algebraic model to describe the functioning of the
mechanical model and found both models useful in producing counterin-
tuitive results and leading to an understanding he would not have achieved
otherwise.

USES OF MATHEMATICAL MODELS

Just as there are many kinds of models, there are many ways in which models can be used in science and natural resource management. Thus there can be no single set of specific instructions about how to build and use models. In the place of such instructions, I offer two guidelines as keys to successful model use:

1. Define the objective of the modeling effort clearly—that is, how is the model to be used in the conduct of science or management?
2. Develop the model by extracting those features of the system that are essential to the objective.

These general guidelines, which have been presented elsewhere (Conley and Nichols 1978; Nichols 1987), represent some of my only views on models that have not changed over the last 20 years.

Classes of Model Use

In a very basic sense, all mathematical models are used to project the consequences of hypotheses. Just as statisticians sometimes distinguish between scientific and statistical hypotheses, one way of classifying models is based on their correspondence with scientific or statistical hypotheses. *Scientific hypotheses* represent stories about how a system works or responds to management actions; *scientific models* are used to project the consequences of such hypotheses. We may have a conceptual model of how a population responds to changes in harvest regulations, for example, but most such models will not be so simple that we can use them directly to project responses to harvest via computations (or other processes) carried out in our heads. The scientific model can be viewed as the "calculating engine" (Lewontin 1963) needed to project the consequences of a scientific hypothesis.

   Statistical hypotheses are derived from scientific hypotheses and represent stories about not just the underlying system of interest but also the quantities that are relevant to the system's behavior and can be observed. Thus the *statistical model* projects how the observable quantities or data should appear if the system is operating in a manner consistent with the corresponding statistical—and hence scientific—hypothesis. The statistical model's construction will be based not only on the underlying scientific hypothesis but also on aspects of sampling design and data collection.

   In this view, scientific models are used to project system dynamics, whereas statistical models are used to project dynamics of observable quantities under one or more scientific hypotheses. Statistical model projections are used for estimating quantities of interest and discriminating among competing hypotheses—that is, to address the question "Which statistical, and hence scientific, hypothesis corresponds most closely to the data?"

In addition to this classification of models as scientific or statistical, we can focus on the classes of problems addressed. There are three classes of problems—and hence three classes of model use—in natural resource science and management: theoretical, empirical, and decision-theoretical. Empirical and decision-theoretical uses typically require both scientific and statistical models; theoretical uses may require only scientific models.

Theoretical Uses

Theoretical models are used to investigate system responses and trajectories that are possible under specific hypotheses. These uses do not include comparison of model predictions with data or observation. Indeed, the absence of any confrontation of predictions and data is the distinguishing feature of theoretical model use. This use of *theoretical* is consistent with Lewontin's (1968:3) view of theoretical population biology as "the science of the possible" and with the views expressed in Caswell's (1988) essay on theory and models in ecology. Can density-dependent migration stabilize a particular kind of metapopulation system? Can populations governed by a specific set of nonlinear-dynamic equations exhibit chaotic behavior? Such questions can be addressed by using the appropriate mathematical models. If these questions are based on a priori hypotheses, then this theoretical use of models constitutes one kind of hypothesis test and fits within the general framework of the Popperian, single-hypothesis approach to science.

Note that this use of *theoretical* has nothing to do with whether or not the model is being used to address applied or management-oriented questions. In fact, theoretical model use can be very important in decision-theoretical approaches to managing natural resources—for example, models with substantial mechanistic differences may lead to very similar management policies. From the manager's perspective, it would be unwise to devote resources to learning which model corresponds most closely to reality, because this distinction is not relevant to management decisions (Johnson et al. 1993; Williams and Johnson 1995). Competing models can be subjected to optimization algorithms, and the resulting management policies can then be compared. This kind of theoretical model use should precede efforts to distinguish among competing models for management purposes.

Even when different models do lead to different management actions, it is useful to assess the management value of discriminating among their associated hypotheses. A robust, nonadaptive policy may perform very well—in terms of the value of the objective function (say, number of animals harvested in the case of harvest management)—regardless of which model provides the best approximation of reality (Hilborn and Walters 1992). Modeling and optimization can be used to estimate the "expected value of perfect information" in order to decide whether it is worthwhile trying to discriminate among the competing hypotheses (Hilborn and Walters 1992; Johnson et al. 1993). From a pragmatic management perspective, therefore, modeling exercises that are "theoretical" in the sense of involving no confrontation with data can be extremely useful.

Empirical Uses

By *empirical* uses of models, I mean using models to predict a system's behavior for the purpose of comparing the predictions with realized system behavior. This confrontation of model predictions with data is used to discriminate among competing hypotheses. When defined in this way, empirical model use essentially involves "doing science." Although various writers have identified multiple approaches to "doing science" (Hilborn and Mangel 1997), here I want to focus on two approaches and specify the role of models in each.

Single-Hypothesis Approach. This approach is frequently associated with Popper (1959, 1963, 1972) and an influential paper by Platt (1964) on strong inference. The approach is outlined in the following steps:

1. Develop a hypothesis.
2. Deduce testable predictions.
3. Carry out a suitable test.
4. Compare the test results with predictions.
5. Reject or retain the hypothesis.

Mathematical models are typically used in steps 2 and 4. Scientific models are used in step 2 to deduce predictions from the scientific hypothesis. Statistical models are used in the comparison of test results with these predictions (step 4). Advocates of this approach sometimes emphasize that use of a critical experiment in step 3 is most likely to yield strong inferences (Platt 1964). In my view, however, it is the a priori hypothesis, rather than the nature of the test, that is the defining feature of this approach to science.

In the situation where we reject the hypothesis, we have two options (Figure 2.1). One option is simply to develop a completely new hypothesis. The other option is to revise the original hypothesis in a manner that would cause it to be consistent with those aspects of the test results that were at deviance with predictions and resulted in rejection of the original hypothesis. This revised hypothesis would then be tested.

In the situation where we fail to reject the tested hypothesis, we again

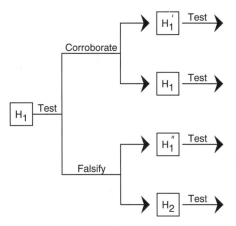

Figure 2.1. Schematic representation of the single-hypothesis approach to scientific inquiry. H_1 denotes the original hypothesis tested. H_1' denotes an extension or elaboration of H_1. H_1'' denotes a revision of H_1 designed to account for those aspects of test results that deviated from predictions of H_1. H_2 is a new hypothesis.

have two options (Figure 2.1). Recognizing that a hypothesis can be corroborated but can never be *proved* to be true (Popper 1959, 1963), we might subject the hypothesis to still another test, using either the same or different predictions as those tested initially. Alternatively, we might extend or otherwise modify the hypothesis and then develop a test focused on the extension or modification.

If we proceed in the stepwise manner outlined in Figure 2.1, we may eventually reach a hypothesis that withstands repeated tests and efforts at falsification—that is, it is predictive. Such a hypothesis becomes our provisional truth in that we view it as our best approximation of reality (at least for the time being).

Multiple-Hypothesis Approach. This approach is usually traced to a paper by Chamberlin (1897) on multiple working hypotheses (Platt 1964). Multiple auxiliary hypotheses are also an important part of the scientific research programs described by Lakatos (1970). My own ideas about a multiple-hypothesis approach to doing science have come primarily from the literature of adaptive management (Walters 1986; Johnson et al. 1993; Williams 1996a), but these ideas pertain whether or not the motivation to learn involves management. The approach can be outlined in the following steps:

1. Develop a set of competing hypotheses.
2. Derive prior probabilities associated with these hypotheses.
3. Use associated models to deduce testable predictions.
4. Carry out a suitable test.
5. Compare the test results with predictions.
6. Compute new probabilities for the hypotheses.

Models again feature prominently in this approach. Scientific models corresponding to the different hypotheses are used to deduce competing predictions (step 3). Statistical models are then used in the comparison of test results with predictions (step 5) as well as in the computation of new probabilities for the competing hypotheses (step 6). Because the approach outlined here is not as widely known as the single-hypothesis approach to science, some of the steps require explanation.

The prior probabilities of step 2 can be viewed as measures of our relative faith in the different hypotheses. Let $P(H_i)$ denote the probability associated with hypothesis H_i. These probabilities are relative in the sense that the probabilities for all the n members of the hypothesis set sum to 1:

$$\sum_{i=1}^{n} P(H_i) = 1$$

Comparing test results with predictions of the different models (step 5) leads to an updating of the associated probabilities (step 6). This updating can be accomplished by using a likelihood-based approach in conjunction with Bayes' theorem. (See, for example, Hilborn and Mangel 1997.) Define $\mathcal{L}(\theta_i \mid \text{data})$ as the likelihood function of the parameters (θ_i) of the statistical model under hypothesis H_i given the data resulting from a relevant experiment or set of observations. The likelihood function gives the "likelihood" (this is a probability for discrete random variables) that the random variables constituting the data assume a particular set of values (see Mood et al. 1974). This probability is obtained by evaluating the likelihood function at the maximum-likelihood estimates of the parameters of the statistical model corresponding to H_i, where these estimates are the values of the parameters that maximize the likelihood function given the observed data. The likelihoods corresponding to the different hypotheses in the set can be computed directly by using the single data set in conjunction with the statistical models associated with H_i. Given the set of prior probabilities ($P[H_i]$), the single set of data resulting from the test or observations, and the likelihoods for the different hypotheses, $\mathcal{L}(\theta_i \mid \text{data})$, we can compute updated probabilities for the different hypotheses, $P'(H_i)$, as

$$P'(H_i) = \frac{\mathcal{L}(\theta_i \mid \text{data}) P(H_i)}{\sum_{i=1}^{n} \mathcal{L}(\theta_i \mid \text{data}) P(H_i)} \qquad [2.1]$$

(See, for example, Hilborn and Mangel 1997:204.) These updated probabilities, $P'(H_i)$, then become the prior probabilities for the next test or confrontation with data.

Learning can be viewed as occurring via the change in probabilities associated with the different hypotheses (Figure 2.2). These hypotheses are viewed as competing for our faith and confidence, and each test or confrontation of data and model-based predictions leads to a change in proba-

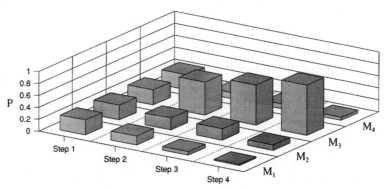

Figure 2.2. Hypothetical changes in probabilities associated with four hypotheses under the multiple-hypothesis approach to scientific inquiry. *P* denotes probability; M_i denotes the model associated with hypothesis *i*. An investigation (such as an experiment) occurs between each pair of steps, and comparison of model-based predictions with test results leads to changes in the probabilities associated with the different models (using an approach such as Equation 2.1, for example). All four hypotheses begin with equal probabilities at step 1 (we have no prior knowledge permitting us to discriminate among them), and our investigations lead to high probabilities associated with M_3 and its corresponding hypothesis.

bilities. If the set of competing hypotheses contains at least one hypothesis that provides a reasonable approximation of reality, we expect the probability to increase for the hypothesis providing the best approximation and decrease for the other hypotheses. The accumulation of probability for model 3 in our example (Figure 2.2) reflects increasing relative faith in hypothesis 3 as an approximation of reality.

Popper's Natural Selection of Hypotheses Analogy. In one of his discussions of the single-hypothesis approach to science, Popper (1959:108) wrote: "We choose the theory which best holds its own in competition with other theories; the one which, by natural selection, proves itself the fittest to survive." Popper (1972:261) later expanded on this analogy and noted that "the growth of our knowledge is the result of a process closely resembling what Darwin called 'natural selection'; that is, *the natural selection of hypotheses:* our knowledge consists, at every moment, of those hypotheses which have shown their (comparative) fitness by surviving so far in their struggle for existence; a competitive struggle which eliminates those hypotheses which are unfit." Candidate hypotheses are subjected to falsification efforts. Some survive the testing; others do not.

Popper's analogy can also be applied to the multiple-hypothesis approach to science. Instead of focusing attention on a single hypothesis (analogous to an individual or a genotype) and whether or not it can survive the various confrontations with data we are able to contrive, our interest turns to the hypothesis probabilities, $P(H_j)$, which can be viewed as analogous to gene frequencies. Just as natural selection events bring about adaptive changes in gene frequencies within the population, our tests and experiments bring about changes in the probabilities associated with the different hypotheses within the set. Changes in gene frequencies reflect the action of natural selection; changes in hypothesis probabilities reflect our learning about the relative predictive abilities of the different hypotheses and their models. Other sources of variation influence changes both in gene frequencies (environmental variation, for example, and the "drift" associated with the stochastic nature of fitness components) and in hypothesis probabilities (environmental variation, for example, and partial observability [state variables are typically not known but are estimated]). But our focus here is on natural selection and learning, respectively, as determinants of change.

Recommendations Based on the Multiple-Hypothesis Approach. Because the multiple-hypothesis approach to science is not as widely used as the single-hypothesis approach, less thought has been devoted to it by those interested in scientific methodology. Here I want to make two methodological recommendations that emerge from a multiple-hypothesis view of science.

The first recommendation is simply a reiteration of the view that science is a progressive endeavor. This view has been expressed frequently by scientists over the ages. In 1637, Descartes wrote: "I hoped that each one would publish whatever he had learned, so that later investigations could begin where the earlier had left off" (Lafleur 1960:46). That modern ecologists pay some attention to the previous work of others is evidenced by the perfunctory paragraph or so on background found in the introduction of most scientific papers. Authors of review papers frequently take previous work very seriously and try to develop overall generalizations, or answers to questions, based on prior work on a topic. But it may be possible, sometimes, to account more formally for what has been learned by previous workers by developing prior probabilities for competing hypotheses based on past research. The key to such an endeavor is the development of explicit scientific models associated with members of the hypothesis set. With these models it should be possible to develop predictions for each hypothesis corresponding to every past experiment or investigation. Comparing these predictions with the actual observations would then permit computation of revised hypothesis probabilities (as in Equation 2.1) based on the results of each test. The ability to carry out this suggestion formally depends on the level of detail provided in the reporting of past work. But even when such detail is less than ideal, it may still be possible to revise hypothesis probabilities based on a slightly less formal approach. "Wish I didn't know now what I didn't know then" (Seger 1980) is not a reasonable perspective for a scientist. My recommendation is simply to take full advantage of knowledge gained from past work. The multiple-hypothesis approach offers a means of doing this via the development of prior probabilities for the competing hypotheses to be considered in our investigations.

The second recommendation involves study design and statistical methodology and emerges from a consideration of the optimal control methods used in adaptive management (Walters 1986; Johnson et al. 1993; Nichols et al. 1995; Williams 1996a). As noted by Hilborn and Mangel (1997), the historical development of the single-hypothesis approach to science was accompanied by corresponding development of associated statistical methods. A great deal of thought has been devoted to the design of experiments intended to result in the rejection or tentative acceptance of an a priori null hypothesis (Fisher 1947, 1958; Cox 1958). After ensuring the critical elements (such as randomization and replication) needed for reliable inference, the designer of an experiment frequently turns to the question of test power—the probability of rejecting the null hypothesis when it is indeed false. Power is frequently viewed as an optimization criterion in experimental design (Skalski and Robson 1992), and efforts are made to maximize power given fixed values for other test characteristics (such as selected significance level, α, and specified effect size or difference to be detected).

With a multiple-hypothesis approach, design criteria based on the rejection of a single hypothesis are no longer relevant. Instead of maximizing test power, we want to maximize discrimination ability. We seek a design that will produce data with the greatest ability to discriminate among the competing hypotheses. Active adaptive management makes use of optimal stochastic control methods to develop management policies that are optimal with respect to a specified objective function. (See Walters 1986, Johnson et al. 1993, Nichols et al. 1995, Williams 1996a, and Chapters 6 and 10 of this volume.) We should be able to use the methods developed to solve optimal stochastic control problems (as in Bellman 1957; Williams 1982, 1989, 1996a, 1996b; Lubow 1995; and Chapter 6 of this volume), in conjunction with objective functions that specify discrimination among competing hypotheses, to develop optimal designs. We might specify the prior probabilities for the competing hypotheses as the state variables of interest in our objective function, for example, and seek to minimize a diversity index such as the Shannon-Wiener H' (Krebs 1972). For a fixed number of hypotheses in the model set, diversity indices such as H' are minimized when one of the $P(H_j)$ approaches 1 and the remaining $P(H_j)$ approach zero (that is, when we are confident that one of the hypotheses approximates reality better than all the others). Although other approaches can be envisioned, my basic recommendation is simply to exploit optimal stochastic control methods to assist in the design of studies directed at discriminating among multiple hypotheses.

Decision-Theoretical Uses

In *decision-theoretical* uses, scientific models are used to project the consequences of hypotheses about how a system behaves in order to derive wise, or even optimal, management actions. Models are used to project a system's responses to the various management actions that could be employed in order to assist in deciding which action is most appropriate. Just as two approaches to doing science were discussed under empirical model uses, two analogous approaches to decision-theoretical model uses will be identified and discussed.

Single "Best Model" Approach. This approach to making management decisions is common in natural resource management and relies on a single model judged to be the best available for predicting a system's response to management actions. With this approach we begin with:

1. An objective function (a formal statement of management objectives)
2. A favorite hypothesis (and corresponding scientific model) for the managed system
3. A set of available management options (actions that can be taken to achieve management objectives)
4. A monitoring program providing time-specific information about system state and other variables relevant to the objective function

Armed with these prerequisites, we can implement the single "best model" approach to management with the following iterative steps:

1. Observe the current state of the system.
2. Update model parameter estimates, if appropriate, based on current information from step 1.
3. Derive the optimal management action.
4. Implement management action and return to step 1.

Step 2 usually requires a statistical model, whereas step 3 relies on a scientific model for the system. Given the objective function and information on the current state of the system, the scientific model is used to derive the management action most likely to meet management objectives. In some cases, the scientific model may be used to project the consequences of the various management actions, and the management decision is then based on these projected consequences. In other cases, optimization algorithms (Williams 1982, 1989, 1996a, 1996b; Lubow 1995) are used to identify the management option that is optimal with respect to objectives. Implementation of the management action (step 4) drives the system to a new state, and the process begins again.

Multiple-Model Approach. This approach to making management decisions is most commonly associated with adaptive management. (See Walters 1986; Johnson et al. 1993, 1997; Williams 1996a; and Chapters 6 and 10 of this volume.) Prerequisites for this approach are:

1. An objective function
2. A model set consisting of the scientific models associated with competing hypotheses about how the managed system responds to management actions
3. Prior probabilities associated with the different hypotheses (and thus their models) in the model set
4. A set of available management options
5. A monitoring program providing time-specific information about system state and other variables relevant to the objective function

Implementation of the multiple-model approach to management then involves the following iterative steps:

1. Observe the current state of the system.
2. Update model probabilities based on current information from step 1.
3. Derive the optimal management action.
4. Implement management action and return to step 1.

Information about the current state of the system (step 1) is provided the monitoring program. The estimated state of the system at time t is compared with the predictions made at time $t - 1$ by each of the models, and model probabilities are revised (step 2). Model probabilities are updated using a process based on the statistical models (such as Equation 2.1) such that probabilities for models predicting well increase whereas probabilities for models predicting poorly decrease. Derivation of the optimal management action (step 3) typically requires use of the methods of optimal stochastic control (Bellman 1957; Anderson 1975; Williams 1982, 1989, 1996a, 1996b; Lubow 1995; Chapter 6 of this volume) in conjunction with the competing scientific models. Implementation of the optimal management action (step 4) then drives the system to a new state, and the entire process is repeated.

Learning Through Management. Growth of knowledge in the general field of wildlife management has not been as rapid as we would like (Romesburg 1981, 1991). Many have argued that one path to more rapid learning is to make better efforts to learn through our management. (See, for example, Holling 1978; Walters and Hilborn 1978; Macnab 1983; Walters 1986; Murphy and Noon 1991; Sinclair 1991; Johnson et al. 1993, 1997; Lancia et al. 1996; Williams 1997; and Chapters 6 and 10 of this volume.) I agree—and would add that learning should occur through either the single-model or multiple-model approach to management.

Under the single-model approach, the predicted response of the system to the prescribed management actions is compared with the observed (estimated) response. Based on this comparison, the scientific model and its associated hypothesis are either retained for future use or rejected and replaced by a new hypothesis and model. Thus learning occurs in the same manner as under the single-hypothesis approach to science. Under the multiple-model approach to management, comparing the model's predictions with observed system response leads to changes in model probabilities— that is, to learning.

In the cases of the single-model approach to management and "passive adaptive management" (Walters and Hilborn 1978; Walters 1986; Hilborn and Walters 1992; Williams 1996a; Chapter 10 of this volume) using multiple models, learning occurs as a by-product of efforts to meet management objectives. In the case of "active adaptive management" (Walters and Hilborn 1978; Walters 1986; Hilborn and Walters 1992; Williams 1996a) using multiple models, optimal management decisions are solutions to the "dual-control problem" (Walters and Hilborn 1978) of trying to learn (because of the resultant ability to better achieve management objectives in the future) and achieve short-term payoffs simultaneously.

I have typically associated some of the general ideas about adaptive management with work conducted in the 1970s and synthesized by Holling (1978) and Walters and Hilborn (1978). With respect to influence on managers, this association is probably appropriate. As a historical note, however, consider the following quote from Beverton and Holt (1957:436): "It is the changes produced in the fisheries by the regulations themselves . . . that provide the opportunity of obtaining, by research, just the information that we may have been lacking previously. Thus the approach towards optimum fishing, and the increase in knowledge of where the optimum lies, can be two simultaneous and complementary advances; the benefits to the fisheries of such progress can hardly be exaggerated." With characteristic insight, Beverton and Holt recognized the nature of the dual-control problem and recommended an adaptive management approach to solving it.

DETERMINANTS OF MODEL UTILITY

As noted earlier, the first guideline for model use is to define the objective of the modeling effort, and the second is to develop the model by extracting those features of the modeled system that are critically relevant to the objective. In the preceding section we focused on the first guideline and categorized (theoretical, empirical, decision-theoretical) and examined the different objectives and associated uses of models in ecology and natural resource management. Here I want to discuss the selection of critical system features for inclusion in the model (the second guideline)—a process that will ultimately determine the model's utility. This section will be organized by three dichotomies that merit consideration in model development: simple versus complex, mechanistic versus descriptive/phenomenological, and more versus less integrated parameters. Although they are presented as dichotomies, each pair of terms can be used to define a continuum. The task of the modeler is to decide the optimal position on each continuum relative to the model's intended use. These dichotomies are not the only issues that should be considered during model development. They are simply a convenient way of illustrating the kinds of considerations that I believe to be important when developing a model.

Simple vs. Complex

Every modeler must face a question about model complexity (Levins 1966; Walters and Hilborn 1978). By definition, the process of modeling involves abstraction and simplification and thus entails a loss of information when going from the true system to a model of it. The modeling process can be viewed as a filter. When the full information about the real system is passed through the filter, we would like to retain the variables and processes that are essential to our objectives and restrict our loss of information to those variables and processes least relevant to our objectives. We are simply trying to match the model's complexity to its use.

I believe that biologists have a natural tendency to create models that are more complex than necessary. At one time, for example, I used a detailed simulation model of an alligator population to draw general inferences about relative effects of size-specific and age-specific harvest on the population's dynamics (Nichols et al. 1976). My model included various components of reproductive and survival rates, but many of my general objectives could have been met by using a simpler population projection matrix (Nichols 1987). Some biologists take this tendency to favor complex explanations too far—to the point where modeling itself is viewed as a useless endeavor because no model can incorporate nature's complexity. Referring

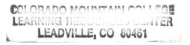

to the science of geographical ecology, MacArthur (1972:1) wrote: "The best person to do this is the naturalist. . . . But not all naturalists want to do science; many take refuge in nature's complexity as a justification to oppose any search for patterns." Our tendency to focus on complexity is quite understandable. The central guiding paradigm of all the biological sciences is Darwinian evolution by natural selection, and the raw material for this process is natural (and heritable) variation. As young ecologists, we were taught to focus on differences, rather than similarities, between individual organisms, between organisms and their behaviors in different habitats, between species, and so forth and then to build selective stories to explain these differences. (See the discussion in Gould and Lewontin 1979.)

To take an extreme view of variation and complexity, the behavior or fate of an individual organism at a particular point in space and time is a unique event that is of no use in predicting the behavior or fate of another organism (or even the same one) at a different point in space and time. In this view biologists are involved in descriptive work, and perhaps in a posteriori storytelling, but not in science. I prefer the scientific view that some generalization is possible and some biological phenomena should be at least stochastically predictable. This view leads us back to modeling—and to the recommendation that we should try to select for our model only those aspects of system complexity that are essential to the objective of the modeling effort, thus trying to match the model's complexity to its intended use.

Mechanistic vs. Descriptive/Phenomenological

By *descriptive/phenomenological* models I mean those that define relationships between variables without incorporating the underlying mechanisms responsible for these relationships. *Mechanistic* models are those that depict causative relationships between variables in the sense that changes in one variable are directly responsible for changes in the other. Certainly this distinction lies in the eye of the beholder: all models can be viewed as descriptive and phenomenological in some sense, and most models can probably be seen as mechanistic from some perspectives. I will try to illustrate this dichotomy with the following example, described in more detail elsewhere (Johnson et al. 1993).

Different hypotheses about the effects of hunting mortality on annual survival rates of mallard ducks can be incorporated into the following equation (Anderson and Burnham 1976; Burnham et al. 1984; Nichols et al. 1984):

$$S_i = \theta(1 - \beta K_i) \qquad\qquad [2.2]$$

where S_i is the probability that a bird alive at the beginning of the hunting season in year i is still alive at the beginning of the hunting season the next year, $i + 1$. Usually θ is viewed as the annual probability of surviving in the complete absence of hunting, and K_i is the probability that a bird alive at the beginning of the hunting season in year i dies as a result of hunting during the subsequent season. Finally, β denotes the slope of the relationship between annual survival and hunting mortality rate. If $\beta = 1$, then Equation (2.2) corresponds to the completely additive mortality hypothesis under which hunting and nonhunting mortality sources act as independent competing risks. If $\beta = 0$, at least for some values of K_i (for $K_i < c$, for example, where c reflects a threshold value), then Equation (2.2) corresponds to the completely compensatory mortality hypothesis under which variation in hunting mortality (below c) brings about no corresponding variation in annual survival (Anderson and Burnham 1976; Burnham et al. 1984; Nichols et al. 1984).

Recent analyses of band recovery data for North American mallard ducks have produced very different estimates of the slope parameter β for different decades of data that were analyzed. One post hoc explanation that has been offered for this difference involves mallard abundance. Density-dependent nonhunting mortality has been postulated as the most likely mechanism underlying the compensatory mortality hypothesis (Anderson and Burnham 1976; Nichols et al. 1984), so density-dependent responses to changes in hunting mortality would be expected to differ in years of high and low mallard abundance.

Johnson et al. (1993) recommend considering the following model:

$$S_i = \theta_i(1 - K_i) \qquad\qquad [2.3]$$

where we model θ_i as

$$\theta_i = \frac{e^{a + bN_i(1 - K_i)}}{1 + e^{a + bN_i(1 - K_i)}} \qquad\qquad [2.4]$$

where N_i is the number of mallards alive at the beginning of the hunting season in year i and where a and b are model parameters.

We attribute the failure of Equation (2.2)—as evidenced by the different estimates of β for different time periods—to the fact that it is descriptive and not mechanistic with respect to density dependence. If Equations (2.3) and (2.4) provide a good mechanistic model, then no single value of β in Equation (2.2) would be expected to perform well in a model and Equation (2.2) would not represent abstraction of the essential features of the modeled system. The true relationship between annual survival and hunting mortality may not be well represented by Equations (2.3) and (2.4) either, of course, and they may also omit some essential feature of the system's response to hunting. The main point here is that if density depend-ence really does underlie the compensatory mortality phenomenon, then Equations (2.3) and (2.4) are likely to provide a more mechanistic model than Equation (2.2). Equation (2.2) may perform reasonably well over cer-tain ranges of system-state variables—for example, for sets of years over which mallard abundance was similar to abundance during the period when Equation (2.2) parameters were estimated—but would not be expected to perform well for other levels of mallard abundance (Johnson et al. 1993).

My general recommendation regarding this dichotomy is this: Tend toward more mechanistic models, as they are more likely to provide better predictions when state and environmental variables assume values outside the observed historical ranges (or outside ranges used in estimating model parameters). The notion of mechanistic models is closely related to the idea of extracting essential features of the modeled system, as we are interested in essential mechanisms. Models that are mechanistic in ways that are not essential to the purpose of modeling (in our example, physiological models of the death process as steel pellets enter the body cavity of a mallard duck) have no intrinsic value.

More vs. Less Integrated Parameters

The degree of integration of model parameters reflects the degree to which components of a process are aggregated into a single parameter or modeled with separate parameters. The concept is easily explained via example. In animal population ecology, the finite rate of increase (λ) of a population (defined, for example, as the ratio of population sizes in two successive years) is sometimes used to model population change. I view λ as an inte-grated parameter in the sense that it integrates effects of survival, reproduc-tion, and movement on the population. In the case of a population closed to movement (say, an island population), the modeler might choose to decompose λ into two parameters: an annual survival rate and a reproduc-tive rate. For still other modeling purposes, it is best to decompose annual survival rate into component survival probabilities corresponding to differ-ent seasons of the year and to decompose reproductive rate into functional components such as probability that an adult breeds, clutch size, hatching success, and brood survival.

Depending on the hypothesis and the purpose of the modeling effort, any of these three parameterizations (λ; survival and reproductive rates; components of survival and reproductive rates) might be appropriate. If we have a very general hypothesis that imposition of a certain set of hunting regulations will not cause a decline in population size, then use of the integrated parameter λ in the corresponding model may be appropriate. As the primary focus of this general hypothesis is on changes in abundance, details about responses of the different survival and reproductive rate components may not be needed in the modeling effort. In fact, incorporating these components may make the modeling more difficult (stories must be developed about possible changes in each component that result from the hunting regulations) and will increase information needs for the purposes of model development and testing. Assume, however, that our a priori hypothesis concerns the effects of hunting mortality on mallard survival and follows the model of Equations (2.3) and (2.4). This hypothesis is difficult to test using only the population growth rate, λ, because this integrated parameter is also influenced by reproductive rates. Some predictions of the hypothesis can be tested using the annual survival rate, S_i, but the predictions that are most specific to the hypothesis of interest (for example, about the density dependence of seasonal survival, θ_i) are best tested with estimates of θ_i, b, and $(1 - K_i)$ of equations (2.3) and (2.4).

By analogy with the term *sufficient statistic,* which has a precise statistical meaning (Mood et al. 1974), Levins (1966, 1968) introduced the term *sufficient parameter.* Levins (1966: p. 429) noted that a sufficient parameter was "a many-to-one transformation of lower level phenomena" and thus emphasized integration and aggregation in his discussion of the term. But by analogy with "sufficient statistic," it is reasonable to think of a sufficient parameter as one that contains all the information needed to accomplish the function for which the model was intended. In the foregoing examples, λ might be a sufficient parameter for some models involving changes in animal abundance but would not be sufficient for testing mechanistic hypotheses about density-dependent seasonal mortality. So if we develop models for the empirical use of comparing predictions of competing hypotheses under some sort of treatment or manipulation, the models should include a parameter structure that accommodates the treatment/manipulation and yields predictions useful in discriminating among the competing hypotheses. Thus we return to the second general determinant of a model's utility and simply note that the degree to which model parameters are integrated or aggregated should reflect the model's intended use.

HYPOTHESES, MODELS, AND SCIENCE

According to the scientific approaches described here, learning is conditional on, and accomplished relative to, a priori hypotheses and their associated models. Perhaps this point is obvious to many readers, but often it is not adequately appreciated. Under a single-hypothesis approach to science (or management), our inferences are restricted to the a priori hypothesis and its associated model-based predictions. Our scientific process results in a decision about whether we reject, or provisionally retain, our a priori hypothesis. Similarly, the multiple-hypothesis approach to science and management is conditional on the a priori set of hypotheses and their corresponding models. The prior probabilities associated with the different hypotheses and their models are relative in the sense that they sum to 1. Changes in the hypothesis probabilities (learning) are relative as well and are entirely conditional on the members of the hypothesis set. This conditional nature of learning is true even if our set contains no hypotheses that provide reasonable approximations of reality.

These considerations suggest that we should be devoting much more thought and effort to the development of a priori hypotheses and the associated model set. Because of historical emphasis in our field, our research papers frequently begin with the statement of a statistical null hypothesis to be tested and thus lend the appearance of reasonable science. I am not claiming that such a statement of a null hypothesis is necessarily a bad thing (but see Chapter 5 of this volume). Yet its value to science depends on the nature of the alternative hypothesis (and thus on the underlying scientific hypothesis being tested). Testing a statistical null hypothesis of "no difference" or "no variation" against an omnibus alternative of "some difference" or "some variation" is not likely to be useful. Instead, we should be basing our statistical hypothesis tests on specific numerical, or at least directional, predictions based on an a priori scientific hypothesis and its associated model.

The utility of experimentation has been sold well to ecologists: today we tend to view manipulations and perturbations as inherently good and useful to the scientific endeavor. Although experimentation can indeed be an extremely powerful means of learning about natural systems, the a priori scientific hypothesis is just as important to experimentation as it is to descriptive studies. Manipulations conducted simply to "see what happens" are not likely to be nearly as useful to science as those conducted to "see what happens relative to model-based predictions." Thus the conditional nature of all scientific learning argues that we devote substantial effort to ensuring that our hypothesis set includes useful and plausible hypotheses and corresponding models. It also follows that when experience with a hypothesis set indicates that it contains no real front-runners or good predictors, we should devote additional effort to developing new hypotheses for future incorporation in the set.

In the preface to his Princeton monograph in population biology, Fretwell (1972:viii) noted: "A discussion of philosophy is, or should be, a plea for tolerance, not gratuitous advice. Whatever works should be acceptable." I end with this quote as a reminder to the reader not to take my recommendations too seriously. They deserve consideration, but nothing more. Just as the process of model building involves extraction of those features of the system that are critical to the model's intended use, I recommend that readers of this chapter extract from these recommendations only those that are likely to be useful in their own use of models in the science and management of natural resources.

ACKNOWLEDGMENTS

I thank F. A. Johnson and W. L. Kendall for helpful discussion and K. Boone for preparing the figures. I thank M. J. Conroy, A. B. Franklin, K. H. Pollock, T. M. Shenk, and B. K. Williams for constructive criticism of various forms of this chapter. I followed many, but not all, of their suggestions. I alone am responsible for any errors and misconceptions that remain.

REFERENCES

Anderson, D. R. 1975. Optimal exploitation strategies for an animal population in a Markovian environment: A theory and an example. *Ecology* 56:1281–1297.

Anderson, D. R., and K. P. Burnham. 1976. *Population Ecology of the Mallard. VI: The Effect of Exploitation on Survival.* Resource Publication 125. Washington, D.C.: U.S. Fish and Wildlife Service.

Bellman, R. 1957. *Dynamic Programming.* Princeton: Princeton University Press.

Beverton, R. J. H., and S. J. Holt. 1957. *On the Dynamics of Exploited Fish Populations.* London: HMSO.

Burnham, K. P., G. C. White, and D. R. Anderson. 1984. Estimating the effect of hunting on annual survival rates of adult mallards. *Journal of Wildlife Management* 48:350–361.

Caswell, H. 1988. Theory and models in ecology: A different perspective. *Ecological Modelling* 43:33–44.

Chamberlin, T. C. 1897. The method of multiple working hypotheses. *Journal of Geology* 5:837–848.

Chapman, R. N. 1928. The quantitative analysis of environmental factors. *Ecology* 9:111–122.

Conley, W., and J. D. Nichols. 1978. The use of models in small mammal population studies. Pages 14–35 in D. P. Snyder, ed., *Populations of Small Mammals Under Natural Conditions.* Pittsburgh: University of Pittsburgh Press.

Constantino, R. F., J. M. Cushing, B. Dennis, and R. A. Desharnais. 1995. Experimentally induced transitions in the dynamic behavior of insect populations. *Nature* 375:227–230.

Cox, D. R. 1958. *Planning of Experiments.* New York: Wiley.

Fisher, R. A. 1947. *The Design of Experiments.* 4th ed. New York: Hafner.

———. 1958. *Statistical Methods for Research Workers.* 13th ed. London: Oliver & Boyd.

Fretwell, S. D. 1972. *Populations in a Seasonal Environment*. Princeton: Princeton University Press.

Gould, S. J., and R. C. Lewontin. 1979. The spandrels of San Marco and the Panglossian paradigm: A critique of the adaptationist programme. *Proceedings of the Royal Society of London* B205:581–598.

Hawking, S. W. 1988. *A Brief History of Time*. New York: Bantam Books.

Hilborn, R., and M. Mangel. 1997. *The Ecological Detective: Confronting Models with Data*. Princeton: Princeton University Press.

Hilborn, R., and C. J. Walters. 1992. *Quantitative Fisheries Stock Assessment: Choice, Dynamics, and Uncertainty*. New York: Routledge.

Holling, C. S., ed. 1978. *Adaptive Environmental Assessment and Management*. Chichester: Wiley.

Johnson, F. A., B. K. Williams, J. D. Nichols, J. E. Hines, W. L. Kendall, G. W. Smith, and D. F. Caithamer. 1993. Developing an adaptive management strategy for harvesting waterfowl in North America. *Transactions of the North American Wildlife and Natural Resources Conference* 58:565–583.

Johnson, F. A., C. T. Moore, W. L. Kendall, J. A. Dubosky, D. F. Caithamer, J. R. Kelley Jr., and B. K. Williams. 1997. Uncertainty and the management of mallard harvests. *Journal of Wildlife Management* 61:202–216.

Krebs, C. J. 1972. *Ecology*. New York: Harper & Row.

Lafleur, L. J., trans. 1960. *"Discourse on Method" and "Meditations,"* by R. Descartes. New York: Liberal Arts Press.

Lakatos, I. 1970. Falsification and the methodology of scientific research programmes. Pages 91–195 in I. Lakatos and A. Musgrave, eds., *Criticism and the Growth of Knowledge*. New York: Cambridge University Press.

Lancia, R. A., et al. 1996. ARM! for the future: Adaptive resource management in the wildlife profession. *Wildlife Society Bulletin* 24:436–442.

Levins, R. 1966. The strategy of model building in population biology. *American Scientist* 54:421–431.

———. 1968. *Evolution in Changing Environments*. Princeton: Princeton University Press.

Lewontin, R. C. 1963. Models, mathematics, and metaphors. *Synthese* 15:222–244.

———. 1968. Introduction. Pages 1–4 in R. C. Lewontin, ed., *Population Biology and Evolution*. Syracuse: Syracuse University Press.

Lubow, B. C. 1995. SDP: Generalized software for solving stochastic dynamic optimization problems. *Wildlife Society Bulletin* 23:738–742.

MacArthur, R. H. 1972. *Geographical Ecology*. New York: Harper & Row.

Macnab, J. 1983. Wildlife management as scientific experimentation. *Wildlife Society Bulletin* 11:397–401.

Mertz, D. B. 1972. The *Tribolium* model and the mathematics of population growth. *Annual Review of Ecology and Systematics* 3:51–78.

Mood, A. M., F. A. Graybill, and D. C. Boes. 1974. *Introduction to the Theory of Statistics*. 3rd ed. New York: McGraw-Hill.

Murphy, D. D., and B. R. Noon. 1991. Coping with uncertainty in wildlife biology. *Journal of Wildlife Management* 55:773–782.

Neyman, J. 1957. "Inductive behavior" as a basic concept of philosophy of science. *Revue Institute Internationale de Statistique* 25:7–22.

Neyman, J., T. Park, and E. L. Scott. 1956. Struggle for existence. The *Tribolium* model: Biological and statistical aspects. Pages 41–79 in J. Neyman, ed., *Proceedings of the Berkeley Symposium on Mathematical Statistics and Probability.* 3rd ed. Berkeley: University of California Press.

Nichols, J. D. 1987. Population models and crocodile management. Pages 177–187 in G. J. W. Webb, S. J. Manolis, and P. J. Whitehead, eds., *Wildlife Management: Crocodiles and Alligators.* Chipping Norton, NSW: Surrey, Beatty & Sons.

Nichols, J. D., L. Viehman, R. H. Chabreck, and B. Fenderson. 1976. *Simulation of a Commercially Harvested Alligator Population in Louisiana.* Louisiana Agricultural Experiment Station Bulletin 691. Baton Range: Louisiana Agricultural Experiment Station.

Nichols, J. D., M. J. Conroy, D. R. Anderson, and K. P. Burnham. 1984. Compensatory mortality in waterfowl populations: A review of the evidence and implications for research and management. *Transactions of the North American Wildlife and Natural Resources Conference* 49:535–554.

Nichols, J. D., F. A. Johnson, and B. K. Williams. 1995. Managing North American waterfowl in the face of uncertainty. *Annual Review of Ecology and Systematics* 26:177–199.

Park, T. 1948. Experimental studies of interspecies competition. I: Competition between populations of the flour beetles, *Tribolium confusum* Duval and *Tribolium castaneum* Herbst. *Ecological Monographs* 18:265–308.

Pearson, O. P. 1960. A mechanical model for the study of population dynamics. *Ecology* 41:494–508.

Pease, C. M., and J. J. Bull. 1992. Is science logical? *BioScience* 42:293–298.

Platt, J. R. 1964. Strong inference. *Science* 146:347–353.

Popper, K. R. 1959. *The Logic of Scientific Discovery.* New York: Harper & Row.

———. 1963. *Conjectures and Refutations: The Growth of Scientific Knowledge.* New York: Harper & Row.

———. 1972. *Objective Knowledge.* Oxford: Clarendon Press.

Porter, W. P., J. W. Mitchell, W. A. Beckman, and C. B. DeWitt. 1973. Behavioral implications of mechanistic ecology: Thermal and behavioral modeling of desert ectotherms and their microenvironment. *Oecologia* 13:1–54.

Romesburg, H. C. 1981. Wildlife science: Gaining reliable knowledge. *Journal of Wildlife Management* 45:293–313.

———. 1991. On improving the natural resources and environmental sciences. *Journal of Wildlife Management* 55:744–756.

Seger, R. 1980. *Against the Wind.* New York: Columbia Records.

Sinclair, A. R. E. 1991. Science and the practice of wildlife management. *Journal of Wildlife Management* 55:767–773.

Skalski, J. R., and D. S. Robson. 1992. *Techniques for Wildlife Investigations.* San Diego: Academic Press.

Skellam, J. G. 1972. Some philosophical aspects of mathematical modelling in empirical science with special reference to ecology. Pages 13–28 in J. N. R. Jeffers, ed., *Mathematical Models in Ecology.* Oxford: Blackwell Scientific.

Tracy, C. R. 1976. A model of the dynamic exchanges of water and energy between a terrestrial amphibian and its environment. *Ecological Monographs* 46:293–326.

Wade, M. J., and C. J. Goodnight. 1991. Wright's shifting balance theory: An experimental study. *Science* 253:1015–1018.

Walters, C. J. 1986. *Adaptive Management of Renewable Resources.* New York: Macmillan.

Walters, C. J., and R. Hilborn. 1978. Ecological optimization and adaptive management. *Annual Review of Ecology and Systematics* 9:157–188.

Williams, B. K. 1982. Optimal stochastic control in natural resource management: Framework and examples. *Ecological Modelling* 16:275–297.

———. 1989. Review of dynamic optimization methods in renewable natural resource management. *Natural Resources Modeling* 3:137–216.

———. 1996a. Adaptive optimization and the harvest of biological populations. *Mathematical Biosciences* 136:1–20.

———. 1996b. Adaptive optimization of renewable natural resources: Solution algorithms and a computer program. *Ecological Modelling* 93:101–111.

———. 1997. Logic and science in wildlife biology. *Journal of Wildlife Management* 61:1007–1015.

Williams, B. K., and F. A. Johnson. 1995. Adaptive management and the regulation of waterfowl harvests. *Wildlife Society Bulletin* 23:430–436.

Chapter 3

Statistical Models: Keys to Understanding the Natural World

Gary C. White

Statistical models are models that are used for interpreting data. The process of fitting a model to data in a statistically rigorous fashion is termed *parameter estimation*. There are two main applications of models: for conceptualizing systems and for predicting the real world. Conceptual models provide a tool to think about a system. An example of a conceptual model is the logistic population growth model, $dN/dt = rN(1 - N/K)$, which represents a simplistic description of density dependence in population ecology. This model offers an abstract framework to conceptualize density dependence and includes a mathematical definition of concepts such as a population's intrinsic rate of growth and carrying capacity. Except in limited situations, the model is biologically naive—that is, it has no concept of generations, age classes, gender, or reproductive status. Yet this conceptual model has made an enormous contribution to population ecology because it captures the notion that density causes changes in the population's rate of growth.

Unlike conceptual models, statistical models require data. I define statistical models as models used to make statistical inferences from data—in other words, models that define parameters to be estimated from data. The most common statistical model has one parameter—the mean, μ, for which we obtain an estimate, $\hat{\mu}$ (or more commonly $\bar{x}$)—but this model has little conceptual value from a biological perspective. Parameters are unknown numerical quantities or constants in the model for which we desire estimates. Linear regression models, $y = a + bx$, are also used for parameter estimation where the parameters a and b are estimated as $\hat{a}$ and $\hat{b}$, respectively, and begin to provide a useful conceptual model from a biological view. Here the main parameter of interest might be the slope of the line (b) and whether its estimate indicates an increasing or decreasing trend in the variable y. Still, this model assumes a linear relationship between x and y over their entire range—an unlikely possibility for most biological relations where thresholds and asymptotes are the norm. Other statistical models are analysis of variance (ANOVA) models, used to test hypotheses with observed data. Usually ANOVA models are also linear and lack general biological realism, but they are often adequate to make inferences for a range of behavior of the system being studied. Biologists can conceive of conceptual models that are useful abstractions of the real world and can be considered to define a reasonable biological theory. When these conceptual models are used to make statistical inferences from data, they become statistical models.

Statistical models fulfill three important functions. First, if we do not accept the model as a useful abstraction of the real world, we can test it with the data. That is, we can evaluate whether the model is consistent with the data—or, vice versa, whether the model fails to capture the essence of the data and hence should be rejected. Second, if we do accept the model as a useful abstraction of the real world, we can use it to evaluate the quality of our data. Reliability of the observed data can be judged by the quality of the fit of the model. In this situation, we infer that the data are inadequate if they are not consistent with the model. Third, if we do accept the model as a useful abstraction of the real world, we can use it to make inferences from our observed data (given that the data are adequate). These inferences may be in the form of parameter estimates such as survival rates, a population's intrinsic rate of growth, or the rate coefficients for the kinetics of a contaminant in the environment. With our model now equipped with parameters estimated from data, it offers predictive power for further observations of the real world. This philosophy of modeling was expressed by Aber (1997) in his critique of why ecologists do not trust their models: "Whenever possible, models should include realistic, empirically based parameterizations that tie the model as closely as possible to experimental data."

As we shall see, biologically realistic models, including complex theoretical models, can also be treated as statistical models, and their parameters can be estimated from observed data. This chapter presents examples of fitting models to data and the inferences resulting from this process, including population dynamics, growth, kinetics, capture–recapture, and band recovery models. The fitting of theoretical models to data constitutes a bridge between theory and data in ecology. My objective here is to illustrate the usefulness of fitting conceptual models to data and thus converting a conceptual model to a statistical model. In the following pages I explore methods of parameter estimation, as well as model selection and testing, and illustrate the paradigm shift from hypothesis testing to parameter estimation (Johnson 1999). As examples we shall consider a simple population dynamics model, growth curves, kinetic models of tritium transport, and complex population models involving covariates. A similar philosophy of fitting models to data is espoused by Hilborn and Mangel (1997).

Parameter Estimation Methods

Assume we have a reasonable conceptual model with unknown parameter values, and we have collected data useful in estimating these parameters. We want to estimate the parameters of this model from these sample data.

The principal tool for estimating parameters in modern statistics is the method of maximum likelihood. Much of modern statistical theory rests on Fisher's likelihood principle. Fisher (1922, 1925) presented the method of maximum likelihood as an omnibus procedure for estimating parameters from sample data. Likelihood theory is used to assess the fit of the data to the model and to test a variety of hypotheses. Parameter estimators, and likelihood-based inference in general, have excellent properties such as little or no bias and maximum efficiency. This theory is the backbone of general statistical inference used in nearly every area of science.

Most readers are probably familiar with least-squares estimation—that is, estimating parameter values by minimizing the squared differences between model predictions and observed data. If the differences (errors or residuals) between the model predictions and observed values are assumed to be normally distributed with a mean of zero, then least-squares estimates are identical to maximum-likelihood estimates. In general, however, least-squares estimates are not the same as maximum-likelihood estimates. Maximum-likelihood estimation requires that we have a biological model with parameters to be estimated as well as a probabilistic model to explain the variability observed in our data. This probabilistic model is our descriptor of the random variation observed in the data. Common examples are the normal distribution for regression and ANOVA models, the lognormal distribution for skewed data, the binomial distribution for survival data and other discrete data with only two possible values, and the multinomial distribution for discrete data with more than two values.

The likelihood function, $\mathcal{L}$(parameters | data), is the probability of the observed data viewed as a function of the parameters (Edwards 1972). The function is read as "the likelihood of the unknown parameters given the observed (sample) data." The objective is to find the vector of parameter values that maximizes the likelihood function. That is, parameter estimates are selected to make the sample data seem "most likely" given the statistical model. Consider the simple case of estimating the survival probability (S) from a sample of radio-collared animals. Assume that n animals were collared and y of them lived through the interval. Then:

$$\mathcal{L}(S \,|\, y, n) = (\tfrac{n}{y}) S^y (1 - S)^{(n-y)}$$

The likelihood function involves the estimable parameter S and the data y and n. This model assumes that each animal has the same survival probability and that the fates of the n animals are independent (that is, unrelated). From the likelihood, S is estimated as the value of S that maximizes the likelihood—in this case, $\hat{S} = y/n$ (Figure 3.1). For the case where more than one parameter is estimated, the maximum-likelihood estimates of each are the vector of parameter values that maximizes the likelihood function.

The sampling variance, often expressed as the standard error of the estimator, is a measure of the precision or repeatability of the estimator and is usually a function of sample size and other unknown parameters. For a likelihood function that contains only one parameter, the sampling variance estimator can be derived as the negative inverse of the second partial derivative of the log-likelihood function evaluated at the maximum-likelihood estimate. Thus the larger the second partial derivative, the smaller the variance (Figure 3.1). In the radio-collar example,

$$\text{var}(\hat{S}) = -\left[E\!\left(\frac{\partial^2 \ln \mathcal{L}(S \,|\, y, n)}{\partial S^2} \right) \right]^{-1}$$

which is estimated by

$$\hat{\text{var}}(\hat{S}) = -\left[\left(\frac{\partial^2 \ln \mathcal{L}(S \,|\, y, n)}{\partial S^2} \right) \right]^{-1}_{S=\hat{s}}$$

The expectation operator (E) in these equations is necessary for the theoretical derivation of the estimator. In practice, we assume that sample sizes are large enough to provide the "expected" values of the random variables in the formula. The maximum-likelihood procedure produces the common estimator of the variance of a binomial proportion:

$$\hat{\text{var}}(\hat{S}) = \frac{\hat{S}(1 - \hat{S})}{n}$$

If the likelihood has more than one parameter to be estimated, the sampling

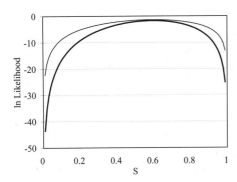

Figure 3.1. Examples of a ln likelihood function for a survival estimation model. The top curve (thin line) and bottom curve (thick line) are the ln likelihood for $n = 10$ and $y = 6$, and for $n = 20$ and $y = 12$, respectively. For both likelihoods, the maximum is obtained at $\hat{S} = 0.6$. The larger sample size of 20 results in a "narrower" function—resulting in a larger second partial derivative with respect to S and hence a smaller sampling variance.

variances and covariances can be estimated from the negative of the matrix of mixed second-order partial derivatives of the log-likelihood function. The resulting matrix, expressed as expected partial derivatives, is called the information matrix

$$-E\left(\frac{\partial^2 \ln \mathscr{L}(\boldsymbol{\theta}\,|\,\text{data})}{(\partial\theta_i)\,(\partial\theta_j)}\right)$$

and is evaluated at the unknown true parameter value, $\boldsymbol{\theta}$. Estimates of variances are achieved by computing the inverse of the information matrix and replacing the true parameter values by their maximum-likelihood estimates:

$$\hat{\text{var}}(\hat{\boldsymbol{\theta}}) = \left[-\left(\frac{\partial^2 \ln \mathscr{L}(\boldsymbol{\theta}\,|\,\text{data})}{(\partial\theta_i)\,(\partial\theta_j)}\right)\right]^{-1}_{\boldsymbol{\theta}\,=\,\hat{\boldsymbol{\theta}}}$$

In ecological modeling, the model's sensitivity to the parameter values is typically evaluated (Aber 1997). Sensitivity is measured by the partial derivative of some model output with respect to a parameter. The estimated sampling variance derived from the method of maximum likelihood provides much the same information as the sensitivity analysis in that the model's output is insensitive to parameters with large sampling variances.

The method of least squares is another standard way of estimating parameters. When the differences between the model's predictions and the sample data are assumed to be normally distributed, the method of least squares is identical to the method of maximum likelihood. But for other assumptions about the variability observed in the data, the two methods are not the same. The least-squares method is typically implemented in linear and nonlinear regression packages, where the model's deviations from the data can be assumed to be normally distributed—making the method identical to maximum likelihood.

A third approach to parameter estimation is the Bayesian method. This method assumes some prior statistical distribution of the estimable parameters combined with the likelihood of the data (the same as described for the maximum-likelihood method) to derive the posterior statistical distribution of the estimable parameter: posterior probability is proportional to the likelihood times the prior probability. The Bayesian method is appealing when we have information describing the prior distribution of the parameters of interest. Typically, however, the prior distribution is unknown and we have only subjective information. The use of "uninformative" priors results in the same estimates as if the method of maximum likelihood had been used. Because of the fundamental theoretical differences between the two methods, however, the interpretation of the resulting estimates is quite different. For an excellent review of Bayesian inference in ecology, see Ellison (1996), ver Hoef (1996), Wolfson et al. (1996), Ludwig (1996), Taylor et al. (1996), Edwards (1996), and Dennis (1996). An overview of Bayesian statistics relative to the approaches discussed here can be found in Malakoff (1999).

The three methods described here are rigorous statistical estimation procedures founded on solid statistical theory. Parameters in many models, however, are fit by ad hoc methods (not founded on statistical theory). The method of "maximum satisfaction" is predominant in this arena, where the parameters are adjusted until the model's fit to the observed data satisfies the user. This method has no known optimal statistical properties; its only value is the user's satisfaction. But estimates satisfying one user are often unsatisfactory to another. Such estimates lack any rigorous theory to support their use and are clearly subjective.

MODEL FIT AND MODEL SELECTION

In the preceding examples my aim has been to verify (or at least assume) that the most general model fits the data. The most general model is the one with the largest number of parameters—that is, the model with the most flexibility to fit the observed data. The fit of the general model is usually assessed with a goodness-of-fit test appropriate for the data being analyzed. Then, by using objective model selection techniques such as AIC (Akaike 1973; Sakamoto et al. 1986; Shibata 1989; Burnham and Anderson 1992, 1998), the selected model provides parsimony (economy or simplicity) in the number of parameters estimated from the data.

Akaike's Information Criterion (AIC) is defined as $-2 \ln \mathcal{L}(\text{parameters} \mid \text{data})$

+ 2K, where K is the number of parameters estimated in the model. For small samples, AIC_c is defined as

$$-2 \ln \mathscr{L} (\text{parameters} \,|\, \text{data}) + 2K + \frac{2K(K+1)}{n-K-1}$$

where n is the sample size. The model with the smallest value of AIC (or AIC_c) for the list of models being considered is selected as the most parsimonious representation of the data. That is, AIC can be regarded as a trade-off between the fit of the model to the data (the likelihood) versus the number of parameters. With AIC the goal is to select the model with the least number of parameters that represents the data adequately—the principle of parsimony. The most parsimonious model that explains the data is selected as the best model.

For the special case of the normal distribution—and particularly for least-squares estimation where the errors can be assumed normally distributed so that least-squares estimates are the same as maximum-likelihood estimates—the log likelihood is (Burnham and Anderson 1998):

$$-\frac{1}{2}n \ln \left(\sum_{i=1}^{n} (y_i - \hat{y}_i)^2 \right)$$

for the case where the errors for all observations (y_i) are assumed to have constant variance. Note that for the normal distribution an additional parameter must be included as being estimated: σ^2, the variance of the errors. Thus K is the number of parameters optimized in the least-squares process, plus 1 for the variance.

AIC values are relative. Thus only the relative difference between models is needed. This relative difference is defined as $\Delta_i = AIC_i - \min AIC$, or the difference between the AIC for model i and the model with the minimum AIC value for the R models considered. Typically AIC_c values are used instead of AIC. With these Δ_i values, Burnham and Anderson (1998) define Akaike weights for the R models being considered as

$$w_i = \frac{\exp(-\frac{1}{2}\Delta_i)}{\sum_{r=1}^{R} \exp(-\frac{1}{2}\Delta_r)}$$

The Akaike weights (w_i) provide a measure of the weight of evidence in favor of model i as being the best model for the situation at hand given the R models considered (Burnham and Anderson 1998). Values of $w_1 = 0.5$ and $w_2 = 0.25$, for example, would imply that model 1 had twice the support as the best model over model 2. Thus Akaike weights provide a likelihood for each model being the best model given the models that were considered.

Another approach to assessing model fit is often advocated for ecological models (Aber 1997): use a portion of the data for developing the model and the remainder for validating the model (see Chapter 7 in this volume). The motivation behind this approach is that validation of the model requires independent data and cannot be properly done with the same data used to estimate the parameters. The concept of assessing validation in this context, however, is that the model is a realistic representation of the natural world. Assessing goodness-of-fit by contrast, is a statistical concept about testing whether the assumptions of the methods being used are met by the data.

POPULATION DYNAMICS EXAMPLES

As a starting example, let us use simple biological models for a simple set of data to determine if population growth is density-dependent or density-independent. Consider the growth of a ring-necked pheasant (*Phaisianus colchicus*) population introduced to an island off the coast of the state of Washington. Initially, in 1937, two cocks and six hens were introduced, after which the population increased over time (Figure 3.2).

Lack (1954) commented: "The figures suggest that the increase was slowing down and was about to cease, but at this point the island was occupied by the military and many of the birds were shot." The dashed line in Figure 3.2 represents density-independent population growth—that is, the model $N(t) = N_0 e^{rt}$. The solid line represents density-dependent population growth—that is, the model

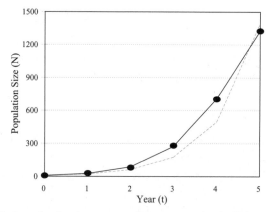

Figure 3.2. Growth of a pheasant population on an island off the coast of Washington State (from Bulmer 1994 after Lack 1954). The dots represent the population size, the solid line the fit of the density-dependent population model, and the dashed line the fit of the density-independent population model.

$$N(t) = \frac{K}{1 + \left(\dfrac{K}{N_0} - 1\right)e^{-rt}}$$

The density-dependent model provides a better fit of the data, but then it should do so because it has two parameters compared to only one for the density-independent model. Is the improvement in fit from the more complex model meaningful—and, therefore, is density dependence supported by these data? Was Lack correct in suggesting that growth had indeed slowed down?

To answer these questions we must construct a statistical test of the null hypothesis that the two models fit equally well. First, assuming that the differences between the observed and predicted values are normally distributed, compute the sum of squared differences for each model (that is, the sum of squared errors, or SSE):

Model	SSE
Density independence	59,600.0
Density dependence	142.8

Clearly the difference in SSE suggests a difference in fit. To test this, construct an extra SS F test as follows:

$$F_{df_I - df_D, df_D} = \frac{\dfrac{(SSE_I - SSE_D)}{(df_I - df_D)}}{\dfrac{SSE_D}{df_D}}$$

where SSE_D is the sum of squared errors for the density-dependent model, SSE_I is the sum of squared errors for the density-independent model, and df_D and df_I are the respective degrees of freedom of the two models. The F statistic equals 1249.2 with 1 and 3 degrees of freedom ($P < 0.001$). The improvement in model fit easily justifies the increase in model complexity. Hence Lack was correct. The parameter estimates for the density-dependent model are $\hat{r} = 1.224$ (SE = 0.00532) and $\hat{K} = 2077.9$ (SE = 39.438); for the density-independent model, the estimates are $\hat{r} = 1.032$ (SE = 0.01681).

This test was developed assuming that the deviations from the model predictions are normally distributed (hence the estimate is maximum-likelihood estimates), which is suspect given the range of values in the data. This assumption can be changed by fitting a model with multiplicative (and hence lognormal) errors or by randomization or permutation tests. For multiplicative errors (where the difference between the log of the predicted value and the log of the observed value is squared), the F test is 38.2 ($P =$

0.009)—still supporting the conclusion that the population was exhibiting density dependence and Lack was correct.

With the alternative philosophy of not testing a statistical hypothesis, but estimating parameter values and using AIC_c model selection (Burnham and Anderson 1998), the AIC_c value for the density-independent model is 64.98 (number of parameters = 2) and for the density-independent model 54.81 (number of parameters = 3), giving Akaike weights of 0.0062 and 0.9938, respectively. Therefore, the weight of the evidence from the data strongly supports the density-dependent model by more than 100 times. This example illustrates two key concepts. First, we are able to estimate parameters of biological interest—carrying capacity. Second, we rigorously evaluated a biological hypothesis about density dependence versus density independence.

The Ricker stock-recruitment model is an example of a model commonly fit to population data to make inferences about the management of a population. W. E. Ricker (1954) invented this equation to model fishery stocks with a discrete population. (See also Ricker 1975:282.) Using the same notation as earlier, the Ricker curve is

$$N_{t+1} = N_t \exp\left[R_0\left(1 - \frac{N_t}{K}\right)\right]$$

where N_t represents the parent stock and N_{t+1} are recruits. The density dependence in this model becomes stronger at higher densities due to the exponential function. This model was fit to data provided by Hilborn and Walters (1992:243) on Skeena River sockeye salmon recruitment (Figure 3.3). The method of maximum likelihood was used assuming normally distributed errors. Hilborn and Walters (1992) describe the traditional approach to fitting this curve via a linear regression of log(recruits/stock) on stock.

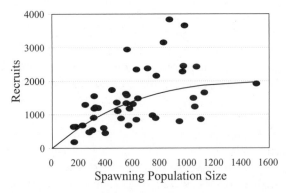

Figure 3.3. Recruitment of sockeye salmon from the Skeena River, British Columbia (Hilborn and Walters 1992). The fitted model is the Ricker curve (Ricker 1954).

A more elaborate example involving two populations is provided by Pascual and Karieva (1996), who fit the population sizes of Gause's (1964) experimental cultures of *Paramecium aurelia* and *P. caudatum* to the Lotka-Volterra differential equation model. Interestingly, they consider the approach of fitting complex models to data new. (Their article was published in the "Concepts Emphasizing New Ideas to Stimulate Research in Ecology" section of the journal.)

Another example of fitting population data is provided by Pascual et al. (1997), who fit a collection of models to Serengeti wildebeest (*Connochaetes taurinus*) population abundances and survival data. Although they could not select a "best" model from the ones they fit to the data, the models resulted in very different implications for management. They concluded that model selection methods based on the parsimony principle were not practical for judging the value of alternative models. Rather than blame the model selection methods, I suggest that these data lacked the information needed to distinguish between the models. Only time series of total population size as well as some adult survival rates and age ratios were available; there was no manipulation of population size to learn how density dependence operated in the population. Shenk (1997) demonstrated with simulations that reliable detection of density dependence in a time series of population sizes requires manipulation—that is, the amount of information available in the data is increased by manipulating population size and letting the population respond. In the wildebeest data set, the lack of manipulation makes distinguishing between similar models unlikely, which is the conclusion based on the model selection procedures.

The foregoing models illustrate how parameters important to the population dynamics of a species can be estimated from observed data with maximum-likelihood and least-squares estimators. Moreover, these examples show how mechanisms influencing population growth, such as density dependence, can be elucidated from observations from the populations and their importance evaluated relative to the alternative hypothesis of density-independent population growth.

GROWTH CURVES: EXAMPLES

The next example illustrates how the deviations between the observed value and the models' predictions may reflect variation in the process rather than sampling or measurement error. This case from the literature is provided by fitting models to the growth data of animals, usually with sigmoid or S-shaped curves. The experimental protocol is to weigh animals periodically during their time of growth, usually from the time they are born or hatched until maturity. The animal's mass has been estimated with a number of different models, but the Richards equation (Richards 1959) as modified by Brisbin et al. (1986a) allows most of these models as special cases:

$$\frac{dW}{dt} = \frac{2(m + 1)}{T(1 - m)} \left(W_\infty^{1-m} W^m - W\right)$$

where W_∞ is the asymptotic mass of the animal (where growth levels off), m is the shape parameter of the curve, and T measures the time required for the major part of growth and, for comparative purposes, probably represents the period of development as well as any parameter derived from a function that reaches some asymptote, or point of leveling off (Richards 1959).

Although the integrated form of this equation could be fit directly to the observed data, a conceptual problem arises. The parameter estimation method assumes that the deviations between the predicted and observed data are independent across time and, moreover, that the differences between observed and predicted values are attributed to sampling errors, that is, errors in observing the mass of the animal. Both of these assumptions are unrealistic. As an animal grows, the process is cumulative. Suppose a mallard duck is sick during week 3 of an eight-week sequence of measurements. During week 3, the duck does not gain the usual amount of weight because of the disease. When the illness is over, the duck resumes its growth, possibly even with compensation. The fit of the growth curve to the observed data would have large residuals during week 3, however, and would basically try to smooth out the anomaly of the illness. The problem is that the model assumes independence of the observations and does not recognize the underlying biological process as cumulative (Figure 3.4).

White and Brisbin (1980) developed a growth curve model based on the Richards model where the variation in the growth process is treated as the stochasticity in the model-fitting process, not the presumed sampling variation of the preceding example. The model

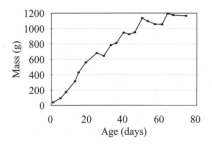

Figure 3.4. Example of the growth of a mallard duck (Brisbin et al. 1986a). Mass is assumed to be measured without error (that is, variability in the observations is assumed to come from variation in the growth process). Thus the declines in mass indicate the animal was losing mass and suggest that a model which incorporates variation in the growth process is required.

$$\frac{W_{i+1} - W_i}{t_{i+1} - t_i} = \frac{2(1 + m)}{T(1 - m)} (W_\infty^{1-m} W^m - W) + e_i$$

predicts the next observation at time t_{i+1} in terms of the current observation at time t_i. This model now handles the hypothetical week of illness in the example. Parameters are estimated with the maximum-likelihood method assuming the errors (e_i) are normally or lognormally distributed. This model assumes that the animals are weighed without error—that is, that the observed mass values are measured without error relative to the deviations expected in the growth process. Thus the errors (e_i) represent variation in the growth process, not sampling variation. As such, the variance of the e_i provides an estimate of the process variance of the growth mechanism.

An extension of this modeling approach was used to compare the impact of environmental contaminants on the growth of ducks. With appropriate controls, PCBs were fed to mallards and wood ducks (Brisbin et al. 1986a) and cadmium to wood ducks (Brisbin et al. 1986b). The three parameter estimates describing the growth of each individual were considered together (that is, they were used as a multivariate vector) to test for effects of the contaminants. For both contaminants, the shape of the growth curve, as measured by the m parameter, was affected but the asymptotic weight of the ducks was not. This experimental design gets at the question of the effects of the contaminant during a time of stress—that is, growth—of the organism. Thus the experimental approach is effective at detecting chronic effects of contaminants.

CONTAMINANT TRANSPORT: EXAMPLE

The next example illustrates how multiple variables can be used to estimate a common set of parameters from observed data. The transport of materials in ecosystems is another common problem where modeling is routinely applied, usually as kinetics or compartment models. These models are generally sets of linear differential equations linking the compartments. As an example (White et al. 1983), consider the flow of tritium (^3H, an isotope of hydrogen) from a source (S) through honeybees (*Apis mellifera*) (B) into their honey (H):

$$\frac{dB}{dt} = k_1 S + k_3 H - (k_2 + k_4)B$$

$$\frac{dH}{dt} = k_2 B - (k_3 + k_5)H$$

where the compartments look like Figure 3.5.

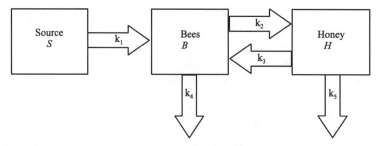

Figure 3.5. Compartment model of a system where the flow of tritium (^{3}H), an isotope of hydrogen, moves from a source (S) through honeybees (*Apis mellifera*) (B) into their honey (H) with transfer coefficients of $k_1, k_2, \ldots, k_5$.

In a 35-day controlled experiment (White et al. 1983), bees were provided with a source of water containing tritium. The concentration in the tritium source (pCi/ml) was modeled as

$$S = \begin{cases} 378.17 + 1.029t - 0.00173t^2 & t \leq 358 \\ 703.82 - 2.388t + 0.00209t^2 & 358 < t \leq 766 \\ -399.04 + 0.979t & t > 766 \end{cases}$$

where t is in hours. Observed values in the tritium source were fitted to a set of polynomial equations to yield this set of equations, which provide the input to the model for bees and honey. Compartments were assumed to have a constant volume, so modeling concentrations does not invalidate the model.

The five unknown parameters ($k_1, k_2, \ldots, k_5$) were estimated with the method of maximum likelihood assuming normally distributed errors and restricting the parameter estimates to nonnegative values. The resulting fit of the model to the observed data is adequate, judging from the predicted and observed values in Figure 3.6. One of the interesting findings was that

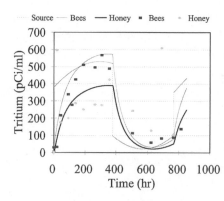

Figure 3.6
Example of fitting kinetics models to compartment data (from White et al. 1983). The source compartment provided tritium to honeybees, which then transferred the tritium to their honey. Predicted values are represented by lines, and observed values are represented by symbols.

$k_5 = 0$. The assumption is that honey sealed in the wax comb prevents tritium from evaporating. The resulting model was then applied to field data to interpret the uptake of tritium from an effluent stack. Of the three hives used to monitor the stack, only two were obtaining tritium from this source.

ESTIMATING POPULATIONS FROM CLOSED CAPTURE–RECAPTURE DATA: EXAMPLE

Estimators of population size have been based on different assumptions. Otis et al. (1978) and White et al. (1982) presented five different models for population estimation based on individual heterogeneity, behavioral responses to capture, and time variation. Models have been developed as well by Chao (1988, 1989), Chao et al. (1992), and Pollock and Otto (1983). This example demonstrates how estimators of population size for closed populations from mark/recapture data from multiple-attribute groups cannot only estimate capture and recapture parameters in common across the groups but also estimate population sizes for each of the groups separately. Further, this example uses covariates to improve the estimates of capture probability.

In this example, capture–recapture data from Coulombe (unpublished data in Otis et al. 1978) are used on house mice (*Mus musculus*) in a southern California coastal salt marsh in December 1962. Morning and evening trapping sessions for 5 days resulted in ten trapping occasions. Two age classes (subadults and adults) × two sexes make four groups of animals. In this analysis, the capture and recapture probabilities are modeled in common across the four groups with Program MARK (White and Burnham 1999) in an effort to gain more precise estimates of population size ($\hat{N}_j$) for the four groups and learn where the variation in capture and recapture probabilities arises.

A partial list of the models is shown in Table 3.1. Day-to-day time variation in the capture probabilities is important, as the smallest AIC_c models all have time-specific capture probabilities. Differences in the morning and evening capture probabilities were modeled with a constant "pm" effect. Models that combined the capture and recapture probabilities for subadults but left the adults separate had smaller AIC_c values than models with four age × sex groups. As a result, the lowest AIC_c model had 25 parameters compared to 48 for the most general model. The best model had three groups with five "day-effect" parameters plus a "pm effect," plus a "recapture effect" for each group, making 21 parameters for modeling the capture–recapture effects. Moreover, the four estimates of $\hat{N}$ are included, making 25 total parameters. Efforts at modeling the group effect as additive to the time effect did not result in

Table 3.1. Results of Modeling Capture and Recapture Parameters of Mark/Recapture Data

Model	AIC_c	Delta AIC_c	Akaike weights	No. of parameters	Deviance
$\{p[(sa=)^*(am + pm)^*t] = c[(sa=)(am + pm)^*t + (sa=)^*c]\}$	1120.093	0	0.52206	25	802.493
$\{p[(am + pm)^*t] = c[(am + pm)^*t + g^*constant]\}$	1120.959	0.866	0.33859	32	788.854
$\{p[(subadults=)^*t) = c[(subadults=)^*t]\}$	1123.36	3.267	0.10193	34	787.077
$\{p(g^*t) = c(g^*t + g^*constant)\}$	1126.522	6.429	0.02097	48	760.763
$\{p(age^*t) = c(age^*t) + (age^*constant)\}$	1127.598	7.505	0.01225	26	807.939
$\{p(g^*t) = c(g^*t)\}$	1129.742	9.649	0.00419	44	772.46
⋮	⋮	⋮	⋮	⋮	⋮
$\{p(\cdot) = c(\cdot)\}$	1187.212	67.119	0	5	910.395

Source: From Coulombe (unpublished data in Otis et al. 1978).

Note: Model descriptions are for initial capture (*p*) and recapture (*c*) probabilities. Codes used in naming models: "sa=" means sexes equal in subadults but adults differ by sex (resulting in three sex × age classes); "g" means four sex × age classes; "am + pm" means an additive effect between morning and evening capture occasions; "constant" is an additional effect on initial capture probability to produce the recapture probability. All models include estimates of population size (*N*) for four groups.

smaller AIC_c values, suggesting that the effect of day-to-day variation was different across the four groups. The results for this model are shown for subadults (both sexes combined) in Figure 3.7. Reducing the number of parameters improved the precision of the estimates of $\hat{N}$ for subadults.

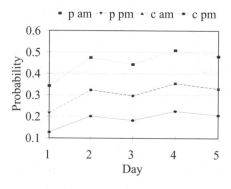

Figure 3.7
Estimates of capture (*p*) and recapture (*c*) probabilities of subadult house mice from a southern California salt marsh. The evening capture probabilities are nearly identical to the morning recapture probabilities, so the two lines fall on top of one another.

ESTIMATING SURVIVAL RATES FROM BAND
RECOVERY DATA: EXAMPLE

This example illustrates the use of environmental covariates in models to increase the precision of estimates of survival rates of sage grouse (*Centrocercus urophasianus*). The Colorado Division of Wildlife (CDOW) began a long-term banding study of the sage grouse population in North Park in 1973. Through 1987, CDOW personnel placed unique bands on 5317 sage grouse as part of this banding study. With few exceptions throughout the length of the study, dates of banding were from the first week in March through the third week in May. Most band recoveries came from birds that hunters had shot and reported; some recoveries came from reports of banded birds found dead.

Zablan (1993) constructed band recovery matrices for each age and sex class using only recoveries of dead birds, for each age and sex class, number banded, and band recoveries by hunting season. These recovery matrices were used in Program MARK (White and Burnham 1999) to test for differences in survival and reporting rates due to age and sex and to calculate estimates of annual recovery and survival rates by sex and age class. Here we use just the results from males to illustrate the estimation of survival rates with covariates included in the model.

Program MARK is a numerical maximum-likelihood program developed to estimate parameters for band recovery data using procedures analogous to those described by Lebreton et al. (1992) for Cormack-Jolly-Seber models. The Brownie et al. (1985) models were reparameterized to separate effects of survival from recovery by replacing the recovery rate, f_i, of their models by $(1 - S_i)r_i$, with r_i the reporting rate or the probability of a band being reported, given that the bird has died. Thus survival and reporting rates were modeled independently. Following the model notation of Lebreton et al. (1992), we developed models incorporating age (*a*), time (*t*), and trend (*T*) effects for both survival (*S*) and reporting (*r*) rates. Examples illustrating the model notation are $\{S(a)r(a)\}$ where both survival and reporting rates are only a function of age, $\{S(t)r(t)\}$ where survival and reporting rates are only a function of time (in this case years), and $\{S(a^*t)r(a^*t)\}$ where survival and reporting rates are a function of both age and time. Models additive on the logit scale were also considered, such as $\{S(a + T)r(a + T)\}$, giving parallel variation for each age group for survival and reporting rates on the logit scale. Numerical maximum-likelihood procedures were used to evaluate whether measured weather variables had any effect on annual survival of male sage grouse. Annual spring and winter precipitation and temperature were incorporated as covariates in a logistic model to estimate survival as

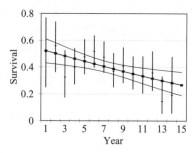

Figure 3.8. Estimated survival of sage grouse for the models $\{S(a^*t)r(a^*T)\}$ (vertical bars are 95% confidence intervals; the horizontal line indicates the estimate) and $\{S(a^*T)r(a^*T)\}$ (the thick solid line connects estimates; thin lines indicate 95% confidence intervals).

$$S_t = \frac{\exp(\beta_0 + \beta_1 W_t)}{1 + \exp(\beta_0 + \beta_1 W_t)}$$

where W_t is the appropriate weather variable for a particular year t and β_0 and β_1 are unknown parameters estimated by numerical maximum likelihood to predict annual survival S_i. The models being tested ranged from a two-parameter model, $\{S(\cdot)r(\cdot)\}$, which includes one reporting rate and one survival rate for both age classes over all years (with $\beta_1 = 0$), to $\{S(a^*w)r(a^*t)\}$, which allows 34 parameters—including year-specific reporting rates for subadults and adults and weather-related (year-specific, that is, $\beta_1 \neq 0$) survival rates for subadults and adults.

The maximum-likelihood methods used in Program MARK generate the log-likelihood function value, degrees of freedom (df), and AIC (Sakamoto et al. 1986; Burnham and Anderson 1992, 1998) for each model tested. The smaller the AIC value, the more appropriate that model is for the observed data. The results (Table 3.2) suggest that none of the four weather covariates provides a good explanation of the variation in survival because all have larger AIC values than the more parsimonious models. The lowest AIC model, $\{S(a^*T)r(a^*T)\}$ in Table 3.2, suggests a decline in survival through time (Figure 3.8). An analysis-of-deviance test constructed from models $\{S(a^*t)r(a^*T)\}$, $\{S(a^*T)r(a^*T)\}$, and $\{S(a)r(a^*T)\}$ indicates that the model with a negative trend in survival also explains a significant proportion of the variation of survival through time ($F_{2, 26} = 17.26$; $P < 0.001$).

LESSONS

I have presented examples of fitting complex models to data—that is, bringing models to bear on data in a formalized manner. Model parame-

Table 3.2. Analysis of North Park Male Grouse Band Recovery Data Incorporating Weather Variables.

Model	AIC_c	Delta AIC_c	Akaike weights	No. of parameters	Deviance
$\{S(a^*T)r(a^*T)\}$	4405.051	0	0.40175	8	127.752
$\{S(a + T)r(a^*T)\}$	4407.923	2.872	0.09557	7	132.633
$\{S(T)r(a^*T)\}$	4411.969	6.918	0.01264	6	138.686
$\{S(a + T)r(a + T)\}$	4413.549	8.498	0.00574	6	140.267
$\{S(a^*T)r(a + T)\}$	4415.029	9.978	0.00274	7	139.739
$\{S(T)r(T)\}$	4415.422	10.371	0.00225	4	146.152
$\{S(a + T)r(T)\}$	4416.998	11.947	0.00102	5	145.723
$\{S(a + T)r(T)\}$	4416.998	11.947	0.00102	5	145.723
$\{S(a^*T)r(T)\}$	4418.977	13.926	0.00038	6	145.695
$\{S(a^*T)r(a)\}$	4429.233	24.182	0	6	155.951
$\{S(a)r(a)\}$	4430.725	25.674	0	4	161.455
$\{S(a + st)r(a)\}$	4431.624	26.573	0	5	160.349
$\{S(a + sp)r(a)\}$	4431.655	26.604	0	5	160.38
$\{S(a + wp)r(a)\}$	4431.672	26.621	0	5	160.397
$\{S(a + wt)r(a)\}$	4432.684	27.633	0	5	161.409
$\{S(wp)r(a)\}$	4436.079	31.028	0	4	166.809
$\{S(st)r(a)\}$	4436.384	31.333	0	4	167.114
$\{S(sp)r(a)\}$	4436.632	31.581	0	4	167.362
$\{S(wt)r(a)\}$	4437.446	32.395	0	4	168.176
$\{S(a + t)r(a + t)\}$	4441.578	36.527	0	31	117.767
$\{S(t)r(t)\}$	4447.707	42.656	0	29	127.964
$\{S(a^*t)r(a^*t)\}$	4467.033	61.982	0	58	87.855

Note: Results of fitting models incorporating age (a), winter and spring temperature (wt, st), winter and spring precipitation (wp, sp), time (t), trend (T), and constant ($\cdot$) to band recovery data from male adult and subadult sage grouse banded in North Park, Colorado. To conserve space, some of the models' fit to the data are not reported.

ters were estimated by a rigorous statistical method: maximum likelihood. Selection between competing models has been demonstrated as well, with both traditional hypothesis testing methods and newer information-theoretical approaches. These examples demonstrate that:

- Statistical methods can be used to estimate parameters and select the best models from a list of candidates.
- These same methods allow an evaluation of hypotheses suggested by the model.
- Modern personal computers have the power and capacity to estimate parameters for realistic models and large data sets.
- Software exists for personal computers to fit models to data and provide parameter estimates.

Ecologists should more frequently fit their theoretical models to data and evaluate the model's appropriateness to the data in a rigorous, statistical manner. The gap between theory and data need not be as wide as in the past.

References

Aber, J. D. 1997. Why don't we believe the models? *Bulletin of the Ecological Society of America* 78:232–233.

Akaike, H. 1973. Information theory and an extension of the maximum likelihood principle. Pages 267–281 in B. Petrov and F. Czakil, eds., *Proceedings 2nd International Symposium on Information Theory*. Budapest: Akademiai Kiado.

Brisbin, I. L., Jr., G. C. White, and P. B. Bush. 1986a. PCB intake and the growth of waterfowl: Multivariate analyses based on a reparameterized Richards sigmoid model. *Growth* 50:1–11.

Brisbin, I. L., Jr., G. C. White, P. B. Bush, and L. A. Mayack. 1986b. Sigmoid growth analyses of wood ducks: The effects of sex, dietary protein, and cadmium on parameters of the Richards model. *Growth* 50:41–50.

Brownie, C., D. R. Anderson, K. P. Burnham, and D. S. Robson. 1985. *Statistical Inference from Band Recovery Data: A Handbook*. 2nd ed. Resource Publication 156. Washington, D.C.: U. S. Fish and Wildlife Service.

Bulmer, M. 1994. *Theoretical Evolutionary Ecology*. Sunderland, Mass.: Sinauer.

Burnham, K. P., and D. R. Anderson. 1992. Data-based selection of an appropriate biological model: The key to modern data analysis. Pages 16–30 in D. R. McCullough and R. H. Barrett, eds., *Wildlife 2001: Populations*. New York: Elsevier Applied Science.

———. 1998. *Model Selection and Inference: A Practical Information-Theoretic Approach*. New York: Springer-Verlag.

Chao, A. 1988. Estimating animal abundance with capture frequency data. *Journal of Wildlife Management* 52:295–300.

———. 1989. Estimating population size for sparse data in capture–recapture experiments. *Biometrics* 45:427–438.

Chao, A., S.-M. Lee, and S.-L. Jeng. 1992. Estimating population size for capture–recapture data when capture probabilities vary by time and individual animal. *Biometrics* 48:201–216.

Dennis, B. 1996. Discussion: Should ecologists become Bayesians? *Ecological Applications* 6:1095–1103.

Edwards, A. W. F. 1972. *Likelihood: An Account of the Statistical Concept of Likelihood and Its Application to Scientific Inference*. Cambridge: Cambridge University Press.

Edwards, D. 1996. Comment: The first data analysis should be journalistic. *Ecological Applications* 6:1090–1094.

Ellison, A. M. 1996. An introduction to Bayesian inference for ecological research and environmental decision-making. *Ecological Applications* 6:1036–1046.

Fisher, R. A. 1922. On the mathematical foundation of theoretical statistics. *Philo-*

sophical Transactions of the Royal Society of London, Series A: Mathematical and Physical Sciences 222:309–368.

———. 1925. Theory of statistical estimation. *Proceedings of the Cambridge Philosophical Society* 22:700–725.

Gause, G. F. 1964. *The Struggle for Existence.* New York: Hafner. Originally published in 1934.

Hilborn, R., and M. Mangel. 1997. *The Ecological Detective: Confronting Models with Data.* Princeton: Princeton University Press.

Hilborn, R., and C. J. Walters. 1992. *Quantitative Fisheries Stock Assessment—Choice, Dynamics, and Uncertainty.* New York: Chapman & Hall.

Johnson, D. H. 1999. The insignificance of statistical significance testing. *Journal of Wildlife Management* 63:763–772.

Lack, D. L. 1954. *The Natural Regulation of Animal Numbers.* Oxford: Clarendon Press.

Lebreton, J.-D., K. P. Burnham, J. Clobert, and D. R. Anderson. 1992. Modeling survival and testing biological hypotheses using marked animals: A unified approach with case studies. *Ecological Monographs* 62:67–118.

Ludwig, D. 1996. Uncertainty and the assessment of extinction probabilities. *Ecological Applications* 6:1067–1076.

Malakoff, D. 1999. Bayes offers a "new way" to make sense of numbers. *Science* 286:1460–1464.

Otis, D. L., K. P. Burnham, G. C. White, and D. R. Anderson. 1978. Statistical inference from capture data on closed animal populations. *Wildlife Monograph* 62:1–135.

Pascual, M. A., and P. Kareiva. 1996. Predicting the outcome of competition using experimental data: Maximum likelihood and Bayesian approaches. *Ecology* 77:337–349.

Pascual, M. A., P. Kareiva, and R. Hilborn. 1997. The influence of model structure on conclusions about the viability and harvesting of Serengeti wildebeest. *Conservation Biology* 11:966–976.

Pollock, K. H., and M. C. Otto. 1983. Robust estimation of population size in closed animal populations from capture–recapture experiments. *Biometrics* 39:1035–1049.

Richards, F. J. 1959. A flexible growth function for empirical use. *Journal of Experimental Botany* 10:290–300.

Ricker, W. E. 1954. Stock and recruitment. *Journal Fisheries Research Board of Canada* 11:624–651.

———. 1975. *Computation and Interpretation of Biological Statistics of Fish Populations.* Bulletin 191. Ottawa: Fisheries Research Board of Canada.

Sakamoto, Y., M. Ishiguro, and G. Kitagawa. 1986. *Akaike Information Criterion Statistics.* Tokyo: KTK Scientific Publishers.

Shenk, T. M. 1997. Detecting density dependence in natural populations. Ph.D. dissertation, Colorado State University, Fort Collins.

Shibata, R. 1989. Statistical aspects of model selection. Pages 215–240 in J. C. Williams, ed., *From Data to Model.* New York: Springer-Verlag.

Taylor, B. L., P. R. Wade, R. A Stehn, and J. F. Cochrane. 1996. A Bayesian approach to classification criteria for spectacled eiders. *Ecological Applications* 6:1077–1089.

ver Hoef, J. M. 1996. Parametric empirical Bayes methods for ecological applications. *Ecological Applications* 6:1047–1055.

White, G. C., and I. L. Brisbin Jr. 1980. Estimation and comparison of parameters in stochastic growth models for barn owls. *Growth* 44:97–111.

White, G. C., and K. P. Burnham. 1999. Program MARK: Survival estimation from populations of marked animals. *Bird Study* 46 (suppl.):120–138.

White, G. C., D. R. Anderson, K. P. Burnham, and D. L. Otis. 1982. *Capture–Recapture and Removal Methods for Sampling Closed Populations.* LA-8787-NERP. Los Alamos, N.M.: Los Alamos National Laboratory.

White, G. C., T. E. Hakonson, and K. V. Bostick. 1983. Fitting a model of tritium uptake by honey bees to data. *Ecological Modelling* 18:241–251.

Wolfson, L. J., J. B. Kadane, and M. J. Small. 1996. Bayesian environmental policy decisions: Two case studies. *Ecological Applications* 6:1056–1066.

Zablan, M. A. 1993. Evaluation of sage grouse banding program in North Park, Colorado. M.S. thesis, Colorado State University, Fort Collins.

Chapter 4

Theoretical and Statistical Models in Natural Resource Management and Research

Marc Mangel, Øyvind Fiksen, and Jarl Giske

The world is filled with uncertainty. Processes inherently fluctuate. Indeed, the observation system between us and the natural world contains so many sources of uncertainty that even if the processes are certain, the observations are usually uncertain. If we understand theory to be going beyond the data (Peters 1991; Rigler and Peters 1995), then any model—whatever its construction or underlying structure—is a form of ecological theory. Nevertheless, it is possible to classify models broadly as statistical, theoretical, or logical.

Statistical models arise in the analysis of data (regression, ANOVA, nonparametric tests, and the like). They are post hoc models (done after the data are collected) and allow the analysis of data. *Theoretical models* posit mechanisms and thus lead to predictions even before data are collected. There are two main reasons for exploring theoretical rather than statistical models: because we wish to understand nature or because the environment is so variable that statistical relationships will not hold. When mechanistic models lead to predictions that disagree with the data, we must rethink the logic of the model or question the data's quality or validity. Statistical relationships are valuable in situations with low variability—that is, when the model may be expected to work in situations and populations different from the situation of measurement. The way temperature affects growth rate, for instance, may be studied in a laboratory and applied to temperatures in other laboratories and in the field. Statistical models must be treated with caution, however, as soon as the relationship may be influenced by individual behavior. This is particularly true for estimates of natural growth, reproduction, and mortality rates, which are heavily influenced by the activity level and habitat selection of the individuals (Aksnes 1996). To model such phenomena in natural environments, we need theoretical considerations.

Logical models are mathematics motivated by the natural world. An example of the distinction between a logical and a theoretical model is the Euler-Lotka model. According to this model, if a population consists of identical individuals for whom fecundity and survival are deterministic variables of age, then the population will grow by a constant rate and reach a stable age distribution. This was first proved via mathematical arguments by Lotka (1925). As a logical statement it is not open to experimental verification, and it holds true within the realms of mathematics. Biologists, however, may investigate whether this model is a good approximation for real populations. For biologists, therefore, the Euler–Lotka model is a theory for population dynamics. Since it does not fit well with observations, an alternative theory for population dynamics has been developed that includes variable environments, individual variability, and stochasticity (Tuljapurkar 1990; Tuljapurkar and Caswell 1997).

Ludwig (1995) has proposed that natural resource management involves at least two paradoxes connected to uncertainties in nature and models:

- Management for sustained yield cannot be optimal.
- Effective management models cannot be realistic.

The source of these paradoxes is "statistical issues and the relationship between models and data" (p. 516). The implication of these paradoxes, particularly the second, is that "statistical considerations generally invalidate any but the simplest aggregated models as management tools" (p. 516). In this chapter we investigate some of the conceptual issues that underlie the paradoxes proposed by Ludwig. Our goal is to lead the reader to a deeper appreciation of the care that must be taken when connecting models and data.

Theoretical Models, Prediction, and Parameter Estimation

When using theoretical models, we posit mechanisms that connect the independent and dependent ecological variables. Among theoretical models it is fruitful to treat "why" (ultimate/functional) questions and "how" (proximate/mechanistic) questions separately. Models dealing with ultimate questions address the causes of a phenomenon—which for biology means that these models should be founded in the theory of evolution by natural or artificial selection. Models dealing with proximate questions address how a mechanism operates and resolve the process to a desired level. In estimating mortality, for example, we could construct mechanistic models of the environmental factors that influence mortality risk (visibility, smell, sound, density dependencies). Alternatively, we could construct theoretical models of how Individuals are predicted to act in response to a mortality risk (find the tradeoff between predation risk and feeding rate, for example, as in Werner and Gilliam 1984). By combining these models we can calculate the mortality rate.

Two points, however, are generally unappreciated: a theoretical model is almost guaranteed to be wrong, and there can be many theoretical models of the same phenomenon. For example, the long-standing discussion about "testing the optimality assumption" in behavioral ecology (Gray 1987; Pierce and Ollason 1987; Parker and Maynard-Smith 1990; Brandon and Rausher 1995; Orzack and Sober 1994, 1996) by comparing the predictions of a single theoretical model with data misses the point that there are many optimality models (Hilborn and Mangel 1997; Clark and Mangel 2000). Science progresses by the confrontation of different models with data. The models that are simultaneously the most explanatory (help us understand the data) and predictive (tell us how to find new data by predicting outcomes of new experiments or observations) are the winners and represent our best understanding of the natural world. Theoretical models replace the data of a statistical model by mechanisms, and the best predictions are about new kinds of informative data. We use theoretical models to understand systems and predict their properties.

Data and statistical parameter estimation are components of theoretical models. Ludwig points out, for example, that in order to estimate parameters in a relationship between spawning stock (parents) and recruitment (offspring), we need variation in the spawning stock (see also Myers et al. 1995). Thus it is generally true in fisheries management that the stock cannot be maintained at a single "optimal" level if we need to learn about parameters (Ludwig's Paradox 1). Similarly, instream flow models, which are used to predict habitat preferences of fish, are a case of a deterministic model that is probably better treated as one in which it is necessary to learn about parameters (Ghanem et al. 1995). Modern statistical methods, particularly those based on likelihood and Bayesian approaches, are well suited for estimating the parameters in theoretical models (Hilborn and Mangel 1997).

Theoretical models are intended to be general—that is the point of focusing on mechanisms. The parameters at a particular site may change, but we assume that the mechanisms do not. Thus theoretical models are intellectually transportable. A theoretical model can fail in the obvious way if it makes predictions that are completely at odds with the data. But a theoretical model may fail in a more insidious way: if a model leads to "exactly what we expected," without further understanding or prediction, then it has failed. After all, if the results were expected and there are no new predictions, then we understood the scientific question before constructing the model and the model is therefore superfluous. This is why we model: a model of vertical migration that yields an ordinary pattern of diel vertical migration as output has value if the model's structure explains the forces that are needed to get this result. A good model should explain phenomena at a level previously not understood and should suggest experiments or observations that have not yet been conducted. If we are particularly lucky, then after the model has been developed and analyzed it may be possible to understand the biological situation without recourse to the model (Clark and Mangel 2000, especially chapter 4).

Theoretical models need not be simple. Indeed, the development of high-speed and powerful desktop computing has allowed the construction of individual-based models (Romey 1996; Chapter 12 in this volume) and spatially explicit models (Mason and Brandt 1996) of enormous complexity. They are still theoretical models, however, positing mechanisms to make predictions.

A theoretical model must be able to explain the mechanism and processes of the problem at hand, and its structure and detail must have a biological (or physical) interpretation and be measurable (at least in principle). Formulating a theoretical model—specifying the mechanism, constraints, and parameters—is an exercise by itself, and a fit to data is not the only criterion by which the model is evaluated. Although we can investigate the internal consistency and predictions from a theoretical model, a theory can be tested for relevance to natural phenomena only through normal scientific progression—that is, by formulating alternative hypotheses, outlining critical experiments (or searching for field observations to evaluate hypotheses), and then letting the data adjudicate the hypotheses (Platt 1964; Mangel and Clark 1988; Hilborn and Mangel 1997). We should not evaluate theoretical models solely on how well they fit the data: there are other grounds as well, such as elegance, internal logic, and explanatory power. If a consistent theory does not compare favorably with all the data, we should reconsider the data and the way they were acquired before rejecting the theory. This is especially relevant when no alternative theory is available or when the alternative theory is not consistent or simple or supported by other sources. Natural resource ecology and management is a complex matter. No matter how expanded our model, we cannot expect more than partial overlap between the model and field or laboratory data. This point is related to Ludwig's second paradox: when we need to estimate parameters, smaller (and simpler) management models often perform better than more complicated ones.

In a variant of the approach used here, Loehle (1983) divided the models along a continuum between the "application" model and the "calculation" model. An application model uses laws and theories to make predictions about a phenomenon; a calculation model can be as simple as a statistical regression without any notion of mechanism. Because they are more general and apply to a wider range of situations, application models are superior to calculation models.

In general, theoretical models provide a deeper level of understanding than statistical models. This is not always reflected in the quality of fit to data, however. If we are most interested in a close fit to the data, we should choose a statistical model because it allows us to modify all parts of the model to achieve this goal. As we start to adjust theoretical models, however, they lose their explanatory power and gradually become statistical models. The implication is that science should aim for theoretical models (Giske et al. 1992; Giske 1998)—while always making explicit the processes and parameters that weaken the level of understanding expressed through the model. This is an important part of the modeling process: to clarify what is known and what needs further elaboration. Since theoretical models should be formulated in biologically meaningful terms, they indicate what needs to be measured in order to settle parameter values. Once these values are defined and measured, the modeler is no longer free to change them.

STATISTICAL MODELS AND EFFECTS

Statistical models are typically without a mechanism, although they posit relationships between variables. Imagine a set of data $\{X(i), Y(i); i = 1, \ldots , n\}$, where $X(i)$ are the presumed independent variables and $Y(i)$ are the presumed dependent variables. The statistical model answers the question "Does Y change as X changes?" (or some variant of this); this is what most ecologists do. Even with statistical models, this question can be answered in a number of different ways. That is, there are many statistical models for a phenomenon. In null hypothesis testing, for example, we begin by hypothesizing that there is no relationship between X and Y (the null hypothesis) and then use the data to determine the probability of observing data given the assumption of no relationship. If this probability is small enough, we say the hypothesis of no relationship has been "rejected" (see also Gotelli and Graves 1996). Note that this does not actually deliver the goods. What we would ideally like to know is the probability that a hypothesis (say, that X increases as Y increases) is true given the data. What we get is the probability of observing the data given that the null hypothesis (in this case of no relationship) is true (Cohen 1994; Royall 1997).

Nonparametric statistical methods deal with the data only. Parametric statistical methods posit a statistical relationship such as

$$Y(i) = \beta_0 + \beta_1 X(i) + Z(i) \qquad [4.1]$$

where β_0 and β_1 are constants and $Z(i)$ represents the uncertainty in the system. Alternatively, we might posit a log-linear relationship in which the logarithms of the variables are linearly related. Equation (4.1) is generalized in a relatively straightforward manner when there is more than one kind of independent variable. Suppose that $X_1(i)$ and $X_2(i)$ are two different independent variables. The generalization is

$$Y(i) = \beta_0 + \beta_1 X_1(i) + \beta_2 X_2(i) + Z(i) \qquad [4.2]$$

This is called a model without interactions, because no combinations of X_1 and X_2 appear. There is only one model without interactions but an infinite number of models with interactions because the interaction can be characterized by any function of X_1 and X_2. Hence researchers typically concentrate on models without interactions (see also Hilborn and Mangel 1997). Bradford et al. (1997), for example, used a combination of statistical models to develop predictions about the relationship between abundance of coho salmon (*Oncorhynchus kisutch*) smolts and stream characteristics such as length, gradient, valley slope, latitude, and minimum and maximum flows.

Statistical models are driven by data. For this reason they are specific to the location and the system studied. Their details are not intellectually transportable, although the general approach may be. Indeed, Roughgarden et al. (1994) argue that we should view ecology more as an earth science (in which every setting is unique and controlled as much by geological transport processes as by biological species interactions) than as a molecular biological science (in which every experiment is reproducible anywhere). But care must be taken. Kozel and Hubert (1989), for example, identified the physical and biological factors that appeared to control the density of brook trout (*Salvelinus fontinalis*) in drainages in Wyoming. They found a suite of 18 variables that were significantly ($p < 0.05$) correlated with brook trout standing stock and developed individual regression equations for each of them. They also discovered 25 significant correlations between the variables, but they provided little theoretical underpinning for the statistical relationships. Fine so far; this is a statistical model. Now consider their last sentence: "The relationships presented by us can be used as standards for comparison when assessing abundance of brook trout in streams altered by human activity or when determining mitigation objectives for such streams." By advocating not the approach but the relationships, they changed a statistical model into a theoretical model with little evidence that this change is valid.

AVOIDING THE PITFALLS

There are a number of ways to avoid getting trapped by Ludwig's paradoxes, which remind us of the care that must be taken when connecting models and data.

Avoid Too Many Uncertain Parameters

Ludwig (1995) points out the dangers of overfitting data and notes: "Having the correct model is not enough: the associated parameters must be well determined" (p. 521). Picking the right size for a model is a developing art (Hilborn and Mangel 1997). This applies to statistical models (Hakanson 1995) and to theoretical models for which parameters must be estimated. If the physical or biological parameters are not known or are measured with great uncertainty, it is even more important to keep the number of parameters low. With well-defined and independently measured parameters, this is less critical.

There is always a tradeoff between simplicity and the level of mechanistic description. This is what leads to Ludwig's second paradox. In general, simple models are attractive because of their tractability and transparency and should not be abandoned too quickly due to dissimilarities with empirical studies (although our unease with the model may increase). A mechanistic model of the functional response in fish was developed by Aksnes and Utne (1997), for example, and the derivation clarifies the importance of the optical properties of water in understanding the distribution and dynamics of fish and zooplankton. In this case, the level of elaboration was justified by the influence of the model's details on the predictions—conforming to the rule that we should keep models simple unless there are good reasons to do otherwise.

This argument can also be applied in the discussion of whether a model should be formalized computationally or analytically. With analytical models, we are more likely to be able to control and verify the results directly from the derivation, whereas numerical models may carry flaws in the computer realization that are not easily detected. Analytical models are often more elegant and parsimonious in the sense that they may be resolvable without aid of computers (at least in principle). This is also the limitation of the analytical approach, however, because the simplifications are made at the expense of realism. Numerical models allow much more biological detail and realism and permit investigations of many questions that cannot be asked analytically. General principles can be drawn from numerical modeling through the performance of "computer experiments" and sensitivity analyses (Mangel and Clark 1988; Hilborn and Mangel 1997; Clark and Mangel 2000).

Always Try to Compare Multiple Models with Data

Chamberlin (1897) argued that we should always have multiple working hypotheses. As we have seen, theoretical models almost immediately lead to multiple models as different mechanistic formulations are envisioned. Statistical models can do the same, if we posit different relationships, but without a mechanism. Myers et al. (1995), for example, confronted four different models of recruitment and two different models of uncertainty with more than 250 sets of stock–recruitment data. This method allowed them to determine the most appropriate description of the functional relationship between recruits and spawners and the most appropriate conceptualization of the variability in recruitment.

Gan and McMahon (1990) showed that the Physical Habitat Simulation System (PHABSIM) used for instream flow analysis actually consists of a large number of different logical and statistical models (based on which subprogram is used), assumptions about how velocity, depth, and substrate are related to weighted usable area (WUA), type of velocity profile, type of velocity equation, and bed material. Using a single set of hydraulic data and preference curves, they investigated 23 combinations of variables and discovered (Figure 4.1) a nearly tenfold range in predictions of WUA for fry and juvenile brown trout (*Salmo trutta*). They noted (p. 233) that the "results are shown to vary greatly according to the particular combination of options selected, so unless calculations are founded on biologically realistic assumptions, the potential within PHABSIM for the 'fudging' of results is considerable." Thus it is essential to have agreement on biological assumptions before computations are done (Mangel et al. 1996). It is even more important, however, to evaluate the models by confrontation with data (Hilborn and Mangel 1997).

The same is possible for statistical models. Rahel et al. (1996), for example, used a statistical model to predict habitat loss and population fragmentation in the North Platte River drainage by constructing statistical relationships between geographic area lost based on air temperature, stream

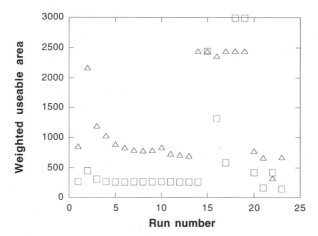

Figure 4.1. Gan and McMahon (1990) investigated different predictions of weighted usable area (WUA), computed from PHABSIM, for brown trout (*Salmo trutta*) fry (squares) and juveniles (triangles). Different assumptions in the underlying logical model are used in different runs of the program. Note that the WUA for fry may differ by a factor of 10 and for juveniles by a factor of nearly 8.

distance lost based on air temperature, and stream distance lost based on water temperature. They noted that the three approaches gave different predictions of the amount of habitat loss due to climate warming and then used theoretical methods to sort out some of the variation in the predictions of the statistical model. Lek et al. (1996) conducted a similar study, using statistical models involving up to eight variables, to relate environmental parameters and trout abundance.

Always Be Thinking of Alternative Models

Logical models are tested with mathematics. Theoretical models are tested by experimentation and observation. The models we use in management and ecology are often complex. For these, it is better to test each of the major assumptions rather than try to test the predictions of the models. This has to do with the incomplete overlap between model and environment and the hopeless task of measuring the relevant environmental complexity in an instant. We should always recognize that the model may miss a key feature of the natural system—even one that drives the full behavior of the system.

An example of this research strategy is the study of eutrophication in the North Sea (Aksnes et al. 1995). Starting from the Holling equation describing the feeding rate in animals, Aksnes and Egge (1991) developed a mech-

anistic model for nutrient uptake in phytoplankton. Parameters were estimated for two groups of algae (diatoms and flagellates) such that the parameters (which have precise biological interpretations) were fixed from measurements (Aksnes et al. 1995). Simultaneously, many series of enclosure
experiments were conducted with a wide range of nutrients (Egge and
Aksnes 1992; Egge et al. 1994), and the time series of phytoplankton abundance was compared with predictions from the model. No tuning of the
parameters was allowed, since the intention was to develop a general tool
for the study of eutrophication. The model has now been incorporated into
a three-dimensional physical model of the North Sea and applied to investigate issues related to eutrophication and management (Aksnes et al. 1995;
Baliño 1996).

Similarly, from the predictions of a model of an experiment studying
migration and allocation patterns in *Daphnia magna,* Fiksen (1997) suggested
that the daphnids maximized rate of increase (r) rather than net reproductive
rate (R_0). In the model (and experiment), growth was a function of temperature, with 98 percent of the variance explained by temperature. Mortality
risk from fish was an encounter-based model with measurable parameters
such as image area, ambient light, and predator density. The model did not
match the data very well without the assumption of decreasing mortality
with increasing size, which would occur if there were invertebrate predators
present or if the daphnids live according to this potential threat. Thus with
well-defined environmental forcing and physiological response, the model
and the data could be used to investigate assumptions about the shape of the
predation risk and the optimality criterion. By further mechanistic modeling and corresponding fixation of parameters, the number of assumptions
was reduced and the model improved for applications.

In summary, then, instead of talking about models being false or true,
we should talk of good or bad models—evaluated by their explanatory
power and ability to predict observations. In practice, models that are considered good (often the simplest models) are not rejected even if observations do not confirm their validity (Lotka-Volterra models of population
dynamics, for example). Some models are retained even though there are
hardly any observations that fit the predictions (Fagerstrøm 1987). Finally,
models and theories tend to be used as long as there is no better theory to
apply (Lakatos 1978; Hilborn and Mangel 1997). For this reason we should
always be thinking about alternative models.

Don't Go Where the Data Aren't

Both theoretical and statistical models may enter intellectual quicksand
when applied to situations where there are no data. Consider, for example,

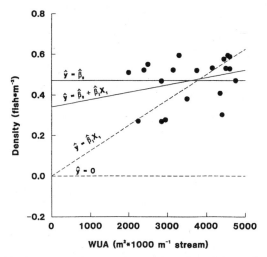

Figure 4.2. Forcing a regression equation to show the origin can be very dangerous if there are no data in that region. Doing so essentially converts a statistical model to a logical model, perhaps unintentionally. (Reproduced from Cade and Terrell 1997.)

a stock-recruitment relationship between parents in year t (S_t) and offspring in year $t + 1$ (R_t):

$$R_{t+1} = aS_t e^{-f(S_t)} \qquad\qquad [4.3]$$

The parameter a represents maximum per capita reproduction when population size is small; $f(S_t)$ captures the density dependence of reproduction. The form of density dependence has to be estimated. The trouble is that the parameter characterizing behavior at a small population size is usually influenced by observations far from the origin (and vice versa: Levins 1966). As a solution, Myers et al. (1997) propose that we should use only the six observations with the smallest spawner biomass. When a model has a strong theoretical basis, we should not feel obliged by the data to apply a simpler relationship. Rather, we should use the theory to suggest investigations that will find data in an area that is relevant for discrimination among the competing models.

Similar problems arise with statistical models. Cade and Terrell (1997), for example, point out that by forcing a regression through the origin by setting $\beta_0 = 0$ in Equation (4.1) or (4.2), we may generate an apparent relationship between fish density and weighted usable area even though there are no data to support this (Figure 4.2) (see Bourgeois et al. 1996; for examples in evolutionary ecology see Charnov 1993 or Mangel 1996).

Don't Confuse Statistical and Theoretical Models

The error of mixing statistical and theoretical models is called "the error of pseudo-explanation" in Loehle (1987); Dunham and Vinyard (1997) make a similar point. It is possible to conduct an excellent and elegant study using a statistical model but then to conclude wrongly that you have constructed a theoretical model. As we have seen, forcing the regression through the origin adds mechanism to a statistical model (see Cade and Terrell 1997 for ways to avoid this) and thus makes it an implicitly theoretical model. Often a good statistical model will identify relationships that then lead us to think about the mechanisms underlying them. Lanka et al. (1987), for example, found that geomorphic variables alone, used in a statistical (regression) model, predicted the standing stock of trout as accurately as stream habitat variables (see also Nelson et al. 1992). This presents a challenge to understand the mechanistic relationship underlying the statistical discovery.

To be sure, all kinds of models are needed for the solution of ecological problems. As theoretical models become larger and computationally more intensive, they require more parameters, and thus we end up with a hybrid between a theoretical and statistical model. Bartholow et al. (1993), for example, constructed such a model for spatially distinct cohorts of chinook salmon (*Oncorhynchus tshawytscha*). They used theoretical descriptions of life history characteristics and statistical descriptions of flow patterns of the Trinity River (see also Williamson et al. 1993). The fundamental notion here is that flow-dependent physical habitat and water temperature may either increase or limit the carrying capacity of streams. To operationalize this assumption requires careful use of theoretical and statistical models— and knowing which is which (see Gore et al. 1992; Harper et al. 1992; Kershner and Snider 1992). Baker and Coon (1997) used a theoretical model, based on optimal foraging theory, to evaluate habitat suitability criteria for brook trout (*Salvelinus fontinalis*).

To construct an effective model requires specification of mechanisms, processes, and parameters that may not be available. Models are tools to guide further inquiries in the laboratory, in the field, or in the literature (Gabriel 1993). They are not the truth, but they are "the lie that helps us see the truth" (Fagerstrøm 1987).

ACKNOWLEDGMENTS

The work of Marc Mangel was partially supported by Cooperative Agreement NA77FL0433 from the National Oceanic and Atmospheric Administration. The views expressed here are those of the authors, of course, and do not necessarily reflect the views of NOAA or any of its subagencies. The U.S. government is authorized to reproduce and distribute this chapter for governmental purposes. We thank Mike Healey, Don Orth, Carl Walters, and John Williams for conversations about the subject and comments on the chapter and thank two anonymous referees for comments.

REFERENCES

Aksnes, D. L. 1996. Natural mortality, fecundity, and development time in marine planktonic copepods: Implications of behaviour. *Marine Ecology Progress Series* 131:315–316.

Aksnes, D. L., and J. K. Egge. 1991. A theoretical model for nutrient uptake in phytoplankton. *Marine Ecology Progress Series* 70:65–72.

Aksnes, D. L., and J. Giske. 1993. A theoretical model of aquatic visual feeding. *Ecological Modelling* 67:233–250.

Aksnes, D. L., and A. C. W. Utne. 1997. A revised modeling of the visual range in fish. *Sarsia* 82:137–147.

Aksnes, D. L., K. B. Ulvestad, B. M. Baliño, J. Berntsen, J. K. Egge, and E. Svendsen. 1995. Ecological modelling of coastal waters: Towards predictive physical-chemical-biological simulation models. *Ophelia* 41:5–36.

Baker, E. A., and T. G. Coon. 1997. Development and evaluation of alternative habitat suitability criteria for brook trout. *Transactions of the American Fisheries Society* 126:65–76.

Baliño, B. M. 1996. Eutrophication of the North Sea, 1980–1990: An evaluation of anthropogenic nutrient inputs using a 2D phytoplankton model. Ph.D dissertation, University of Bergen.

Bartholow, J. M., J. L., Laake, C. B., Stalnaker, and S. Williamson. 1993. A salmonid population model with emphasis on habitat limitations. *Rivers* 4:265–279.

Bourgeois, G., R. A., Cunjak, D. Caissie, and N. El-Jabi. 1996. A spatial and temporal evaluation of PHABSIM in relation to measured density of juvenile Atlantic salmon in a small stream. *North American Journal of Fisheries Management* 16:154–166.

Bradford, M. J., G. C. Taylor, and J. A. Allan. 1997. Empirical review of coho salmon smolt abundance and the prediction of smolt production at the regional level. *Transactions of the American Fisheries Society* 126:49–64.

Brandon, R. N., and M. D. Rausher. 1995. Testing adaptationism: A comment on Orzack and Sober. *American Naturalist* 148:189–201.

Cade, B. S., and J. W. Terrell. 1997. Comment: Cautions on forcing regression equations through the origin. *North American Journal of Fisheries Management* 17: 225–227.

Chamberlin, T. C. 1897. The method of multiple working hypotheses. *Journal of Geology* 5:837–848.

Charnov, E. L. 1993. *Life History Invariants.* New York: Oxford University Press.

Clark, C. W., and M. Mangel. 2000. *Dynamic State Variable Models in Ecology: Methods and Applications.* New York: Oxford University Press.

Cohen, J. 1994. The earth is round ($p<0.05$). *American Psychologist* 49:997–1003.

Dunham, J. B., and G. L. Vinyard. 1997. Incorporating stream level variability into analyses of site level fish habitat relationships: some cautionary examples. *Transactions of the American Fisheries Society* 126:323–329.

Efron, B., and R. J. Tibshirani. 1993. *An Introduction to the Bootstrap.* New York: Chapman & Hall.

Egge, J. K., and D. L. Aksnes. 1992. Silicate as regulating nutrient in phytoplankton competition. *Marine Ecology Progress Series* 83:281–289.

Egge, J. K., Ø. Fiksen, D. L. Aksnes, T. Harboe, A. Jacobsen, and Ø. Rykkelid. 1994. Summary of data from enclosure experiments at Espegrend in 1986–1993. IFM-Rapport 36/1994. Bergen: University of Bergen.

Fagerstrøm, T. 1987. On theory, data, and mathematics in ecology. *Oikos* 50:258–261.

Feynman, R. P. 1965. *The Feynman Lectures on Physics.* San Francisco: Freeman.

Fiksen, Ø. 1997. Allocation patterns and diel vertical migration: Modeling the optimal *Daphnia. Ecology* 78:1446–1456.

Gabriel, W. 1993. Models on diel vertical migration. *Archiv für Hydrobiologie Beihefte Ergebnisse der Limnologie* 39:123–136.

Gan, K., and T. McMahon. 1990. Variability of results from the use of PHABSIM in estimating habitat area. *Regulated Rivers: Research and Management* 5:233–239.

Ghanem, A., P., Steffler, F. Hicks, and C. Katapodis. 1995. *Two-Dimensional Finite Element Modeling of Flow in Aquatic Habitats.* Water Resources Engineering Report 95-S1. Edmonton: Department of Civil Engineering, University of Alberta.

Giske, J. 1998. Evolutionary models for fisheries management. Pages 377–386 in T. Pitcher, D. Pauly, and P. J. B. Hart, ed., *Re-inventing Fisheries Management.* New York: Chapman & Hall.

Giske, J., H. R. Skjoldal, and D. L. Aksnes. 1992. A conceptual model of distribution of capelin in the Barents Sea. *Sarsia* 77:147–156.

Giske, J., D. L. Aksnes, B. Baliño, S. Kaartvedt, U. Lie, A. G. V. Salvanes, J. T. Nordeide, S. M. Wakili, and A. Aadnesen. 1990. Vertical distribution and trophic interactions of zooplankton and fish in Masfjorden, Norway. *Sarsia* 75:65–81.

Gore, J. A., J. B. Layzer, and I. A. Russell. 1992. Non-traditional applications of instream flow techniques for conserving habitat of biota in the Sabie River of Southern Africa. In P. J. Boon, P. Calow, and G. E. Petts, ed., *River Conservation and Management.* New York: Wiley.

Gotelli, N., and A. Graves. 1996. *Null Models.* Washington, D.C.: Smithsonian.

Gray, R. D. 1987. Faith and foraging: A critique of the paradigm argument from design. Pages 69–140 in A. C. Kamil, J. R. Krebs, and H. R. Pulliam, ed., *Foraging Behavior.* New York: Plenum Press.

Hairston, N. G. 1989. *Ecological Experiments: Purpose, Design, and Execution.* New York: Cambridge University Press.

Hakanson, L. 1995. Optimal size of predictive models. *Ecological Modelling* 78:195–204.

Harper, D. M., C. D., Smith, and P. J. Barham. 1992. Habitats as the building blocks for river conservation assessment. Pages 311–319 in P. J. Boon, P. Calow, and G. E. Petts, ed., *River Conservation and Management.* New York: Wiley.

Harvey, P. H., and M. D. Pagel. 1991. *The Comparative Method in Evolutionary Biology.* New York: Oxford University Press.

Hilborn, R., and M. Mangel. 1997. *The Ecological Detective: Confronting Models with Data*. Princeton: Princeton University Press.

Hosmer, D. W., and S. Lemeshow. 1989. *Applied Logistic Regression*. New York: Wiley Interscience.

Hubert, W. A., and S. J. Kozel. 1993. Quantitative relations of physical habitat features to channel slope and discharge in unaltered mountain streams. *Journal of Freshwater Ecology* 8:177–183.

Kershner, J. L., and W. M. Snider. 1992. Importance of a habitat-level classification system to design instream flow studies. Pages 179–193 in P. J. Boon, P. Calow, and G. E. Petts, ed., *River Conservation and Management*. New York: Wiley.

Kozel, S., and W. A. Hubert. 1989. Factors influencing the abundance of brook trout (*Salvelinus fontinalis*) in forested mountain streams. *Journal of Freshwater Ecology* 5: 113–121.

Krebs, J. R., and N. B. Davies. 1993. *Behavioral Ecology*. Sunderland, Mass.: Sinauer.

Lakatos, I. 1978. *The Methodology of Scientific Research Programmes*. New York: Cambridge University Press.

Lanka, R. P., W. A. Hubert, and T. A. Wesche. 1987. Relations of geomorphology to stream habitat and trout standing stock in small Rocky Mountain streams. *Transactions of the American Fisheries Society* 116:21–28.

Lek, S., A. Belaud, P. Baran, I. Dimopoulos, and M. Delacoste. 1996. Role of some environmental variables in trout abundance models using neural networks. *Aquatic Living Resources* 9:23–29.

Levins, R. 1966. The strategy of model building in population biology. *American Scientist* 54:421–431.

Loehle, C. 1983. Evaluation of theories and calculation tools in ecology. *Ecological Modelling* 19:239–247.

———. 1987. Errors of construction, evaluation, and inference: A classification of sources of error in ecological models. *Ecological Modelling* 36:297–314.

———. 1997. A hypothesis testing framework for evaluating ecosystem model performance. *Ecological Modelling* 97:153–165.

Lotka, A. J. 1925. *Elements of Physical Biology*. Baltimore: Williams & Wilkins.

Ludwig, D. 1995. Uncertainty and fisheries management. *Lecture Notes in Biomathematics* 100:516–528.

Mangel, M. 1996. Life history invariants, age at maturity, and the ferox trout. *Evolutionary Ecology* 10:249–263.

Mangel, M., and C. W. Clark. 1988. *Dynamic Modeling in Behavioral Ecology*. Princeton: Princeton University Press.

Mangel, M., et al. 1996. Principles for the conservation of wild living resources. *Ecological Applications* 6:338–362.

Mason, D. R., and S. B. Brandt. 1996. Effects of spatial scale and foraging efficiency on the predictions made by spatially-explicit models of fish growth rate potential. *Environmental Biology of Fishes* 45:283–298.

Myers, R. A., J. Bridson, and N. J. Barrowman. 1995. *Summary of Worldwide Spawner and Recruitment Data*. Canadian Technical Report of Fisheries and Aquatic Sciences 2020. St. John's, Newfoundland: Department of Fisheries and Oceans, Northwest Atlantic Fisheries Centre.

Myers, R., G. Mertz, and P. S. Fowlow. 1997. The maximum population growth rates and recovery times of Atlantic cod (*Gadus morhua*). *Fisheries Bulletin* 95:762–772.

Nelson, R. L., W. S. Platts, D. P. Larsen, and S. E. Jensen. 1992. Trout distribution and habitat in relation to geology and geomorphology in the North Fork Humboldt River drainage, northeastern Nevada. *Transactions of the American Fisheries Society* 121:405–426.

Orzack, S. H., and E. Sober. 1994. Optimality models and the test of adaptationism. *American Naturalist* 143:361–380.

——— 1996. How to formulate and test adaptationism. *American Naturalist* 148: 202–210.

Parker, G. A., and J. Maynard-Smith. 1990. Optimality theory in evolutionary biology. *Nature* 348:27–33.

Peters, R. H. 1991. *A Critique for Ecology*. New York: Cambridge University Press.

Pierce, G. J., and J. G. Ollason. 1987. Eight reasons why optimal foraging theory is a complete waste of time. *Oikos* 49:111–125.

Platt, J. R. 1964. Strong inference. *Science* 146:347–353.

Rahel, F. J., C. J. Keleher, and J. L. Anderson. 1996. Potential habitat loss and population fragmentation for cold water fish in the North Platte River drainage of the Rocky Mountains: Response to climate warming. *Limnology and Oceanography* 41: 1116–1123.

Rigler, F. H., and R. H. Peters. 1995. *Science and Limnology*. Oldendorf/Luhe, Germany: Ecology Institute.

Romey, W. L. 1996. Individual differences make a difference in the trajectories of simulated schools of fish. *Ecological Modelling* 92:65–77.

Rosland, R. 1997. Optimal responses to environmental and physiological constraints: Evaluations of a model for a planktivore. *Sarsia* 82:113–128.

Roughgarden, J., T. Pennington, and S. Alexander. 1994. Dynamics of the rocky intertidal zone with remarks on generalization in ecology. *Philosophical Transactions of the Royal Society of London* B343:79–85.

Royall, R. 1997. *Statistical Evidence: A Likelihood Paradigm*. New York: Chapman & Hall.

Tuljapurkar, S. D. 1990. *Population Dynamics in Variable Environments*. Lecture Notes in Biomathematics 85. New York: Springer-Verlag.

Tuljapurkar, S. D., and H. Caswell, ed. 1997. *Structured Population Models in Marine, Terrestrial, and Freshwater Systems*. New York: Chapman & Hall.

Werner, E. E., and J. F. Gilliam. 1984. The ontogenetic niche and species interactions in size-structured populations. *Annual Review of Ecology and Systematics* 15:393–425.

Williamson, S. C., J. M. Bartholow, and C. B. Stalnaker. 1993. Conceptual model for quantifying pre-smolt production from flow-dependent physical habitat and water temperature. *Regulated Rivers: Research and Management* 8:15–28.

PART II

Developing and Interpreting Models

CHAPTER 5

Statistical Model Selection: An Alternative to Null Hypothesis Testing

Alan B. Franklin, Tanya M. Shenk,
David R. Anderson, and Kenneth P. Burnham

Model selection is an alternative statistical approach to null hypothesis testing when we wish to evaluate the plausibility of competing hypotheses or models. The primary advantage of the model selection approach is that it allows simultaneous examination of multiple working hypotheses rather than just two (the null and the alternative), as in null hypothesis testing. Moreover, model selection eliminates the need for an uninformative null hypothesis of "no difference" (although it can still be included in this approach). Finally, the model selection approach allows multiple hypotheses to be ranked and quantitatively evaluated in terms of their plausibility in explaining an empirical set of data and, as well, estimates of precision can incorporate the uncertainty about which model best approximates the data.

This chapter presents an overview of model selection based on Kullback-Leibler information (Kullback and Leibler 1951) and likelihood-based inference to evaluate the evidence for alternative scientific hypotheses. The information presented here is not new. For details of the philosophies and mechanisms of model selection see Linkhart and Zucchini (1986), Miller (1990), and Burnham and Anderson (1998). What we present here is a primer on the model selection approach, an outline of the works just cited, and an example of how to apply the approach in analyzing empirical data.

THE DEVELOPMENT OF NULL HYPOTHESIS TESTING

Statistics is a language of science (Zimmerman 1995) that helps us in understanding the natural world. There are different branches of statistical language and diverse interpretations of these branches. For example, there are frequentist and Bayesian branches in statistics (Malakoff 1999; see also Chapter 3 in this volume), each with its own paradigms and philosophies. In general, frequentist statistics has dominated the field of applied statistics.

Null hypothesis testing has been important in the frequentist branch of statistics. Anyone who has taken a course in statistics has been exposed to null hypothesis testing. Indeed, this paradigm has dominated statistical thinking since its inception in the 1920s and 1930s (Royall 1997). Under the paradigm of null hypothesis testing, there are two main philosophies. The first philosophy, attributed to R. A. Fisher (1925), focuses on significance testing, where the degree to which evidence against a null hypothesis is measured in terms of a p-value. The second philosophy, developed under Neyman and Pearson (1933), focuses on the decision aspect of hypothesis testing—that is, whether to reject one of two hypotheses in favor of the other and to do so in terms of Type I and Type II error probabilities. The decision of which hypothesis to support is made according to whether a test statistic falls into a predefined critical region α (usually $\alpha = 0.05$). The result is a decision: "choose H_1" or "choose H_2" (Royall 1997: 63–64). Fisher's philosophy differs from Neyman-Pearson's in two fundamental ways. First, under Fisher's philosophy only the null hypothesis is considered and the alternative hypothesis (H_A) is simply something other than the null. In reality, only the null hypothesis is being tested because the null is the hypothesis of "no effect" (Royall 1997:63); thus one only tests the hypothesis of "no effect" against every other possibility. Second, Fisher's significance testing involves a p-value (Fisher 1958) that has been misused as a measure of evidence against the null hypothesis—for example, small p-values have been interpreted to mean the data provide evidence against the null hypothesis, whereas large p-values do not provide evidence against the null hypothesis. (See Graybill and Iyer 1994:32.) But p-values are an inappropriate metric for strength of evidence (see Royall 1997:8–13, 68–71). There is a key point here: even when the Neyman-Pearson and Fisher significance testing philosophies are combined (Schweder 1988), only two hypotheses can be examined simultaneously under the paradigm of null hypothesis testing. Although multiple tests can be conducted (H_0 versus H_{A1}, H_0 versus H_{A2}, H_0 versus H_{A3}, and so forth), there is no way to rank hypotheses quantitatively when there are more than two p-values.

In addition to his contribution to significance testing in statistics, Fisher also introduced maximum-likelihood estimation in the 1920s. The idea of likelihood differs from probability in statistics in a fundamental way (Edwards 1992) with respect to how hypotheses relate to the empirical data. A hypothesis begins as a concept that can be expressed verbally—such as "the density of cottonwood seedlings decreases as distance from the river's edge increases." This conceptual idea can then be translated into a statistical model. For example, the preceding verbal hypothesis can be formalized as a regression model,

$$Y = \beta_0 - \beta_1 X$$

where Y is the density of cottonwood seedlings measured on plots at varying distances from the river's edge and X is the distance of each plot from the river's edge. The parameters of this model are β_0 (the intercept) and β_1 (the slope). Standard null hypothesis testing would test each parameter of the model separately: H_0: $\beta_0 = 0$ versus H_A: $\beta_0 \neq 0$ for the intercept and H_0: $\beta_1 = 0$ versus H_A: $\beta_1 < 0$ for the slope (Ott 1993:499–500). The interpretation of the p-values resulting from these tests is that they are the probability of observing a sample outcome more contradictory to H_0 than the observed sample result (Ott 1993:231) if H_0 was true. In null hypothesis testing, statistical probability models are based on $P(X|\theta, \text{model})$—the probability of obtaining data X given the parameter θ from the hypothesized statistical model (after Edwards 1992:9). Neither the idea of testing each parameter of the model separately nor the logical interpretation of resulting probabilities is intuitively appealing. Likelihood, by contrast, is expressed as $\mathcal{L}(\underline{\theta}|X, \text{model})$—the likelihood of the model parameters, $\underline{\theta}$, given the data X and the specific statistical model. The interpretation of likelihoods is more logical because the hypothesis is evaluated given the data rather than the data being evaluated given the hypothesis. This interpretation is carried through the model selection paradigm.

Kullback-Leibler information (Kullback and Leibler 1951) is the fundamental basis for the model selection paradigm. Conceptually this quantity, denoted as $I(f, g)$, is the information lost when model g is used to approximate full reality (f). Clearly we would like to use a model that loses as little information as possible as a basis for formal statistical inference. But we have to know reality (f) in order to compute Kullback-Leibler information in real-world situations. Obviously, we never know reality in natural resource (or any other scientific) application. A breakthrough came in 1973 when Hirotugo Akaike derived an estimator of Kullback-Leibler information (Akaike 1973).

His estimator was based on a bias correction of the log-likelihood function at its maximum and is called AIC for Akaike's Information Criterion. Thus likelihood theory is central to model selection (estimation of Kullback-Leibler information), parameter estimation (such as maximum-likelihood estimates), and hypothesis testing (such as likelihood-ratio tests).

THE IDEA OF MULTIPLE WORKING HYPOTHESES

Thomas C. Chamberlin was a geologist and president of the American Association for the Advancement of Science at the end of the nineteenth century (Hilborn and Mangel 1997). In a seminal paper (Chamberlin 1890) that was largely overlooked until the 1960s, he argued that scientists tend to have certain hypotheses that they subjectively favor and tend to promote in their work. In adopting a favorite hypothesis, scientists tend to filter their view of the world in favor of this hypothesis and, when faced with contra-dictory data, tend to reject the contradictory data rather than challenge their favorite hypothesis. This phenomenon simply points out that scientists are human: when faced with an explanation that seems logical and satisfac-tory, it is only human to want to believe in it. To avoid this subjective bias, Chamberlin suggested that creative scientists should consider a number of viable alternative explanations in the form of scientific hypotheses (hence the phrase "multiple working hypotheses") and should even consider alter-natives that contradict their own beliefs if such candidates are feasible and realistic.

Platt (1964) argued that this idea of multiple hypotheses was both an explanation and a cure for many of the problems in science and indeed was at the heart of an approach to science he called *strong inference*. In strong inference, a number of alternative hypotheses are devised and then crucial experiments are set up such that many of these candidates can be excluded. Strong inference is not a requisite for doing science, but it is a requisite for rapid progress in science. In the study of natural resources and ecology, we are probably more guilty than most other branches of science in not fol-lowing the tenets of Chamberlin and Platt (Romesburg 1991). At this point, a reasonable question arises: How do we incorporate the idea of mul-tiple working hypotheses into ecological and natural resource sciences? This question was recently addressed by Hilborn and Mangel (1997) and by Burnham and Anderson (1998). Both proposed that model selection, rather than hypothesis testing, is the mechanistic key to the approach originally proposed by Chamberlin and extended by Platt. Chamberlin and Platt ini-tially proposed the philosophy and rationale for using multiple hypotheses. In this chapter we describe some of the tools outlined by Burnham and Anderson (1998) to provide a strength of evidence for multiple models representing a set of hypotheses. What we cannot supply here is the intuition, imagination, and knowledge needed to actually develop the candidate hypotheses. These hypotheses can come only from resource managers and researchers creatively merging information about their system with possible explanations of the phenomenon of interest. (See also Chapter 11 in this volume.)

THE MODEL SELECTION APPROACH

The model selection approach in statistics has a number of key components:

- Developing an a priori set of candidate models that represent candidate hypotheses
- Assessing goodness-of-fit of data to the assumptions of the underlying statistical model that forms the "backbone" of the models being considered (such as linear regression)
- Fitting the candidate models to the set of data using least squares or maximum likelihood
- Ranking the candidate models in terms of their estimated Kullback-Leibler information
- Examining the highest-ranking models for inference based on strength of evidence using statistical tools derived from Kullback-Leibler information
- Estimating the amount of variation in the data explained by the models selected for inference
- Making formal inferences from the best model in the set and, in some cases, making multimodel inferences

We will discuss each of these components in more detail with an example. Further details on multimodel inference can be found in Buckland et al. (1997) and Burnham and Anderson (1998).

A Unifying Example

To demonstrate the methodology and utility of the model selection approach, consider a fictitious example based on simulated data. Simulated data, where the generating model and its parameters are known, are useful when we want to examine how well different statistical methods perform. For our fictitious example, we generated 10 years of reproductive data from the brown owl on an isolated island in the South Pacific. (Neither the owl nor the place actually exists.) There are only 250 pairs of owls on this island, and the population size has varied little during the 10-year period. Each pair of owls occupies a distinct territory, and for each territory in each year the reproductive outcome is either 0, 1, 2, or 3 young fledged. The distribution of the 0s, 1s, 2s, and 3s, however, does not follow any categorical distribution (such as a Poisson distribution). For each year, the mean annual reproductive output (R) is based on the average across the territories where the sampling variances of R behave similar to a Poisson distribution in that they increase as the mean increases. Thus reproductive output within each year is nonnormally distributed, and the sampling variances of R are heterogeneous (not equal across years).

The people of the island where the owl occurs practice slash-and-burn agriculture—that is, they periodically cut small patches of forest and burn the plot to grow crops. A scientist has been working in the field on the brown owl for the past 10 years and has sampled the same 50 territories (out of the total 250 territories) each year. By sampling the same 50 territories each year, the field scientist has introduced a lack of independence in the estimates of R between years: the outcome on a territory in a given year may affect the outcome there in the following year. This lack of independence cannot be resolved in the design of the field study, however, because of logistic constraints. In examining the preliminary data, the field scientist has noticed that reproductive output has declined over time (Figure 5.1) and consults with other scientists about the potential causes for this decline.

One of the consulting scientists, a parasitologist, believes that an increase in a certain bloodsucking fly (the hippoboscid fly) that lives in the plumage of birds is the cause for the decline. He hypothesizes that the agricultural

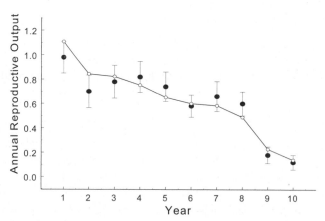

Figure 5.1. Estimates of annual reproductive output for the fictitious brown owl (solid dots) in relation to the known values (open dots connected by solid line) from which the estimates were drawn. Vertical bars are ± one standard error.

practices of the indigenous people have limited the number of cavity nests that the owl uses, thus exposing the young to increased parasite populations as the same nests are used repeatedly. The field scientist had routinely collected parasites while banding young and was able to develop an annual variable called PARA (the mean number of hippoboscid flies per young). A second scientist, a conservation biologist, believes that increasing smoke from the fires used in the slash-and-burn agriculture is negatively affecting survival of the young in the nest prior to fledging. To examine this idea, he developed a variable called FIRE (the acreage burned each year). The field scientist, however, believes that the cause is weather-related; she has noticed that field seasons have been wetter in the last few years she has conducted fieldwork. She hypothesizes that increased precipitation during the nesting season affects the ability of the nocturnal parents to hunt and provide food for the young. A third scientist, an ornithologist, does not think there is a single cause. Based on conversations with the field scientist and the parasitologist, he proposes that it is a combination of precipitation and parasites. Thus there is some disagreement about the cause of the decline in R for the brown owl. Each scientist, therefore, has developed a hypothesis based on the literature or experience working with the brown owl.

We know the answer to this problem because we simulated the data. In the generating model, mean annual reproductive output was perfectly correlated with precipitation during the breeding season and only slightly correlated with fire and parasites. Thus the generating model is one where reproductive output has a perfect negative linear relationship with precipitation during the breeding season. Expressed as a linear regression, the model used to generate our data is

$$E(R) = \beta_0 - \beta_1 \,(\text{PRECIP}) = 2.00 - 2.00 \,(\text{PRECIP})$$

(with no residual error), where 2.00 is the intercept (β_0) and 2.00 is also the slope on precipitation (β_1). In the real world, none of the scientists know this. In the following sections we outline the process of how the conflicting hypotheses of the scientists were examined in the case of the brown owl.

The Set of Candidate Models

Often wildlife studies involve the collection of data on numerous variables that are then exhaustively searched for patterns and "significant" relationships to some response variable (reproductive output, in our example). This type of analysis is sometimes called *data dredging* (Anderson and Burnham 1999a) and often results in spurious conclusions and selection of fitted models that have more variables than are supported by the data. A valid alternative is to develop a priori hypotheses before analyzing the data

(Burnham and Anderson 1998; Anderson and Burnham 1999a). These a priori hypotheses are based on biological and management considerations and represent plausible candidate models. In fact, they are the multiple working hypotheses that Chamberlin (1890) advocated over a century ago.

In our brown owl example, the ideas advocated by the different scientists were initially expressed as concepts that we then translated into statistical models in the form of linear regression models (Table 5. 1). Apart from their own ideas, the four scientists also agreed to include two additional models of reproductive output. Trend Model 1 represents the hypothesis that reproductive output is declining but not for the reasons suggested by

Table 5.1. Candidate Set of Models Developed to Explain Apparent Decline in Brown Owl Reproduction

Advocate	Concept	Statistical model
Field scientist	Increased precipitation during the nesting season (PRECIP) is negatively associated with annual reproductive output	$R = \beta_0 - \beta_1 \,(\text{PRECIP})$
Parasitologist	Increased parasite loads on young (PARA) are negatively associated with annual reproductive output	$R = \beta_0 - \beta_1 \,(\text{PARA})$
Conservation biologist	Increased acreage burned for farming (FIRE) is negatively associated with annual reproductive output	$R = \beta_0 - \beta_1 \,(\text{FIRE})$
Ornithologist	The combination of increased precipitation and increased parasite loads is negatively associated with annual reproductive output	$R = \beta_0 - \beta_1 \,(\text{PRECIP}) - \beta_2 \,(\text{PARA})$
Trend Model 1	There is a negative linear trend (T) in reproductive output over time but not due to the variables proposed	$R = \beta_0 - \beta_1 \,(\text{T})$
Trend Model 2	There is no trend over time in reproductive output	$R = \beta_0$

Note: The models are presented as the concepts of four scientists and translated into a priori statistical models concerning the causes for decline in annual reproductive output (R) in the fictitious brown owl over a 10-year period.

the four scientists. Trend Model 2 expresses the hypothesis that reproductive output is approximately constant over time. Considered together, the six models presented in Table 5.1 are based on biological and management considerations prior to conducting the analysis and represent different hypotheses about the decline in brown owls during the 10-year study period.

What would have happened if the scientists had decided to employ a data-dredging strategy rather than selecting a set of carefully considered, a priori candidate models? To explore this possibility, we subjected the simulated data to forward, backward, and stepwise regression procedures where each variable was examined for "significance" based on an arbitrary α level (in this case, $\alpha = 0.10$, the default set by the computer program). Although widely used, these procedures lack any theoretical justification (referred to as ad hoc). The resulting model from all three procedures included both precipitation during the breeding season (PRECIP) and parasite loads (PARA):

$$R = \beta_0 - \beta_1 \,(\text{PRECIP}) - \beta_2 \,(\text{PARA})$$

Although it includes one of the variables from the generating model, it contains more parameters than can be accounted for by the data. Thus the model selected by data dredging would lead us to believe that the hypothesis espoused by the ornithologist (see Table 5.1) is the most plausible when in fact it is not the model that was used to generate the sample data.

Goodness-of-Fit

All statistical models used to estimate parameters rely on some underlying distribution. (See Chapter 3 of this volume.) The typical use of linear regression, for example, whether based on likelihood or least-squares estimators, assumes that the residuals are independent, normally distributed, and have constant variance (Graybill and Iyer 1994). Goodness-of-fit testing examines whether the data being considered fit these underlying assumptions. Under the model selection approach, goodness-of-fit is examined with the model having the largest number of parameters. When assumptions underlying the statistical model are known to be violated, these violations must be accounted for. In the brown owl example, we simulated the data to violate two assumptions underlying the typical use of linear regression: independence of observations and homogeneity of variances. Lack of independence will not affect parameter estimates, but estimated standard errors will appear more precise than they should be if the lack of independence between years is not accounted for. One way we can account for these two violations is by using likelihood-based, mixed-effects models

(Littell et al. 1996)—models that include both fixed effects (precipitation, parasite loads, and so forth) and random effects (year, territory). With this type of analysis, the covariances between years (to account for lack of independence) and the proportionality of means with the sampling variances (to account for heterogeneity of variances) can be estimated and incorporated into the analysis. Thus what would be assumption violations in a simple analysis are eliminated by using an appropriate generalized analysis. The lack of normality cannot be dealt with in this manner. Instead we must rely on the robustness of regression and analysis of variance even to severe departures from normality, as is the case with the simulated count data for the brown owl (White and Bennetts 1996).

Model Selection Criteria

Once a set of candidate models is proposed, how do we select the one that best explains our data? We have seen that the ad hoc procedures do not work well. Ideally we want some measure that allows us to state that a certain model is preferred, and by how much, over other models to explain a set of data. There are two further desirable properties of such a model selection criterion: it should be objective (the investigator cannot change the outcome by adjusting subjective inputs to the analysis), and it should have a sound theoretical basis. Objectivity is a key component of this criterion because of the tenets of science. The stepwise model selection procedure we used previously with our simulated data, for example, would not qualify as an objective model selection procedure; a different model would be selected if we changed the α level from 0.10 to 0.20 or to 0.05. Anderson and Burnham (1999b) and Burnham and Anderson (1998) have reviewed a number of alternatives for model selection and conclude that Akaike's Information Criterion (AIC) (Akaike 1973) is an appropriate criterion. AIC is mathematically defined as

$$AIC = -2 \log_e \mathcal{L}(\text{parameters}\,|\,\text{data}) + 2(\text{number of parameters})$$

The first component of AIC represents how well the model fits the data. Recall the definition of the likelihood presented earlier in this chapter: $\mathcal{L}(\boldsymbol{\theta}\,|\,X,\,\text{model})$, the likelihood of the parameters given the data X and the model (hypothesis). Here the hypothesis is represented by the parameters in the statistical model that was translated from the conceptual ideas of the scientists. The likelihood expressed for the model suggested by the field scientist, for example, would be written simplistically as

$$\mathcal{L}\{\beta_0,\,\beta_1,\,\sigma^2\,|\,\text{data and model } R = \beta_0 - \beta_1\,(\text{PRECIP})\} \qquad [5.1]$$

which can be translated as the "likelihood of parameters β_0, β_1, and σ^2 given the data and model $R = \beta_0 - \beta_1$ (PRECIP)." The higher the value of the likelihood, the better the model's fit to the data. The second component of AIC represents a penalty in terms of the number of parameters in the model. Why penalize based on the number of parameters? The reason is based on the principle of parsimony (see Burnham and Anderson 1992), which represents a tradeoff between models having too few parameters and models that have too many. A model such as $\{R = \beta_0\}$ may have too few parameters (only two: β_0 and σ^2), and the estimates of R would be biased relative to the true values. The estimates would be precise, however, because all of the data are being used to estimate the two parameters. A model that estimates parameters for each of the 10 years, such as $R = \beta_0 + \beta_1(\text{Year 2})$ $+ \cdots + \beta_9$ (year 9) may be less biased with an estimate for each year, but it would also be much less precise because the data are divided to estimate 11 parameters (ten β plus σ^2). Thus as the number of parameters increases, bias is reduced but precision is lost. As the number of parameters decreases, bias worsens as precision improves. AIC balances this tradeoff between bias and precision. Within the set of candidate models, the model having the lowest AIC is the "best" model in terms of estimated Kullback-Leibler information. That is, AIC is an estimate of the expected, relative Kullback-Leibler information lost when a model is used to approximate reality. These ideas of parsimony and penalty for too many parameters in a model become by-products of estimating Kullback-Liebler information using AIC.

When $n/K < 40$ (where K is the number of parameters and n is the sample size), AIC poorly estimates Kullback-Leibler. In this case, a second-order version of AIC, AIC_c, should be used (Hurvich and Tsai 1989):

$$AIC_c = AIC + \frac{2K(K+1)}{n - K - 1} \qquad [5.2]$$

In our example, we would use AIC_c because the sample size we are ultimately dealing with is $n = 10$ years.

Ranking of Candidate Models

Both AIC and AIC_c can be used to rank models within a set of candidate models such as these proposed in Table 5.1. Once ranked, however, how good is the "best" model relative to the second-ranked model or even the third-ranked model? To resolve this question, there is an additional tool, Akaike weights (Buckland et al. 1997), that can be assigned to each model i in a set containing M candidate models:

$$w_i = \frac{\exp(-\frac{\Delta_i}{2})}{\sum_{m=1}^{M} \exp(-\frac{\Delta_i}{2})} \qquad [5.3]$$

where Δ_i is the difference between model i and the model with the lowest AIC (or AIC_c) value. The weights for all models in the candidate set sum to 1 and, for each model i, represent the likelihood of that model given the data. This idea of the likelihood of the model given the data, and hence these model weights, has been suggested for many years by Akaike (1978, 1979, 1980, 1981, 1983). Strength of evidence for model i versus model j can be expressed as the ratio w_i/w_j. This ratio addresses the question "How much more likely is model i than model j given these data?"

Now we have the tools to rank and examine the likelihood of each model in our candidate set for the brown owl. The results of this exercise are shown in Table 5.2. First we were able to rank the proposed hypotheses in terms of their plausibility, using AIC_c, and find that the model stemming from the hypothesis proposed by the field scientist $\{R = \beta_0 - \beta_1$ (PRECIP)$\}$ is the most plausible given the data. Although this model also happens to be the generating model ("truth"), we reiterate that the objective when using AIC is to select the best approximating fitted model given the data. What was the likelihood of this model relative to the other models in the candidate set—or, in other words, were any of the other models similarly likely to be the best model selected by AIC_c? To answer this question we examine the Akaike weights in Table 5.2 and find that the best model is highly likely as well, with no other models coming close in terms of their relative likelihood. Remember that the Akaike weights for all the models in the candidate set sum to 1. Therefore, the best model has almost all (0.933) of the weight associated with it. In terms of strength of evidence, the best model is 23 times (0.933/0.040) more likely than the second-ranked model. Thus we conclude that the model representing the hypothesis proposed by the field scientist is the most plausible. But how good a model is it? It may be the best model out of the set of models proposed by the scientists. But if it does not explain much of the variation in annual reproductive output, it is not a very good model. We address this question in the next section.

Table 5.2. Ranking and Weighting of the Set of Candidate Models

Model	$K^\dagger$	AIC_c	Rank	Δ_i	Akaike weights
$R = \beta_0 - \beta_1$ (PRECIP)	3	1053.80	1	0.00	0.933
$R = \beta_0 - \beta_1$ (PRECIP) $- \beta_2$ (PARA)	4	1060.10	2	6.30	0.040
$R = \beta_0 - \beta_1$ (T)	3	1062.10	3	8.30	0.015
$R = \beta_0$	2	1062.60	4	8.80	0.011
$R = \beta_0 - \beta_1$ (FIRE)	3	1068.70	5	14.90	0.001
$R = \beta_0 - \beta_1$ (PARA)	3	1069.80	6	16.00	0.000

† K is the number of parameters—in this case, the number of β plus σ^2.

How Good Is the Best Model?

There are a number of ways to assess how good a model is in terms of explaining the data. In the model selection approach (as in hypothesis testing), it is plausible to have inappropriate models in the candidate set; AIC will select the best of these models. Although the best model selected by AIC will be the best of the lot examined, it may still be a poor model in terms of explaining the data. Therefore, we want to further examine our best selected model for the brown owl. First we want to examine the precision of the estimated regression coefficient for PRECIP ($\hat{\beta}_1$) and see whether the 95 percent confidence interval for this parameter overlaps zero. If the interval overlaps zero considerably, there is little support for the trend in reproductive output being due to changes in precipitation. In the case of our best model $\{R = \beta_0 - \beta_1 \text{ (PRECIP)}\}$, $\hat{\beta}_1 = -0.196$ with $\hat{SE}(\hat{\beta}_1) = 0.021$ and 95 percent confidence intervals of $-0.237, -0.155$. In this case, the parameter both is precise and has a 95 percent confidence interval that indicates the slope is quite different from zero.

Next we want to find out how much variation in reproductive output is explained by the best model. To do this we use a variance-components analysis (see Chapter 3 in this volume). Here we are interested in the total temporal variation ($\sigma^2_{\text{temporal}}$) and how much of that variation is explained by the best model (σ^2_{model}). The percentage of variation explained by the best model can then be calculated as

$$\% \text{ variation explained} = \frac{\hat{\sigma}^2_{\text{model}}}{\hat{\sigma}^2_{\text{temporal}}} \times 100 \qquad [5.4]$$

Without going into details about the variance-components analysis, we simply note that it can easily be done as a by-product of our mixed-effects modeling with the simulated brown owl data (see Franklin et al. 2000). The best model selected by AIC_c explains all of the temporal variation (Table 5.3) after separating out the annual sampling variance. This model also has

Table 5.3. Variance-Components Analysis for Total Temporal Variation and the Amount and Percentage of Variation Explained by Various Models

Type of variation	$\hat{\sigma}^2$	%[†]
Total temporal ($\sigma^2_{\text{temporal}}$)	0.0619	–
Explained by model $\{\beta_0 - \beta_1 \text{ (PRECIP)}\}$	0.0619	100.0
Explained by model $\{\beta_0 - \beta_1 \text{ (PRECIP)} - \beta_2 \text{ (PARA)}\}$	0.0619	100.0

[†]Percentage of temporal variation explained by the model.

precise estimates different from zero and explains a considerable amount of the process variation in annual reproductive output for the brown owl. Thus it is a good model.

Moreover, the model selected by using stepwise procedures also explains a large amount of variation (Table 5.3). This illustrates why using the amount of variance explained is a poor criterion for selecting the best model. As parameters are added to a model—even totally useless parameters—the amount of variance explained will increase. We know that the variable PARA is essentially random noise in our simulated data and adds little to explaining the data because we made it that way. But if we had chosen it for inference, we would be ascribing some biological meaning to the presence of parasites and their effect on brown owls.

ADVANTAGES OF THE APPROACH

The increased use of statistical model selection to explain data is relatively new to natural resource management. In this chapter we have outlined the concepts and procedures used in the model selection approach based on Kullback-Leibler information and likelihood-based inference to select the best model from a set of candidates. We also contrasted this model selection approach with traditional null hypothesis testing. For further clarification, we demonstrated the model selection approach through an example of simulated data where we knew the generating model. For the philosophy, statistical details, and theory behind the model selection approach we have outlined here, we urge readers to review Burnham and Anderson (1998).

The statistical model selection approach not only eliminates the arbitrary limitations of null hypothesis testing, such as significance level and tests of null hypotheses, but also embraces the concept of multiple working hypotheses as first proposed by Chamberlin (1890). Rarely is there a single, simple, true model that explains a natural phenomenon. To avoid being misled by individual biases, scientists and managers should develop a set of candidate models to explain the phenomenon of interest. Developing a set of plausible, creative candidate models is the key to the quality of inference that can be drawn from the data. Incorporating ideas from the resource managers and researchers involved with the problem is critical to the development of the best set of models.

Statistical model selection offers a valid, comprehensive approach to evaluating the evidence for alternative scientific hypotheses given the data. Whatever information is supported by the data, the entire set of candidate models is incorporated in the final inference—through selection of the best model, ranking of candidate models, and strength of evidence for the best and competing models in the candidate set. Such an approach yields valid inferences following objective analysis of a broad spectrum of a priori hypotheses.

ACKNOWLEDGMENTS

We thank Mark Bakeman, Monica Bond, and Tom Ryan for their excellent comments on previous drafts of this manuscript.

REFERENCES

Akaike, H. 1973. Information theory as an extension of the maximum likelihood principle. Pages 267–281 in B. N. Petrov and F. Csaki, eds., *Second International Symposium on Information Theory*. Budapest: Akademiai Kiado.

————. 1978. A Bayesian analysis of the minimum AIC procedure. *Annals of the Institute of Statistical Mathematics* 30:9–14.

————. 1979. A Bayesian extension of the minimum AIC procedure of autoregressive model fitting. *Biometrika* 66:237–242.

————. 1980. Likelihood and the Bayes procedure. Pages 143–203 in J. M. Bernardo, M. H. De Groot, D. V. Lindley, and A. F. M. Smith, eds., *Bayesian Statistics*. Valencia: University Press.

————. 1981. Modern development of statistical methods. Pages 169–184 in P. Eykhoff, ed., *Trends and Progress in System Identification*. Paris: Pergamon Press.

————. 1983. Information measures and model selection. *International Statistical Institute* 44:277–291.

Anderson, D. R., and K. P. Burnham. 1999a. General strategies for the analysis of ringing data. *Bird Study* 46(suppl.):S261–S270.

————. 1999b. Understanding information criteria for selection among capture–recapture or ring recovery models. *Bird Study* 46 (suppl.):S14–S21.

Buckland, S. T., K. P. Burnham, and N. H. Augustin. 1997. Model selection: An integral part of inference. *Biometrics* 53:603–618.

Burnham, K. P., and D. R. Anderson. 1992. Data-based selection of an appropriate biological model: The key to modern data analysis. Pages 16–30 in D. R. McCullough and R. H. Barrett, eds., *Wildlife 2001: Populations* London: Elsevier Applied Science.

————. 1998. *Model Selection and Inference: A Practical Information-Theoretic Approach*. New York: Springer-Verlag.

Chamberlin, T. C. 1890. The method of multiple working hypotheses. *Science* (old series) 15:92. Reprinted in 1965 in *Science* 148:754–759.

Edwards, A. W. F. 1992. *Likelihood*. Expanded ed. Baltimore: Johns Hopkins University Press.

Fisher, R. A. 1925. Theory of statistical estimation. *Proceedings of the Cambridge Philosophical Society* 22:700–725.

————. 1958. *Statistical Methods for Research Workers*. 13th ed. New York: Hafner.

Franklin, A. B., D. R. Anderson, R. J. Gutiérrez, and K. P. Burnham. 2000. Climate, habitat quality, and fitness in northern spotted owl populations in northwest California. *Ecological Monographs* 70: 539–590.

Graybill, F. A., and H. K. Iyer. 1994. *Regression Analysis: Concepts and Applications.* Belmont, Calif.: Duxbury.

Hilborn, R., and M. Mangel. 1997. *The Ecological Detective: Confronting Models with Data.* Monographs in Population Biology 28. Princeton: Princeton University Press.

Hurvich, C. M., and C.-L. Tsai. 1989. The impact of model selection on inference in linear regression. *American Statistician* 44:214–217.

Kullback, S., and R. A. Leibler. 1951. On information and sufficiency. *Annals of Mathematical Statistics* 22:79–86.

Linkhart, H., and W. Zucchini. 1986. *Model Selection.* New York: Wiley.

Littell, R. C., G. A. Milliken, W. W. Stroup, and R. D. Wolfinger. 1996. *SAS System for Mixed Models.* Cary, N.C.: SAS Institute.

Malakoff, D. 1999. Bayes offers a "new" way to make sense of numbers. *Science* 286: 1460–1464.

Maurer, B. A. 1998. Ecological science and statistical paradigms: At the threshold. *Science* 279:502–503.

McCullagh, P., and J. A. Nelder. 1989. *Generalized Linear Models.* 2nd ed. London: Chapman & Hall.

Miller, A. J. 1990. *Subset Selection in Regression.* London: Chapman & Hall.

Neyman, J., and E. S. Pearson. 1933. On the problem of the most efficient tests of statistical hypotheses. *Philosophical Transactions of the Royal Society Series A* 231:289–337.

Ott, R. L. 1993. *An Introduction to Statistical Methods and Data Analysis.* Belmont, Calif.: Duxbury.

Platt, J. R. 1964. Strong inference. *Science* 146:1–7.

Romesburg, H. C. 1991. On improving the natural resources and environmental sciences. *Journal of Wildlife Management* 55:744–756.

Royall, R. 1997. *Statistical Evidence: A Likelihood Paradigm.* London: Chapman & Hall.

Schweder, T. 1988. A significance version of the basic Neyman-Pearson theory for scientific hypothesis testing. *Scandinavian Journal of Statistics* 15:225–242.

White, G. C., and R. E. Bennetts. 1996. Analysis of frequency count data using the negative binomial distribution. *Ecology* 77:2549–2557.

Zimmerman, M. 1995. *Science, Nonscience, and Nonsense: Approaching Environmental Literacy.* Baltimore: Johns Hopkins University Press.

••••••••••••••••••••••

Chapter 6

Simulation Models and Optimal Decision Making in Natural Resource Management

Michael J. Conroy and Clinton T. Moore

Renewable resource management typically involves, at its core, an optimization problem of intrinsically dynamic systems. Viewed this way, management involves three elements: quantifying an objective, often involving multiple resources and inherent tradeoffs; defining system dynamics, including components of uncertainty and detail such as spatial resolution; and specifying a decision, including possible dynamic and spatial aspects. Williams (1989) has compared the major features of optimization and simulation, and Conroy and Noon (1996) have discussed them in relation to spatially explicit models.

THE OPTIMAL CONTROL PROBLEM

Much, if not all, of natural resource management can be described as the formulation of a set of management actions that are expected to result in the achievement of a desired objective. An *objective function* is simply a mathematical statement that describes, in terms of measurable system attributes or *system states* (such as population abundance), values ascribed to possible outcomes following a decision. *Optimal control* is the problem of finding a set of actions that maximize or minimize the objective function. The resulting set of actions through time is known as an *optimal policy*—frequently termed an *optimal strategy* when the system is stochastic (Dreyfus and Law 1977; Lubow 1995). In most cases, natural resource managers must consider not only the immediate consequences of a decision (such as this year's harvest) but also the decision's impact on the future condition of the resource and its value (future harvest opportunities). Given this long-term view, the objective function must now explicitly incorporate the value of future system states, which of course are not presently observable. To do this we must have a mathematical model for *system dynamics* that describes the relationship between certain management actions and these future system states given the current system state and assumptions about system behavior. Our model may be *deterministic*—that is, each combination of management actions leads to the same trajectory of the system through time—or, more realistically, *stochastic,* in which case intervening random events (such as environmental variation or demographic processes) cause the system to deviate from a completely predictable path. Often decisions are made and resource systems are monitored at discrete points in time—for example, once a year—and thus it may be appropriate to model system dynamics in discrete time as

$$\mathbf{X}(t + 1) = \mathbf{X}(t) + f(\mathbf{X}, \mathbf{Z}(t), \mathbf{U}(t), t) \qquad [6.1]$$

where $\mathbf{X}(t)$ is a vector describing the system state (abundance of several species, habitat conditions) at time t, $\mathbf{Z}(t)$ is a vector of random variables, and $\mathbf{U}(t)$ is a vector of management actions taken at time t. The variable t may denote any discrete unit of time. In this discussion we refer to the interval $(t, t + 1)$ as a *time step.* A general form for the objective function is

$$J = \sum_{t=t_0}^{T} V(\mathbf{X}(t), \mathbf{U}(t), t) + V_1(\mathbf{X}(T)) \qquad [6.2]$$

where V is a function describing the value or return from management actions $\mathbf{U}(t)$ and system state $\mathbf{X}(t)$ and where V_1 is a value given by the system state $\mathbf{X}(T)$ at some "terminal time" T, usually taken as the distant future (100 years, for example, or even $T = \infty$). The long-term nature of the decision problem is made explicit in that the objective value is obtained by summing from the present decision time ($t = t_0$) to this distant future time. The optimization problem can be then mathematically formulated as

maximize J
$\{\mathbf{U}(t)\} \in \mathbf{U}$

subject to

$$\mathbf{X}(t + 1) = \mathbf{X}(t) + f(\mathbf{X}(t), \mathbf{Z}(t), \mathbf{U}(t), t) \qquad [6.3]$$
$$\mathbf{X}(t_0) = \mathbf{X}_0$$

where for stochastic systems

$$J = E\left[\sum_{t=t_0}^{T} V(\mathbf{X}(t), \mathbf{U}(t), t + V_1\mathbf{X}(T))\right] \qquad [6.4]$$

that is, the objective is now over the average of the random outcomes influenced by $\mathbf{Z}(t)$.

A number of mathematical approaches may be taken to solve the optimal control problem and are reviewed by Williams (1989). Here we focus on applying two methods—dynamic programming (DP) and forward simulation-optimization (FSO)—to finding optimal solutions for a simple natural resource decision problem. Briefly, optimization approaches such as DP have the advantage of guaranteeing that the resulting decision will be optimal with respect to the objective function. Dynamic programming (Bellman 1957; Dreyfus and Law 1977; Mangel and Clark 1988) works by application of the "principle of optimality," which states that "an optimal policy has the property that, whatever the initial state and decision are, the remaining decisions must constitute an optimal policy with regard to the state resulting from the first decision" (Bellman 1957). The objective form described earlier lends itself to this principle because the objective function is composed of two parts: an "immediate reward" part that starts at t_0 and moves to t_1 and a subsequent part that starts at t_1 and moves to the terminal time T. The optimality principle says that in order for the overall strategy to be optimal (given initial system conditions $\mathbf{X}(t_0)$), the strategy over this second portion must be optimal as well. Dynamic programming then applies the principle to finding the optimal strategy at t_0 by working backward from T; once we arrive at t_0, the overall strategy must now be optimal by definition. The same approach can be extended to stochastic systems by invoking the stochastic form of the state dynamics and objective function (Dreyfus and Law 1977; Lubow 1995).

Dynamic programming is an extremely powerful means of finding optimal solutions for dynamic systems. Indeed, it is guaranteed to provide optimal decisions given the assumptions of the method. It is nearly impossible, however, to include much complexity in the model of system dynamics—particularly if this involves spatial or individual animal components. And although dynamic programming allows for dynamic and stochastic systems typical of natural resource management, this method works only for systems in which there are just a few state variables and decisions. By contrast, simulation models (such as FSO) allow for virtually unlimited modeling of the details of systems, including spatial resolution and individual animal behavior. These methods may be used to seek optimal solutions, but they provide no guarantee that a solution is optimal. Moreover, complex simulation models are often of dubious reliability because of limited validation and difficulties in parameter estimation (Conroy et al. 1995).

In summary, optimization methods such as DP are known to give optimal solutions for problems, but only for simple systems where everything can be specified. Thus these methods are limited in terms of the detail of the systems that can be modeled. Simulation methods such as FSO can accommodate much more detail, but they are not guaranteed to find an optimal solution. Thus a natural question arises for resource managers: To what degree are the approaches comparable in terms of the optimal decision for a given system state and the value of the objective function given the optimal strategy?

A COMPARISON OF METHODS

We approached this question by constructing a simple dynamic problem for which we could specify the parameters but which nonetheless contained the essential elements of dynamic decision making and a tradeoff in natural resource objectives. For this problem we applied both a backward-iteration, stochastic optimization approach (Bellman 1957) and a forward-simulation model with optimal one-time-step decision making (FSO). We then compared the optimal decision and resulting objective function—in this case involving the abundance trajectories of two vertebrate species of interest—in each approach.

An Example System

Although it was simple, we used a model system that was motivated by natural resource management problems encountered in forestlands of the southeastern United States—in particular our experiences at the Piedmont National Wildlife Refuge in Georgia. Our model system contained a 1000-hectare landscape of forest composed of two successional stages: early (0–40 years) and late (40–120 years). These stages might correspond to early succession following clear-cutting and regeneration of loblolly pine (*Pinus taeda*) and older stands following thinning to remove understory and midstory vegetation. Figure 6.1*a* illustrates the habitat dynamics of this system between the two successional stages (that is, habitat states); the proportions indicate the 5-year rates of transition between early and late successional stages. In all of our models, habitat dynamics were completely deterministic. Habitat state dynamics can thus be represented by the expression

$$\mathbf{x}_{t+1} = \mathbf{L}\mathbf{x}_t \qquad [6.5]$$

where

$$\mathbf{x}_t = \begin{bmatrix} x_1(t) \\ x_2(t) \end{bmatrix}$$

is a column vector describing the system habitat state, with $x_i(t)$ representing the number of hectares in forest stage i at time step t and

$$\mathbf{L} = \begin{bmatrix} 0.875 & 0.0625 \\ 0.125 & 0.9375 \end{bmatrix}$$

defining the rate of transition between stages. The values in $\mathbf{L}$ are purely a function of the length of time spent in each stage (40 and 80 years, respectively) and the length of a time step (5 years). Thus every 5 years $5/40 = 0.125$ of the early stage moves to late with $35/40 = 0.875$ remaining in the early successional stage. Likewise $1/16 = 0.0625$ of the late successional stage reverts to early succession with $15/16 = 0.9375$ remaining behind. The columns always sum to 1 because of area conservation (that is, the total acreage of 1000 hectares does not change through time). The acreage in each stage after each 5-year transition is the total of the acreage remaining in that stage from the previous time step plus the acreage moving into the stage. For example, given a distribution of acreage at time $t = 4$ of

$$\mathbf{x}_4 = \begin{bmatrix} 750 \\ 250 \end{bmatrix}$$

the state at time $t = 5$ (that is, in 5 years) will be

$$\mathbf{x}_5 = \mathbf{Lx}_4 = \begin{bmatrix} 0.875 & 0.0625 \\ 0.125 & 0.9375 \end{bmatrix} = \begin{bmatrix} 750 \\ 250 \end{bmatrix} = \begin{bmatrix} 0.875(750) + 0.0625(250) \\ 0.125(750) + 0.9375(250) \end{bmatrix} = \begin{bmatrix} 671.875 \\ 328.125 \end{bmatrix}$$

with $671.875 + 328.125 = 1000$.

The single decision to be made, every 5 years, is what proportion of the late successional stage to harvest in five evenly spaced levels from 0 to 1; there was no harvest in the early stage. The effect of harvest on habitat dynamics is to immediately transfer the indicated proportion of late-stage habitat to the early stage with succession rates continuing as before (Figure 6.1b). Thus the system of equations representing succession dynamics is modified to include harvest

$$\mathbf{x}_{t+1} = \mathbf{L}(\mathbf{H}_t \mathbf{x}_t)$$

where

$$\mathbf{H}_t = \begin{bmatrix} 1 & h_t \\ 0 & (1 - h_t) \end{bmatrix}$$

and h_t is the proportion of the later stage that is harvested, again with no harvest occurring in the early stage. For example, if $h_t = 0.50$ and the ini-

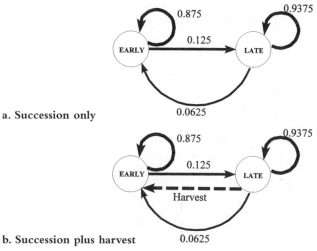

a. Succession only

b. Succession plus harvest

Figure 6.1. Schematic of habitat dynamics for a simple forest management problem. **(a)** Model incorporating succession only. **(b)** Model incorporating succession plus harvest of older stage.

tial stage is defined as in the previous example, the distribution of acreage at $t = 5$ is

$$
\mathbf{x}_5 = \mathbf{L}(\mathbf{H}_4\, \mathbf{x}_4) = \begin{bmatrix} 0.875 & 0.0625 \\ 0.125 & 0.9375 \end{bmatrix} \begin{bmatrix} 1 & 0.5 \\ 0 & 0.5 \end{bmatrix} \begin{bmatrix} 750 \\ 250 \end{bmatrix}
$$
$$
= \begin{bmatrix} 0.875 & 0.0625 \\ 0.125 & 0.9375 \end{bmatrix} \begin{bmatrix} 750 + 0.5(250) \\ 0.5(250) \end{bmatrix}
$$
$$
= \begin{bmatrix} 0.875 & 0.0625 \\ 0.125 & 0.9375 \end{bmatrix} \begin{bmatrix} 875 \\ 125 \end{bmatrix}
$$
$$
= \begin{bmatrix} 773.4375 \\ 226.5625 \end{bmatrix}
$$

We represented population response for the two hypothetical species by species-specific source/sink models (Pulliam 1988; Conroy and Noon 1996). For species 1, early forest was source habitat; for species 2, late forest was source. Upper limits in the source and sink habitats were 0.1 animal/hectare and 0.5 animal/hectare, respectively. Species that could be associated with these respective source and sink habitats for a southeastern pine system might include Carolina wren (*Thryothorus ludovicianus*) for early successional stage and red-cockaded woodpecker (*Picoides borealis*) for late successional stage. The population abundance for each species is determined both by the amount of suitable habitat (that is, acreage in each successional

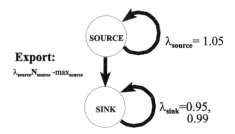

Export:

$\lambda_{source}N_{source} - max_{source}$

Figure 6.2. Schematic model of source/sink population dynamics. Each species increases at the rate of $\lambda = 1.05$ in its source habitat (defined as early forest stage for species 1, late stage for species 2) with a ceiling density specified as 0.1 animal/hectare of source. When density reaches this ceiling, all surplus animals are assumed to emigrate to the sink habitat—up to the ceiling density in the sink of 0.5 animal/hectare of sink (defined as late forest stage for species 1, early stage for species 2). Species decrease at the rate of $\lambda = 0.95$ for species 1 and $\lambda = 0.99$ for species 2 in sink habitats.

stage) present and by the ability of each species to export excess animals from source habitats to sink habitats. For a single species (assuming no density limitation in the sink habitat), population abundance in the source and sink habitats at time $t + 1$ depends on whether the size of the source population, $N_{source}(t)$, is expected to exceed the saturation abundance N^*_{source} at time $t + 1$ given the finite rate of growth of the source population, λ_{source}. If $\lambda_{source} N_{source}(t) < N^*_{source}$ (future population does not exceed saturation abundance), then $N_{source}(t + 1) = \lambda_{source}N_{source}(t)$ and $N_{sink}(t + 1) = \lambda_{sink} N_{sink}(t)$, where λ_{sink} and $N_{sink}(t)$ have analogous meanings to λ_{source} and N_{source}. Otherwise (future population exceeds saturation abundance), then $N_{source}(t + 1) = N^*_{source}$ and $N_{sink}(t + 1) = \lambda_{sink}N_{sink}(t) + \lambda_{source}N_{source}(t) - N^*_{source}$. However, because we also enforce a destiny limit in the sink habitats (0.5 animal/hectare), $N_{sink}(t + 1)$ can never exceed a saturation abundance N^*_{sink}. We assume that each species' growth rates (λ) are uniform within the source or sink habitats. For both species under consideration we set $\lambda_{source} = 1.05$, $\lambda_{sink} = 0.95$ for species 1 (affinity for early forest stages), and $\lambda_{sink} = 0.99$ for species 2 (later forest stages), resulting in greater source-to-sink dispersal rates for the latter species than the former (Figure 6.2).

We introduced random variation into this model by using a discrete lognormal distribution to model variation in λ, as

$$\lambda_i = \overline{\lambda}^{(1 + z_iCV)} \tag{6.6}$$

where λ_i is a value of $\overline{\lambda}$ (as in source habitats), $\overline{\lambda}$ is the mean (1.05) of the distribution from which λ_i is taken, z_i is a standard normal deviate, and CV is the coefficient of variation on the logarithmic scale. We took discrete values of z_i as $\{-2.367, -1.15, 0, 1.15, 2.367\}$ corresponding to approximate

1, 25, 50, 75, and 99 percent quantiles of the standard normal distribution, and $CV = 0.10$ for all runs. Values of z_i were not different between species for source or sink growth. That is, a value of z_i drawn for species 1 source growth was also used as source growth for species 2, and a different z_i drawn for sink growth was applied to both species.

Optimization

We defined the objective for optimization as the 100-year abundances for each species, weighted by a value for each species, and penalized for quasi-extinction of either species:

$$J_T = [N_{1T} (v_1 + \frac{N_{2T} - N_2^{min}}{N_2^{min}}) + N_{2T} (v_2 + \frac{N_{1T} - N_1^{min}}{N_1^{min}})] \quad [6.7]$$

where T is the terminal time period under investigation, v_1 and v_2 are relative values for each species, and N_1^{min} and N_2^{min} are quasi-extinction levels for each species. In our analyses we set the values equal for both species ($v_1 = v_2 = 1.0$) and set quasi-extinction levels to 10 ($N_1^{min} = N_2^{min} = 10$). Given Equation (6.7), if either species declined to extinction the resulting objective value is zero. We evaluated the objective function (Equation 6.7) at $T = 20$ five-year time steps—that is, after 100 years.

For both optimization approaches, we evaluated the expected value of the objective for each state with expectations taken across the random λ_i outcomes. The optimal decision was the one that maximized this expected value. With DP, the optimal decision was obtained by backward iteration from the optimal terminal value to the present—that is, 20 iterations or 100 years. Five state variables described the status of the modeled system at any point in time: amount of early forest habitat (amount of late forest is known by subtraction) and abundances of both species in respective source and sink habitats. We discretized each of the state variables into 11 levels; thus the strategy yielded a decision for each of the 11^5 state combinations. We used Program ASDP, a successor to SDP (Lubow 1995) to perform these computations.

To illustrate the backward-iteration procedure, start with the terminal state of the system. In our case, this is the terminal distribution of habitats between successional stages and the abundance of animals of each species in the sources and sinks. The objective function is then evaluated for each combination of the random λ—in this case illustrated (Figure 6.3) by the five possible values for the source λ. The expected value for each decision is evaluated and the optimal decision selected. This process is repeated for the previous time step and continued until the present time is reached—resulting in an optimal state-specific and time-specific decision strategy (Figure 6.3).

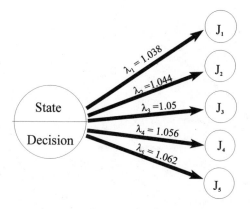

Figure 6.3. Schematic representation of decision making under dynamic programming (DP). The return (J_i) on the objective function is evaluated from the state at time $t = T$ (the terminal state, 100 years in the example) for each combination of random outcomes (in this case illustrated by five possible λ_i for a source population). The optimal state-specific decision is taken as the decision that maximizes the expected value of the objective. Conditioned on this decision, the process is repeated at the previous time step for all possible combinations of states and decisions. The resulting decisions at each previous time, including the current time ($t = 0$), are optimal with respect to the state dynamics and objective function.

With FSO, we began at the present time with a given combination of initial habitat and population states. We evaluated the expected value of the decision for all possible decisions and selected the decision resulting in the optimum for one time step—that is, the best value of the objective over the next 5 years. We then selected random values of λ for the source and sink populations and, implementing the optimal decision, used forward simulation to move to the next time. Figure 6.4 illustrates the basic steps in the FSO algorithm. Given an initial state, then: the objective values for each possible decision are averaged across the random λ; the optimal decision is selected, resulting in the highest expected value of the objective function; random λ are selected to move the system forward one time step; and the process is repeated at the next time step. We used a stochastic forward-optimization procedure written in SAS PROC IML (SAS Institute 1990) to perform these computations.

Simulation of Strategies

We compared the FSO and DP strategies by simulation starting from a range of initial state conditions (243 combinations of habitat and initial population size for each species in each habitat). For each initial state com-

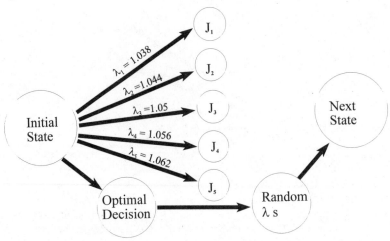

Figure 6.4. Schematic representation of decision making under forward simulation-optimization (FSO). Beginning at an initial state, the objective function return (J_i) is evaluated for each combination of random outcomes (again illustrated by five possible λ_i for a source population) and the decision that is optimal (provides the maximum expected value of the objective) over one time step is selected. Given this decision, random values representing a source λ and a sink λ are selected, which are used with the model of system dynamics to simulate a new state of the system. The process is repeated until the terminal time ($t = 100$ years) is reached.

bination we used identical realizations of random outcomes for λ_i in order to specify the population's trajectory to the next time step conditional on the habitat conditions (influenced by the strategy selected) and the initial population state. We continued this process for 20 iterations, or 100 years, and recorded the value of the objective at the terminal time. For each simulation we kept track of the initial ($t = 0$) harvest decision as being relevant to initiating an "optimal" 100-year strategy as well as the objective values at $T = 20$ resulting from each strategy. We then compared the strategies by computing

$$\frac{J_{20}\,(\text{DP}) - J_{20}\,(\text{FSO})}{J_{20}\,(\text{DP})} \qquad\qquad [6.8]$$

to represent the relative difference of the DP (presumed optimal) strategy compared to the FSO strategy, where J_{20} (DP) and J_{20} (FSO) were obtained from Equation (6.7) evaluated at $T = 20$ under the simulated DP and FSO strategies, respectively. Finally, we replicated this procedure 10,000 times for each of the 243 starting states.

As expected, FSO and DP yielded identical optimal strategies, with

Equation (6.8) equal to zero, for all state combinations at $t = 19$, that is, one time step before the terminal time $T = 20$ (100 years). Although this comparison was not of particular interest and is not reported here, it confirmed that the two procedures were solving the same one-time-step problem. That is, from the perspective of a decision maker at $t = 19$, the one-time-step, "myopic" strategy yielded by FSO is equivalent to a long-term, "farsighted" strategy provided by DP.

As the decision horizon lengthened to 100 years (that is, time starting at $t = 0$ rather than $t = 19$), the two strategies diverged. The 100-year strategies were compared with respect to whether the $t = 0$ harvest decisions differed and the direction of difference if any (Figure 6.5). Under a broad range of initial conditions, FSO yields an optimal strategy that is more aggressive (involves more cutting) than does DP—which makes sense given the myopic nature of FSO. That these myopic strategies are suboptimal with respect to the long-term objective is seen by comparing the simulated 100-year ($t = 20$) objective outcomes (Equation 6.8; Figure 6.6). The results confirm the superiority of the DP strategy. For all state combinations, the average over 10,000 simulations always resulted in positive values for Equation (6.8), although FSO happened to outperform DP in some simulations. The degree of suboptimality of the FSO strategy depended on initial habitat conditions: poorer performance occurred

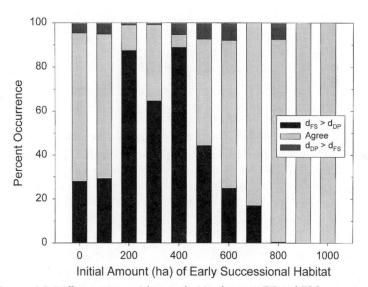

Figure 6.5. Differences in $t = 0$ harvest decision between DP and FSO over state combinations displayed over levels of the habitat state variable. Darkest and intermediate-shaded bar sections represent cases of more and less aggressive cutting strategies, respectively, under FSO compared to DP.

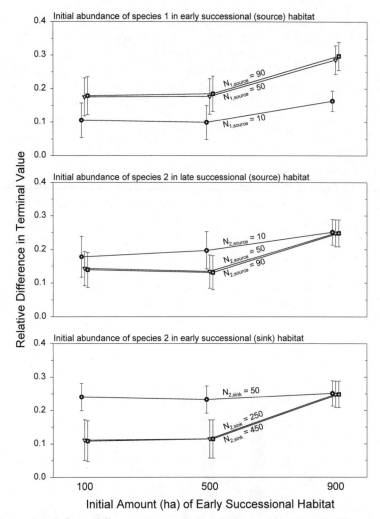

Figure 6.6. Relative differences in expected performance (objective value) between DP and FSO (Equation 6.8) over 10,000 simulation trials displayed over three two-way combinations of initial system states. Error bars around means represent one standard deviation of simulated difference measures over all other initial system states.

when more versus less of the landscape is in early successional habitat. We note, however, that under the worst-case scenario FSO only approached a 30 percent loss in optimality and for a wide range of initial state conditions FSO provided decisions that approached 90 percent of the optimal DP results.

Considerations in Using Optimization versus Simulation

Our example illustrates the benefits of optimization approaches such as DP, which are designed to efficiently solve dynamic problems in which the objective is specified over a long time frame. Because of its backward, iterative approach, DP is able to decompose the time frame into stages and then solve the problem one stage at a time. In contrast, FSO (and simulation in general), by working forward through time, deals with problems that increase geometrically in complexity at each time step. A forward-looking algorithm like FSO is simply incapable of anticipating all the possible pathways that decisions could take through time and therefore becomes increasingly inferior to DP as time horizons lengthen. For the problem just described, FSO would have had to consider decisions over $(5 \times 25)^{20} = 8.7 \times 10^{41}$ decision pathways (5 decision levels, 25 random source and sink λ outcomes, 20 decision periods) from a single starting state of the system—and most problems are more complex. Nonetheless, forward-looking but myopic simulation procedures such as FSO can be useful for exploring complex problems and, as illustrated here, may yield results that are not substantially inferior to DP or other optimization procedures. For complicated systems involving multiple species and spatial components, DP may be incapable of providing solutions at all—due to the "curse of dimensionality" (Bellman 1957)—in which case managers are forced to use simulation or other heuristic approaches.

There is, however, a troubling conceptual issue: we may never be able to assess the cost of moving from truly optimal solutions to solutions obtained by incorporating simulation. Despite the simplicity of our model, stripped of all but the most fundamental elements of long-term, multispecies management, we still faced computational challenges. For a more realistic problem there will not be a benchmark optimal strategy—otherwise we would never consider simulation—so it may never be possible to evaluate the relative performance of simulation-optimization strategies.

Adaptation is the explicit incorporation of information from monitoring, management, and experimentation into decision making. At present, formal coupling of adaptation to optimization is very complex—even for simple systems (Williams 1996). Combining simulation and optimization and incorporating adaptation for complex systems such as ours will require innovative applications of hardware and software and will no doubt require the development of new methods. Our future work will explore how adaptation can best be incorporated into decision problems like those described here. The results of this work should have important implications for the role of monitoring programs in adaptive resource management.

ACKNOWLEDGMENTS

We thank T. M. Shenk, A. B. Franklin, and two anonymous referees for critical comments on an earlier draft. The Georgia Cooperative Fish and Wildlife Research Unit is jointly sponsored by the USGS Biological Resources Division, the University of Georgia, the Georgia Department of Natural Resources, and the Wildlife Management Institute.

REFERENCES

Bellman, R. E. 1957. *Dynamic Programming.* Princeton: Princeton University Press.

Conroy, M. J., and B. R. Noon. 1996. Mapping of species richness for conservation of biological diversity: Conceptual and methodological issues. *Ecological Applications* 6:763–773.

Conroy, M. J., Y. Cohen, F. C. James, Y. G. Matsinos, and B. A. Maurer. 1995. Parameter estimation, reliability, and model improvement for spatially-explicit models of animal populations. *Ecological Applications* 5:17–19.

Dreyfus, S. E., and A. M. Law. 1977. *The Art and Theory of Dynamic Programming.* New York: Academic Press.

Lubow, B. 1995. SDP: Generalized software for solving stochastic dynamics optimization problems. *Wildlife Society Bulletin* 23:738–742.

Mangel, M., and C. W. Clark. 1988. *Dynamic Modeling in Behavioral Ecology.* Princeton: Princeton University Press.

Pulliam, H. R. 1988. Sources, sinks, and population regulation. *American Naturalist* 132:652–661.

SAS Institute. 1990. *SAS/IML Software: Usage and Reference.* Version 6. 1st ed. Cary, N.C.: SAS Institute.

Williams, B. K. 1989. Review of dynamic optimization methods in renewable natural resources management. *Natural Resource Modeling* 3:137–216.

———. 1996. Adaptive optimization and the harvest of biological populations. *Mathematical Biosciences* 136:1–20.

Chapter 7

· ·

Validating and Evaluating Models

Douglas H. Johnson

Models have become a staple of modern wildlife ecology. Virtually every paper published in journals such as *Journal of Wildlife Management* invokes models in one form or another. Journals such as *Ecological Modelling* are devoted exclusively to applying modeling methodology to the ecological sciences. Texts such as Grant et al. (1997) and Starfield and Bleloch (1991) have made modern methods accessible in the classroom, and computer software has brought powerful modeling tools to the desktop.

Models are abstractions of reality. Which features of a real system should you retain in a model? That depends entirely on the model's purpose. If you are in Jamestown, North Dakota, and want to drive to Zap, North Dakota, you need an abstraction of the state that shows features such as highways but not average precipitation; you need a road map, which is one form of a model. If you want to attract ducks to within shooting distance, you need a model with enough features to fool a duck flying over: a decoy. If you want to predict mallard (*Anas platyrhynchos*) recruitment based on information about nest success and wetland conditions in a particular area, you could use a mathematical model that relates recruitment rate to these variables. The appropriate form and content of a model depend entirely on the purpose for which the model is intended.

With the proliferation of models has come a parallel concern about their validity. This chapter addresses the validation issue. I begin by discussing the purposes of models—the key to the notion of validation. Next I present an overview of the kinds of models used, followed by some examples. After discussing two related topics—verification and sensitivity analysis—I turn to validation itself, its diverse definitions, and methods of validation. The chapter concludes with a few final thoughts on validation.

PURPOSES OF MODELS

Uses of models are as diverse as the models themselves. Applications include summarizing information, defining a problem, organizing thinking, and communicating. Most purposes, however, fall into one of three general categories: explanation, prediction, and decision making. Models in these categories differ according to whether our interest is in the system itself, output values from the system, or finding input values, based on assumed knowledge of the other two pieces of the puzzle:

Input → MODEL → Output

Models for *explanatory* purposes seek to explain a system's behavior and understand the phenomena involved. Explanatory models aim to identify the system given input and output conditions. Identifying and understanding the causal mechanisms of the system is important for explanation (Gold 1977). Scientists make the most use of explanatory models, which are sometimes called understanding, learning, causal, or rational models.

Models for *prediction* are used to forecast the outcome of the system being modeled under certain conditions. "What if?" questions are posed to the model. Predictive models seek values of the output based on knowledge of the input conditions and the system. Engineers and managers find these models most useful.

Models for *decision making* are used to prescribe the right input to achieve desired outputs, or to optimize some product of a system, based on an understanding of the system. Also called prescriptive or control models, these models are applied mostly by engineers and managers.

This trichotomy is not perfect, however. Some models may have more than one purpose. Indeed, an explanatory model that truly captures the essence of a system can prove very useful for either prediction or decision making. But prediction and decision making can also be done with a model that has no explanatory value.

KINDS OF MODELS

Models can be classified in numerous ways, including verbal, diagrammatic, physical, and formal (Rubinstein 1975; Starfield and Bleloch 1991; Haefner

1996; Grant et al. 1997). They can be split along various dichotomies as well, such as deterministic versus stochastic, physical versus abstract, dynamic versus static, discrete versus continuous (in time), and spatially homogeneous versus spatially heterogeneous. Model resolution can also vary in scope and detail, from finer grained and intensive to coarse-grained and extensive. For our purposes, however, it is most useful to contrast models as either mechanistic or descriptive.

Mechanistic models are process-oriented. They incorporate components and interactions intended to mimic relevant aspects of the system being modeled. They are also called functional, causal, explanatory, or rational models. Mechanistic models are most useful for explanatory purposes. *Descriptive models* stake no claim to being accurate mimics of the real system: they are intended to simulate relationships between input and output values similar to the real system. They are also called correlational or statistical models (see also Chapter 3 in this volume). Sometimes they are termed phenomenological models, but because they incorporate no phenomena I consider the term inappropriate. Similarly misleading is the phrase "empirical model," which seems to imply that descriptive models have a basis in observations that mechanistic models lack. Descriptive models typically are invoked for predictive or decision-making applications.

Hybrid models between the two extremes are possible, of course. Mechanistic models may make very useful predictions and are especially robust in novel situations—that is, when values of the input variables are outside the range of values used to develop and fit a predictive model (Berryman 1991). Conversely, a predictive model may provide insight into the functioning of the real system that could lead to deeper understanding.

EXAMPLES OF MODELS

To clarify the previous ideas, let's consider a few models. The first one relates scores of elementary school children on a test of arithmetic skills to the students' body weight (Figure 7.1a). The strong correlation between the two variables suggests that this may be a descriptive model that is useful for prediction. It is obviously useless for understanding or managing: parents would not want to try to increase their children's scores by feeding them junk food to increase their weight. The reason why body weight predicts ability so well is that weight increases with age among elementary school children. Another model (Figure 7.1b) relates test scores to age. It too is a good predictive model. But at least part of the reason why older (and heavier) students perform better on the tests is that they have received more training in arithmetic. A more mechanistic model relates test performance to the student's amount of training (Figure 7.1c). This model may not predict as well as the other two, but it does a better

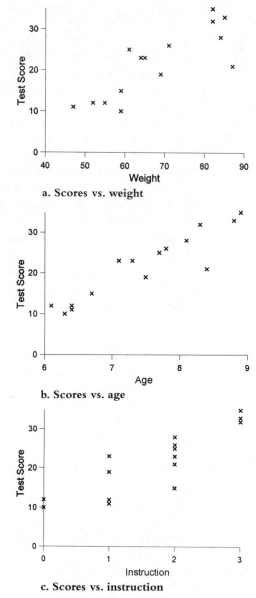

Figure 7.1. (a) Scores of students on a test of arithmetic skills plotted against weight. (b) Scores of students on a test of arithmetic skills plotted against age. (c) Scores of students on a test of arithmetic skills plotted against number of years of instruction.

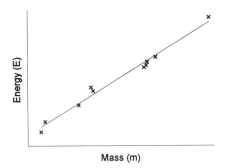

Figure 7.2. Plot of energy against mass.

job of explaining the causal mechanisms that influence test scores—especially for input variables outside the observed range. We might expect a student's performance to improve if he or she receives more training.

Turning to physics, suppose we conducted several experiments that measure energy and mass and obtained the data shown in Figure 7.2. We could then develop a statistical model with good predictive ability. The true model, of course, is $E = mc^2$. This formula represents a mechanistic model, which Einstein obtained without benefit of regression.

In ecology we rarely have such clean and elegant models. Species–area models come fairly close (Figure 7.3). More often, we have statistical or descriptive models. Figure 7.4 shows a model that accounts for renesting in

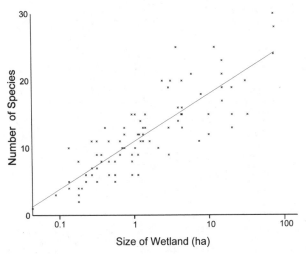

Figure 7.3. Example of a species–area relation showing the number of bird species recorded in semipermanent wetlands in North Dakota and South Dakota plotted against size of wetland.

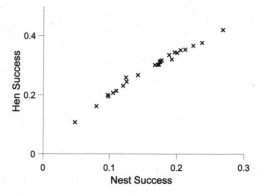

Figure 7.4. Plot of mallard hen success (H) against nest success (P). The linear regression model relating them is $H = 0.03 + 1.54 \times P$.

mallards. If a female mallard is unsuccessful in a nesting attempt, she may try again and, following a second failure, perhaps again (Johnson et al. 1987, 1992). So the probability that a female is successful in hatching a clutch during a breeding season (which we call hen success, H) is related to, but generally higher than, the probability that an individual nesting attempt is successful (nest success, P). This regression model fits the data well ($R^2 = 0.966$), but it does not really explain what is going on. Outside the range of values used to build it, the model does not predict very well. If nest success were 1, for example, the model predicts that hen success would be 1.57—an impossibly large value for a probability.

The process of renesting can be graphically modeled as in Figure 7.5. If

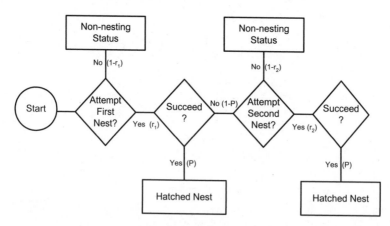

Figure 7.5. Flowchart showing nesting of mallards.

we make some fairly reasonable assumptions about rates of renesting, we end up with this model (Cowardin and Johnson 1979):

$$H = Pe^{(1 - P)^2} \qquad [7.1]$$

This model relates hen success to nest success, as does the regression model, but in a more complex and biologically meaningful way. This is a mechanistic model. It is also fairly elegant, but unlike Einstein's model, it is only approximate. More often, we have to use complex models that involve flowcharts and computer simulation. Such models have numerous components and interrelationships, and their flowcharts would look like Figure 7.5 multiplied many times.

VERIFICATION AND SENSITIVITY ANALYSIS

Verification is sometimes confused with validation, but it is best to distinguish the two concepts (Figure 7.6). Verification is more a mechanical issue. Its aim is to determine if the model behaves as it was intended (Van Horn 1969), that the algorithm or computer code is correct (Haefner 1996), that the modeling formalism is correct, and that ideas are faithfully and accurately translated into computer code or mathematical formulations (Rykiel 1996). Verification also has been called assessing design consistency (House 1974).

Sensitivity analysis is another procedure used to evaluate models but is not itself validation. Sensitivity analysis involves systematically and comprehensively testing to see how changes in the model's parameters affect its output. The key notion is that parameters which cause significant change in a model's behavior should be estimated well (Rykiel 1996). Sensitivity analysis does provide valuable insight into how the model functions and suggests levels of confidence we should have in the model (Grant et al. 1997). Although it has been suggested that sensitivity analysis is appropriate only for predictive models (Bunnell 1989), this procedure can be used with explanatory models to determine the most influential parameters.

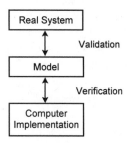

Figure 7.6. Validation relates the model to the real system being modeled; verification relates the model to its computer implementation.

For simple mathematical models, sensitivity analysis can be done analytically. For most models, however, it is necessary to do perturbation analysis with, for example, a fractional factorial design (Starfield and Bleloch 1991). Modelers often vary parameters one at a time. But because the parameters may have interactive effects, they should be varied in combination (Starfield and Bleloch 1991; Henderson-Sellers and Henderson-Sellers 1996). For stochastic models (which can yield different results with the same set of input values), results are more accurate if the stochasticity is eliminated for the sensitivity analysis (Grant et al. 1997).

VALIDATION

Validation is a term that has been applied to a wide variety of attributes of models. Marcot et al. (1983) identified 23 fairly distinct criteria for model validation (including precision, generality, realism, accuracy, robustness, and resolution), and more could be added to their list.

One line of thinking is that models, analogous to hypotheses, can never be proved correct (validated); they can only be invalidated (Holling 1978). Conversely, if a model is corroborated by experience (that is, empirically), it is tentatively accepted until proved false (Popper 1959). By this criterion, a valid model is one that has not failed validation tests (McCarl 1984). Starfield and Bleloch (1991) say that validation in this formal sense is often impossible; it is replaced by an iterative process during which we slowly gain confidence in the model. As more tests are conducted, either the model becomes known to be invalid or else it assumes greater credibility (Rubinstein 1975; McCarl 1984).

Several of the criteria categorized as model validation apply especially to models with explanatory purposes. These criteria include the following: agreement between the real system and the model (Van Horn 1969; Goodall 1972; Power 1993); confidence that an inference about a simulated process is the correct conclusion for the actual process (Van Horn 1969); reasonableness of the model's structure, mechanisms, and overall behavior (Grant et al. 1997); ability to explain the system's behavior (Marcot et al. 1983); the degree to which the model mimics reality as perceived by the developer (McCarl 1984); and the absence of known flaws (Oreskes et al. 1994). The emphasis in these criteria is on the model itself and its veracity, not on output from the model. As learning tools, models may be most valuable when they are clearly wrong (Bunnell 1989)—for the incorrectness encourages further investigation.

Other validation criteria are better suited to models for predictive and decision-making purposes. Among these are the usefulness (Marcot et al. 1983) and accuracy of predictions from the model (Goodall 1972; House

1974; Marcot et al. 1983) and the quantitative correspondence between the model's behavior and the behavior of the real system (Grant et al. 1997). Note the emphasis here on comparison of outputs from the model to those from the real system. A reasonable attitude is "If it ain't broke, don't fix it" (Bunnell 1989).

A third set of criteria is more general and applies equally well to models used for explanatory, predictive, and decision-making purposes. These criteria address the model's *usefulness* (Mankin et al. 1977; Rykiel 1996). Grant et al. (1997), for example, referred to models being good enough to satisfy our needs. Related notions include whether or not the model contributes to better decisions (McCarl 1984) and whether the model has accuracy sufficient for its intended objectives (Rykiel 1996). For explanatory models, Levins (1966) says that the issue is not the truth of the model but whether or not it generates relevant and testable hypotheses. Starfield and Bleloch (1991) note that a model's quality depends not on how realistic it is but on how well it performs in relation to its purpose.

AN ALTERNATIVE TO VALIDATION

Such criteria lead to what I consider a better alternative to the term validation: *evaluation*. By this definition:

> A model has value if it provides better insight, predictions, or control than would be available without the model.

Let us agree that evaluation can be defined as the assessment of a model's usefulness for its intended application. The key notion, then, is that evaluation is specific to the purpose of the model (Bunnell 1989). Thus evaluation relates to the model's potential application and uses, not to the model itself (McCarl 1984; Mayer and Butler 1993). A model suitable for one application may not survive evaluation tests when applied to other uses (Rubinstein 1975). For evaluation, the modeler must specify the purpose of the model, the criteria to be met for the model to be deemed acceptable for use, and the context in which the model is intended to operate (Rykiel 1996).

Evaluation seems a better term than *validation* because *value* is a relative term, whereas *valid* is absolute. Something is either valid or not, but the same thing can have value ranging from none to a little to a great deal. Likewise, models may range widely in their usefulness. Moreover, *valid* is not context-specific but *value* is. A hammer has little value for drilling a hole but great value for pounding a nail. Analogously, a model may have tremendous value for one application but be totally useless for a different one.

EVALUATION METHODS

Many methods traditionally used to validate models apply equally well to the notion of evaluation in that they can be used to compare different models or alternatives. These methods are varied. The easiest way is simply to assume the model is adequate and proceed to implement the results with no evaluation (McCarl 1984). This is certainly the lowest-cost approach (Van Horn 1969).

It is not feasible to develop standard evaluation criteria that apply universally across the range of all models (Mayer and Butler 1993; Grant et al. 1997). Grant et al., however, list several steps in model evaluation. One step is to examine the reasonableness of the model's structure and mechanisms. This step is especially important for mechanistic models, for which our primary interest lies in the mechanisms; it may not be relevant for descriptive models, for which the output is of prime concern. The process is in a sense the same as hypothesis testing in that a model is a collection of hypotheses that we try to disprove. Conversely, Goodall (1972) has argued that, for ecosystem models, testing is not comparable to hypothesis testing because a model is known beforehand to be imperfect; however, nearly all hypotheses that are tested statistically also are known to be false (Johnson 1995, 1999; Cherry 1998). The qualitative reasonableness of the model's overall behavior is important for all types of models (Grant et al. 1997). It is worthwhile checking to see if the model can yield impossible values (such as survival rates that exceed 1) or exhibits other unreasonable behavior. Critical testing involves examining the model under a wide range of input values. Does the model yield plausible results under extreme conditions and combinations (Rykiel 1996)? Often a model can be calibrated to eliminate aberrant behavior.

Another step is to examine the quantitative correspondence between the model's behavior and the real system (Grant et al. 1997). This step is especially relevant for descriptive models and may not apply for uses of mechanistic models. As we shall see, numerous statistical tools are available for this step. Details can be found in Reynolds et al. (1981), McCarl (1984), Mayer and Butler (1993), Haefner (1996), Rykiel (1996), and Grant et al. (1997). Mayer and Butler (1993) class validation techniques into four groups: subjective assessment, visual techniques, measures of deviation, and statistical tests. These methods generally involve a comparison of model output to values of the real system.

Subjective Assessment. One method that does not compare model and true values is the use of expert opinion (McCarl 1984) or determination of face validity: asking knowledgeable persons to assess the model and its behavior (Rykiel 1996). A Turing test—in which knowledgeable persons try to distinguish the model's behavior from that of the real system (Rykiel 1996)—is another subjective method. Subjective tests are clearly prone to personal bias and should be avoided.

Visualization Techniques. This category includes comparing time series of real observations and model results, plotting actual values against predicted values, comparing quantile plots, and graphing differences between actual and predicted values against various input variables. Cleveland (1993) has discussed many techniques, and Tufte (1983) provides an excellent perspective on visualization. Such methods are still subjective, however, and may be misleading (Mayer and Butler 1993; Rykiel 1996).

Measures of Deviation. These methods are applicable when actual data (y) and modeled data ($\hat{y}$) can be paired by time, location, treatment, and so forth (Mayer and Butler 1993). Diverse measures of deviation based on the difference between y and $\hat{y}$ can be used. A useful measure is the root mean square error:

$$\text{RMSE} = \sqrt{\Sigma \, (y - \hat{y})^2}$$

RMSE reflects the absolute difference between actual and model values, is in the same units as these values, and incorporates both bias and imprecision.

Statistical Tests. The fourth class of evaluation methods involves the use of t tests, F tests, contingency tables, correlation coefficients, and other statistical tools to compare actual and model results. See Mayer and Butler (1993) or Grant et al. (1997) for details.

It is best to test a model with data different from those used to build or calibrate the model. Success with new data assures what has been termed *predictive validity* (Power 1993). Simply matching the data used in the model's development ascertains only replicative validity. New data are better for testing than is the reuse of old data (Power 1993). If new data cannot be obtained, an alternative is data splitting: build the model using some of the available data and test the model on the remaining data (Snee 1977; Rykiel 1996). This procedure is also known as historical data validation.

Comparing the average model response to the average response of the actual system is only a beginning. Variation in response may be important as well (Cipra 2000). We can further compare the variances of the two distributions and even the distributions themselves (Goodall 1972). Moreover, we can examine what is termed *event validity* by comparing the occurrences, timing, and magnitude of simulated and actual events (Rykiel 1996).

Theil's inequality coefficient (Theil 1966; Rice and Cochran 1984;

Power 1993) can be used to assess the adequacy of the model's fit. This statistic can be decomposed into components that represent (1) a bias in the model due to differences in the means of predictions and actual values, (2) differences in the variances of the model and the actual system, and (3) imperfect correlation between the model and the system. Theil's coefficient is particularly useful if there are two or more models to be evaluated.

Data for testing a model should be comprehensive and reflect the full range of situations to which the model will be applied (Goodall 1972; McCarl 1984). Sometimes model results are compared not to actual data but to output from another model (Rykiel 1996). Getting comparable results from different models may be reassuring—especially if one of the models already has credibility. And if two models, built on different sets of assumptions, lead to similar conclusions, we have more confidence in the robustness of these conclusions. Different results from two models indicate that at least one of the models is inadequate.

THOUGHTS ON EVALUATION

Different models may fit the data equally well but lead to far different inferences or predictions. Consider, for example, the data in Figure 7.4 showing the success of mallard hens related to success of their nests. They are fit equally well by the regression model in Figure 7.4 and by Equation (7.1). Yet predictions from the two models may be very different. For a value of nest success equal to 1, the regression model predicts hen success to be 1.57. Equation (7.1) yields a hen success value of 1, however, which is biologically more reasonable. Moreover, it is widely recognized that extrapolation beyond the range of data on which a model is based may lead to incorrect conclusions. This caveat is especially critical for descriptive, statistical models as opposed to mechanistic models. A mechanistic model will maintain reasonableness for parameter values outside those from which they were developed better than would descriptive models, as long as the mechanistic models adequately incorporate features of the real system. It is generally argued that models pass validation tests if their results closely match actual system values. It is too often forgotten, however, that the data themselves are fallible and subject to error (McCarl 1984; Rykiel 1996). This situation is especially likely in wildlife ecology—a field with many poorly estimated parameters (Holling 1978).

Model evaluation is a continuing process (Box 1980; Mayer and Butler 1993). A model should be evaluated early and often, not just after it has become operational (Miller et al. 1976; Grant et al. 1997). Evaluation tests can be applied at the design stage, at the implementation stage, and during operation (Rykiel 1996). Validated models may not be valid forever, however, depending on the system of interest (McCarl 1984). Models should be reevaluated and, if necessary, revised or recalibrated as new information becomes available or the settings in which the model is used change. If the model is used regularly, it is worthwhile stepping back occasionally to see if it remains applicable.

Bunnell (1989) cites four excuses for not attempting to evaluate a model. First, evaluation may take too long relative to the need for using the model. This problem is especially likely to arise when we are modeling processes that have long temporal patterns, such as forest succession. Second, the political will to conduct evaluation tests may be lacking—especially if the evaluation involves unpopular decisions. Third, users simply may not care enough about the model to make the effort to evaluate it. And fourth, modelers may not be aware of proper methods of evaluation.

If our testing finds the model invalid (for its intended purposes), we can discard the model and declare it invalid (McCarl 1984; Rykiel 1996). At the other extreme, we can ignore the evaluation results. More realistically, we can qualify the use of the model by restricting its application to situations in which it is appropriate. And finally, we can revise the model. Most simply, the model may be made acceptable by recalibrating it and changing the values of the parameters. More fundamentally, the structure of the model can be modified.

In conclusion, all models are wrong. Some models, however, are useful (Box 1979a, 1979b). Since the discovery that space is curved, Euclidean geometry has been known to be wrong. But for day-to-day applications, it certainly is useful enough. Validation—or, better, evaluation—strives to determine which models are in fact useful.

ACKNOWLEDGMENTS

I am grateful to R. R. Cox Jr., J. W. Grier, W. E. Newton, G. A. Sargeant, two anonymous reviewers, and the editors for valuable comments on the manuscript and thank B. R. Euliss for help with the graphics.

REFERENCES

Berryman, A. A. 1991. Population theory: An essential ingredient in pest prediction, management, and policy-making. *American Entomologist* 37:138–142.

Box, G. E. P. 1979a. Some problems of statistics and everyday life. *Journal of the American Statistical Association* 74:1–4.

———. 1979b. Robustness in the strategy of scientific model building. Pages 201–236 in R. L. Launer and G. N. Wilkinson, eds., *Robustness in Statistics.* New York: Academic Press.

————. 1980. Sampling and Bayes' inference in scientific modelling and robustness. *Journal of the Royal Statistical Society Series* A143:383–430.

Bunnell, F. L. 1989. *Alchemy and Uncertainty: What Good Are Models?* General Technical Report PNW-GTR-232. Portland: USDA Forest Service Pacific Northwest Research Station.

Cherry, S. 1998. Statistical tests in publications of the Wildlife Society. *Wildlife Society Bulletin* 26:947–953.

Cipra, B. 2000. Revealing uncertainties in computer models. *Science* 287:960–961.

Cleveland, W. S. 1993. *Visualizing Data.* Summit, N.J.: Hobart Press.

Cowardin, L. M., and D. H. Johnson. 1979. Mathematics and mallard management. *Journal of Wildlife Management* 43:18–35.

Gold, H. J. 1977. *Mathematical Modeling of Biological Systems—An Introductory Guidebook.* New York: Wiley.

Goodall, D. W. 1972. Building and testing ecosystem models. Pages 173–194 in J. N. R. Jeffers, ed., *Mathematical Models in Ecology.* Oxford: Blackwell.

Grant, W. E., E. K. Pedersen, and S. L. Martin. 1997. *Ecology and Natural Resources Management: Systems Analysis and Simulation.* New York: Wiley.

Haefner, J. W. 1996. *Modeling Biological Systems: Principles and Applications.* New York: Chapman & Hall.

Henderson-Sellers, B., and A. Henderson-Sellers. 1996. Sensitivity evaluation of environmental models using fractional factorial experimentation. *Ecological Modelling* 86:291–295.

Holling, C. S. 1978. *Adaptive Environmental Assessment and Management.* New York: Wiley.

House, P. W. 1974. Diogenes revisited—the search for a valid model. *Simulation* 23: 117–125.

Johnson, D. H. 1995. Statistical sirens: The allure of nonparametrics. *Ecology* 76: 1998–2000.

————. 1999. The insignificance of statistical significance testing. *Journal of Wildlife Management* 63:763–772.

Johnson, D. H., D. W. Sparling, and L. M. Cowardin. 1987. A model of the productivity of the mallard duck. *Ecological Modelling* 38:257–275.

Johnson, D. H., J. D. Nichols, and M. D. Schwartz. 1992. Population dynamics of breeding waterfowl. Pages 446–485 in B. D. J. Batt, A. D. Afton, M. G. Anderson, C. D. Ankney, D. H. Johnson, J. A. Kadlec, and G. L. Krapu, eds., *Ecology and Management of Breeding Waterfowl.* Minneapolis: University of Minnesota Press.

Levins, R. 1966. The strategy of model building in population biology. *American Scientist* 54:421–431.

Mankin, J. B., R. V. O'Neill, H. H. Shugart, and B. W. Rust. 1977. The importance of validation in ecosystem analysis. Pages 63–71 in G. S. Innis, ed., *New Directions in the Analysis of Ecological Systems, Part 1.* La Jolla, Calif.: Simulation Councils.

Marcot, B. G., M. G. Raphael, and K. H. Berry. 1983. Monitoring wildlife habitat and validation of wildlife-habitat relationships models. *North American Wildlife and Natural Resources Conference* 48:315–329.

Mayer, D. G., and D. G. Butler. 1993. Statistical validation. *Ecological Modelling* 68:21–32.

McCarl, B. A. 1984. Model validation: An overview with some emphasis on risk models. *Review of Marketing and Agricultural Economics* 52:153–173.

Miller, D. R., G. Butler, and L. Bramall. 1976. Validation of ecological system models. *Journal of Environmental Management* 4:383–401.

Oreskes, N., K. Shrader-Frechette, and K. Belitz. 1994. Verification, validation, and confirmation of numerical models in the earth sciences. *Science* 263:641–646.

Popper, K. 1959. *The Logic of Scientific Discovery.* New York: Harper & Row.

Power, M. 1993. The predictive validation of ecological and environmental models. *Ecological Modelling* 68:33–50.

Reynolds, M. R., Jr., H. E. Burkhart, and R. F. Daniels. 1981. Procedures for statistical validation of stochastic simulation models. *Forest Science* 27:349–364.

Rice, J. A., and P. A. Cochran. 1984. Independent evaluation of a bioenergetics model for largemouth bass. *Ecology* 65:732–739.

Rubinstein, M. F. 1975. *Patterns of Problem Solving.* Englewood Cliffs, N.J.: Prentice-Hall.

Rykiel, E. J., Jr. 1996. Testing ecological models: The meaning of validation. *Ecological Modelling* 90:229–244.

Snee, R. D. 1977. Validation of regression models: Methods and examples. *Technometrics* 19:415–428.

Starfield, A. M., and A. L. Bleloch. 1991. *Building Models for Conservation and Wildlife Management.* 2nd ed. Edina, Minn.: Burgess.

Theil, H. 1966. *Applied Econometric Forecasting.* Amsterdam: North-Holland.

Tufte, E. R. 1983. *The Visual Display of Quantitative Information.* Cheshire, Conn.: Graphics Press.

Van Horn, R. 1969. Validation. Pages 232–251 in T. H. Naylor, ed., *The Design of Computer Simulation Experiments.* Durham: Duke University Press.

PART III

Applying Models

CHAPTER 8

Population Viability Analysis: Development, Interpretation, and Application

Mark S. Boyce

The theme of this book focuses on valid modeling. If there is one arena in applied ecology where we frequently see abuses of modeling, it is in applications of population viability analysis (PVA). PVA is the process of constructing models to estimate the probability of persistence (or extinction) for a population—typically a threatened or endangered species (Boyce 1992). Analysts often construct viability models with virtually no empirical basis for the ecological mechanisms that drive population fluctuations. Estimates for variables and parameters are often based on low sample sizes, little or no replication, and guesses.

Modeling can be a powerful tool for exploring "what if?" options and framing hypotheses about how a system works. If this were the spirit in which PVA was applied, it could be very useful. In practice, however, viability models are shaping management policy and contributing substantially to the outcome of major resource management decisions (Mace and Lande 1991; Murphy and Noon 1992; Noon and McKelvey 1996). User-friendly software is available that makes PVA modeling easy—even for the construction of remarkably complex models (Boyce 1996). But various software packages yield different results, even with the same data (Mills et al. 1996), and seldom do users have data sufficient to justify the complex models used in many PVA simulations. Rather than testing them in the context of adaptive management (Boyce 1997), researchers are often defensive of their models (Walters 1997). Such approaches stifle the objective development of knowledge.

About eight years ago I prepared a review of PVA (Boyce 1992). Most of what I said in that review, I think, is still applicable today. But I remain concerned about the way in which PVA is being applied to conservation problems. My purpose here is to target a few topics that require additional attention. In the spirit of this volume, I offer caveats and examples that will help people performing PVAs to develop valid models and interpret them correctly.

POPULATION TRAJECTORIES

Time-series models have been used to project populations into the future (Tuljapurkar and Orzack 1980; Boyce and Miller 1985; Dennis et al. 1991). If a population is declining and retains the same trajectory, ultimately it will go extinct. Even constant or increasing populations might go extinct during stochastic (random) excursions that fall below some critical threshold. The beauty of using time series for PVA is that the stochastic theory is well understood and computations are reasonably easy.

In the summer of 1997 the National Marine Fisheries Service (NMFS) posted news releases that the Steller sea lion (*Eumetopias jubatus*) was facing a 100 percent probability of extinction within 60 to 80 years. Details of the analysis were not presented for the popular press, but by inspecting the declining trajectory in numbers of Steller sea lions we easily can see the basis for such a claim (NMFS 1995; Figure 8.1). Indeed, using the diffusion method reviewed by Dennis et al. (1991), we can see that if a population shows a declining trend the probability of extinction is 1. I believe that such a projection for Steller sea lion is naive and alarmist, however. Inspecting the details of population trends, we see that a few local populations are actually increasing—southeastern Alaska, for example—even though the overall trend is dramatically downward (York et al. 1996). Although we do not know the cause for the decline, the most frequently postulated reason relates to conflict with certain types of commercial fishing. A reasonable hypothesis is that fish stocks have been depleted by commercial fishing, thereby reducing the carrying capacity of sea lions. But local populations in areas not heavily fished could be stable or increasing. Incorporating such spatial structure into the population models will greatly reduce the likelihood of extinction (Stacey and Taper 1992; White 2000).

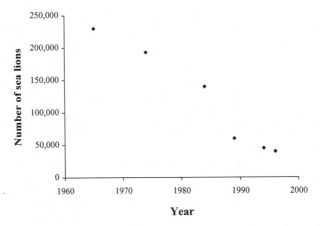

Figure 8.1. Population trajectory of the western stock of Steller sea lions (data from NMFS 1995).

Grizzly bears (*Ursus arctos horribilis*) in the Greater Yellowstone ecosystem have been studied intensively (Knight and Eberhardt 1985; Craighead et al. 1995), and several researchers have used the grizzly bear data to illustrate or contrast PVA methods (Dennis et al. 1991; Foley 1994; Mills et al. 1996). Applying the population trajectory approach to the 1961–1987 time series of counts of females with cubs of the year, Dennis et al. (1991) concluded that the Yellowstone grizzly bear population was "doomed to extinction." This conclusion emerged from the observation that because counts showed a decline over the 27-year interval, the probability of extinction must be 1 (Figure 8.2).

The fallacy in this approach is the implicit assumption that the popula-

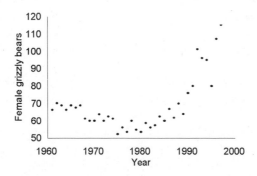

Figure 8.2. Estimated number of adult female grizzly bears in the Yellowstone ecosystem (1961–1997). Adjustments to original counts have been made to account for variation in detectability and search intensity during surveys (Boyce et al. 2001).

tion is driven by a stationary stochastic process. In other words, we are assuming that the mechanism causing the population to decline over the period from 1961 to 1987 will continue to operate in the same fashion in the future. Such stationarity in population processes is seldom the case in conservation applications, however. For grizzly bears, changes in management have affected population trajectories. Around 1970, Yellowstone National Park decided to close the garbage dumps in the park even though many grizzly bears depended on them as a food source (Schullery 1992; Craighead et al. 1995). As a consequence, grizzly bear mortality was high during the 1970s (Knight and Eberhardt 1985). Concern over the declining bear population led to the formation of the Interagency Grizzly Bear Committee in 1983 and the implementation of urgent measures to reduce bear mortality. The data used by Dennis et al. (1991)—which led to the conclusion that the population was doomed to extinction—were gathered only 4 years into the new management regimen. At that point the overall trajectory was still one of population decline. Since 1983, however, the population has increased (Eberhardt et al. 1994; Boyce et al. 2001). Updating the time series with 10 more years of data using the same method as Dennis et al. (1991) for the interval 1961–1997, I found that the probability of extinction declined from 1 to almost zero (3.7×10^{-6}). Because the trend is distinctly nonlinear (Figure 8.2), I calculated the extinction risk for the interval 1983–1997 separately and found an even smaller probability of extinction (7.2×10^{-11}).

Clearly the assumption of stationarity is not valid, and clearly the estimates of extinction probability emerging from such calculations are unreliable. Even when we have good time-series data, extrapolations of population trajectories do not usually constitute valid modeling. The very nature of conservation management aims to alter declines in population or ensure that habitats are preserved. Thus any conservation action is likely to violate the underlying assumption of process stationarity. If the intent is to point out the consequences of continuing on a particular trend, such time-series methods offer useful illustrations. But we must be careful in presentation and interpretation.

I am more optimistic, however, about applications of another time-series approach. Autoregressive (AR) models can be used to characterize population processes (Royama 1992). Second-order or higher AR models can capture the dynamics emerging from a trophic-level interaction—such as a plant/herbivore or predator/prey system. Autoregressive coefficients may then be related to ecological variables in order to characterize complex ecological interactions (Bjørnstad et al. 1995; Stenseth et al. 1996). This is an important development because the statistical theory associated with AR models is understood well. Thus we can develop models that capture some of the true complexity of nature while keeping them simple enough to be statistically defensible. Applications of autoregressive models in PVA have great potential.

DEMOGRAPHIC ANALYSES

Most viability models to date have been structured population models. A common approach is to estimate vital rates and the variances associated with them and then compute a measure of population growth—such as the dominant eigenvalue, λ, of a projection matrix (Forsman et al. 1996). Such estimates of population growth are valid only for the time period over which vital rates were estimated. Results of this sort of analysis face precisely the same problem of interpretation as the population trajectory approach. Simply put: demographic approaches for predicting population trajectories into the future also must assume stationarity of population processes for such projections to be meaningful. But in practice, vital rates change—almost always. As illustrated by the Yellowstone grizzly bear example, the fact that a population might have declined during a time interval gives us little insight into its long-term future.

Another demographic approach commonly used in PVA is sensitivity analysis (Crouse et al. 1987; Meyer and Boyce 1994). Here the basic idea is to calculate the response in population growth rate, λ, resulting from change in a vital rate v, that is $\partial\lambda/\partial v$. By comparing sensitivities, we can find which vital rates result in the greatest population response. For long-lived species with long generation times, we find generally that sensitivity to adult survival is greater than for juvenile survival or reproductive parameters. Conversely, for short-lived species, growth rate sensitivity is highest for fecundity and juvenile survival (Lebreton and Clobert 1991).

Several modelers have suggested that conservation efforts ought to focus on the most sensitive vital rates (Crouse et al. 1987; Lande 1988). This application of sensitivity analysis is problematic for several reasons. First, even though a vital rate might possess high sensitivity, that rate may not vary much and hence may contribute little to variation in population growth. Survival patterns in mammals offer a useful illustration. Even though adult survival may have high sensitivity, it usually varies only a fraction as much as juvenile or subadult survival (Charnov 1986). Thus the contribution to λ from variation in adult survival may be very small. The contribution to variance in population growth from a vital rate is approximately the sensitivity squared times the variance, adjusted for covariance (Brault and Caswell 1993; Nations and Boyce 1997). For populations of large mammals (Gaillard et al. 1998) and seabirds (Nur and Sydeman 1999), the major demographic source of variation in population size tends to be juvenile and subadult survival.

Another consideration relates to the magnitude of vital rates. Consider a decline in grizzly bear adult survival from 96 percent to 94 percent. This is seemingly a small change of only 2 percent in survival. But if cast in the context of adult mortality, this represents a 50 percent increase (from 0.04 to 0.06). So if we compared the consequences of a given magnitude change in a demographic parameter, say 1 percent, we would reach the nonsensical conclusion that population growth is very sensitive to changes in adult survival but not to changes in adult mortality (Nur and Sydeman 2000). This paradox is usually resolved by normalizing sensitivities to create elasticities (de Kroon et al. 1986; Mills et al. 1999).

Further difficulty with simple interpretations of sensitivity analysis emerges because population growth is a nonlinear function of vital rates (Boyce 1977). This means that perturbation of vital rates will influence growth rate relative to the magnitude of perturbation (Meyer and Boyce 1994). For a long-lived species like a grizzly bear, the relation between λ and selected vital rates is shown in Figure 8.3, where the slope of the solid curves

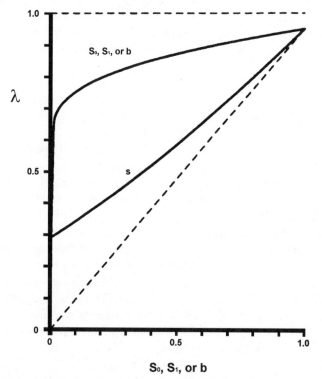

Figure 8.3. Finite population growth factor λ as a function of vital rates of survival and fecundity for a long-lived species. Here s_0 is juvenile survival, s_1 is subadult survival, s is adult survival, and b is fecundity in a Leslie matrix (Meyer and Boyce 1994). The dashed line has a slope of 1. The slope of the curve is the sensitivity, $\partial\lambda/\partial v$.

represents the sensitivities. For a large reduction in juvenile or subadult survival (the top curve in Figure 8.3), for example, we might find the sensitivity to be equal or less than that for adult survival. This seems to contradict Lebreton and Clobert's (1991) observation that sensitivities are ultimately tied to generation time. Reductions in survival ultimately shorten generation time, however, thereby preserving Lebreton and Clobert's generalization.

This discussion of sensitivity analysis has been set in the context of deterministic models (see also Mills et al. 1999). Stochastic model solutions are structurally similar (Nations and Boyce 1997). Instead of the response of λ as a function of vital rates, however, stochastic solutions should be for the response of the long-term growth rate a as a function of vital rates (Tuljapurkar 1989).

Even after sorting out the demographic sources of population fluctuations and sensitivity structure, conservation applications still are not clear. The bottom line is that we must know how effectively we can alter vital rates by management. Although such a management-effectiveness sensitivity analysis is an excellent candidate for adaptive management (Walters 1986; Boyce 1997), I am unaware of any such studies.

VARIATION

Population viability analysis is all about uncertainty and risk (Burgman et al. 1993). Results of a PVA are typically presented as probabilities of persistence or extinction, which should be surrounded by confidence intervals. Major sources of uncertainty in persistence projections are process variance associated with demographic stochasticity, environmental variability (Shaffer 1981), and variation among individuals (White 2000). But something is often overlooked in calculations of uncertainty: sampling variance—that is, variation attributable to estimating a parameter from sample data (see Chapter 3 in this volume). Estimates of stochasticity in the system are always burdened by our limited ability to estimate parameters, and most measures of variance in parameters are confounded with sampling variance. Sampling variability is a component of our uncertainty in the system, and we must think carefully about how to treat it.

One approach is simply to leave the sampling variation confounded with the process variance of parameter estimates—based on the argument that sampling is simply another source of uncertainty that should inflate the variance associated with parameter estimates (Boyce 1994). Such an approach can seriously bias the results, however, because of the way that variance is propagated in the system (Link and Nichols 1994). A more careful approach would be to remove sampling variance from estimates of parameter variation but use the sampling variation to construct variation among iterative runs of the PVA model. If the sampling variance is left confounded with the process variance in parameter estimates, simulations almost certainly will have increased likelihood of extinction. But if sampling variation is extracted and used to base iterations of runs, the consequence of sampling is to expand the confidence intervals surrounding estimates of extinction (or persistence) instead of affecting the estimates themselves (White 2000).

Perhaps the most serious form of uncertainty in PVA occurs when we have no data for certain model parameters. This occurs more frequently than most PVA modelers are willing to admit. One approach is to explore the model's behavior over a range of plausible parameter values and select the parameters that yield the model's behavior most closely mimicking the observed dynamics of the system (Wiegand et al. 1998). A slower way to accomplish the same result would be to invoke adaptive management and revise the model as new data become available (Walters 1986). Moreover, the modeling should help to drive future data collection.

Environmental variation is assumed to increase the risk of extinction (Fagan et al. 1999). Yet some species cannot persist without variation. Aspen (*Populus tremuloides*) on elk (*Cervus elaphus*) winter ranges in the Rocky Mountains requires variation in elk numbers, fire, and climatic fluctuations to persist (Boyce 1990; Romme et al. 1995). Early successional or disturbance-dependent species such as Karner blue butterflies (*Lycaeides melissa samuelis*), sharp-tailed grouse (*Tympanuchus phasianellus*), and Kirtland's warblers (*Dendroica kirtlandii*) require that their habitats be perturbed occasionally to ensure persistence (Boyce and Payne 1997). Populations of such species necessarily will experience demographic variability, and without it they will go extinct. The importance of system variation reinforces the need to model habitats effectively on appropriate spatial scales to anticipate extinction risks (Stacey and Taper 1992).

CHANGING THE PARADIGM FOR PVA

One might fairly ask whether PVA is a worthwhile endeavor. Can we estimate the probability of persistence (or extinction) with sufficient precision or accuracy to be meaningful (Ludwig 1999)? Given the long time horizons over which extinction projections must be made (Marmontel et al. 1997), do we ever have sufficient information to estimate such long-term risks reliably? The answer to both of these questions is no. Therefore, estimates of extinction risk should not be considered as criteria in listing species for protected status—as used, for example, by the IUCN (Mace and Lande 1991; Shackleton 1997). To expect defensible estimates of persistence probability is unrealistic (Taylor 1995), but such expectation misses the true value of PVA. In the words of Hamilton and Moller (1995: 107): "Less reliance should be placed on the predictions of population trends or extinction probabilities than on the model's guidance to the relative efficacy of management actions."

One of the powerful applications of PVA is to develop models for evaluating management alternatives (Thomas et al. 1990; Lindenmayer and Possingham 1996). Moreover, PVA can be a valuable step in adaptive management for threatened or endangered species (Boyce 1997). PVA provides the synthesis and analysis stage from which we can design experimental management and guide the collection of data. Only through such a rigorous interface between PVA modeling, experimental management, monitoring, and reassessment will we gain reliable knowledge with which to manage rare species. Nevertheless, there may be institutional barriers to accomplishing such an approach (Walters 1997). Even though adaptive management protocols were recommended for the northern spotted owl (*Strix occidentalis caurina;* Thomas et al. 1990), the U.S. Fish and Wildlife Service has been unwilling to permit any forest manipulations that might threaten individual owls—despite the long-term ramifications of such experiments (J. W. Thomas, pers. comm.).

One perspective is that most PVAs have been premature and that modeling should await the compilation of a substantial database (Beissinger and Westphal 1998). I disagree. Seldom will we ever secure sufficient data to estimate persistence probability with any rigor. But modeling constitutes a formal statement of hypotheses about how we think the system works. This modeled view of nature always will be wrong. Even so, the process of building a model can be enormously valuable in framing hypotheses, justifying experimental management, and stimulating competing models that ultimately enhance our knowledge. We simply do not understand ecological systems well enough to anticipate all of the information that may be crucial for developing management schemes. So if we demand sufficient data to justify the analysis, seldom will we be able to conduct a PVA.

Models for northern spotted owls offer an illustration. Even had we been compiling monitoring data on northern spotted owls for several years before developing models of owl populations, I doubt we would have had sufficient information with which to make sound management decisions or even form the basis for a useful model. Only after Lande (1987, 1988) proposed his models for northern spotted owls did ecologists and managers begin to think seriously about the possible importance of habitat fragmentation and the threat of an extinction threshold for the species. Subsequent field research on landscape configuration and owl dispersal and distribution has challenged the relevance of Lande's metapopulation models for spotted owls (Meyer et al. 1998). But without Lande's pioneering models, our research efforts would not have asked the right questions. Sometimes models help us to find answers without extensive field investigation. Simulation studies of southern California spotted owls, for example, led to the conclusion that although data on dispersal were meager, they were very unlikely to have important consequences for model predictions (LaHaye et al. 1994).

Modeling has begun to take an exciting new direction involving habitat-based PVAs. Geographic information systems (GIS) have been used to characterize habitat features, and these have been linked to the distribution and abundance of animals using resource selection functions (Manly et al. 1993; Boyce et al. 1994; Mace et al. 1996; Boyce and McDonald 1999). The consequences of landscape management actions can be anticipated by using GIS modeling (Akçakaya and Atwood 1997). Using such landscape models as a foundation for predicting future habitats, PVA modeling can be used to calculate population trajectories over modest time horizons, say 100 years, in ways that are directly linked to land-use management (Boyce 1996). Such spatially explicit modeling can be applied to the design of nature reserves (Lindenmayer and Possingham 1996). Although methodological details require more research and every application will present new challenges, the future of many threatened and endangered species may be dramatically enhanced by this powerful merger of modeling, empirical research, and management.

ACKNOWLEDGMENTS

Thanks to Steve Beissinger, Nadav Nur, and Gary White for permission to cite their unpublished papers. Thanks to Dick Knight, Mark Haroldson, Chris Servheen, and the Interagency Grizzly Bear Study Team for providing unpublished data from the Yellowstone ecosystem.

REFERENCES

Akçakaya, H. R., and J. L. Atwood. 1997. A habitat-based metapopulation model of the California gnatcatcher. *Conservation Biology* 11:422–434.

Beissinger, S. R., and M. I. Westphal. 1998. On the use of demographic models of population viability in endangered species management. *Journal of Wildlife Management* 62:821–841.

Bjørnstad, O. N., W. Falck, and N. Chr. Stenseth. 1995. A geographic gradient in small rodent density fluctuations: A statistical modelling approach. *Proceedings of the Royal Society* B262:127–133.

Boyce, M. S. 1977. Population growth with stochastic fluctuations in the life table. *Theoretical Population Biology* 12:366–373.

————. 1990. Elk winter feeding dampens population fluctuations at the National Elk Refuge. *Western States and Provinces Elk Workshop Proceedings* 1988:18–25.

————. 1992. Population viability analysis. *Annual Review of Ecology and Systematics* 23:481–506.

————. 1994. Population viability analysis exemplified by models for the northern spotted owl. Pages 3–18 in D. J. Fletcher and B. F. J. Manly, eds., *Statistics in Ecology and Environmental Monitoring.* Dunedin, N.Z.: University of Otago Press.

————. 1996. Review of RAMAS/GIS. *Quarterly Review of Biology* 71:167–168.

————. 1997. Population viability analysis: Adaptive management for threatened and endangered species. Pages 226–236 in M. S. Boyce and A. Haney, eds., *Ecosystem Management: Applications for Sustainable Forest and Wildlife Resources.* New Haven: Yale University Press.

Boyce, M. S., and L. L. McDonald. 1999. Relating populations to habitats using resource selection functions. *Trends in Ecology and Evolution* 14:268–272.

Boyce, M. S., and R. S. Miller. 1985. Ten-year periodicity in whooping crane census. *Auk* 102:658–660.

Boyce, M. S., and N. F. Payne. 1997. Applied disequilibriums: Riparian habitat management for wildlife. Pages 133–146 in M. S. Boyce and A. Haney, eds., *Ecosystem Management: Applications for Sustainable Forest and Wildlife Resources.* New Haven: Yale University Press.

Boyce, M. S., J. S. Meyer, and L. L. Irwin. 1994. Habitat-based PVA for the northern spotted owl. Pages 63–85 in D. J. Fletcher and B. F. J. Manly, eds., *Statistics in Ecology and Environmental Monitoring.* Dunedin, N.Z.: University of Otago Press.

Boyce, M. S., B. M. Blanchard, R. R. Knight, and C. Servheen. 2001. Population viability for grizzly bears: A critical review. International Association for Bear Research and Management, Monograph Series 4:1–37.

Brault, S., and H. Caswell. 1993. Pod-specific demography of killer whales (*Orcinus orca*). *Ecology* 74:1444–1455.

Burgman, M. A., S. Ferson, and H. R. Akçakaya. 1993. *Risk Assessment in Conservation Biology.* New York: Chapman & Hall.

Charnov, E. L. 1986. Life history evolution in a "recruitment population": Why are adult mortality rates constant? *Oikos* 47:120–134.

Craighead, J. J., J. S. Sumner, and J. A. Mitchell. 1995. *The Grizzly Bears of Yellowstone: Their Ecology in the Yellowstone Ecosystem, 1959–1992.* Washington, D.C., and Covelo, Calif.: Island Press.

Crouse, D. T., L. B. Crowder, and H. Caswell. 1987. A stage-based population model for loggerhead sea turtles and implications for conservation. *Ecology* 68:1412–1423.

de Kroon, H., A. Plaiser, J. van Groenendael, and H. Caswell. 1986. Elasticity: The relative contribution of demographic parameters to population growth rate. *Ecology* 67:115–143.

Dennis, B., P. L. Munholland, and J. M. Scott. 1991. Estimation of growth and extinction parameters for endangered species. *Ecological Monographs* 61:115–143.

Eberhardt, L. L., B. M. Blanchard, and R. R. Knight. 1994. Population trend of the Yellowstone grizzly bear as estimated from reproductive and survival rates. *Canadian Journal of Zoology* 72:360–363.

Fagan, W. F., E. Meir, and J. L. Moore. 1999. Variation thresholds for extinction and their implications for conservation strategies. *American Naturalist* 154:510–520.

Foley, P. 1994. Predicting extinction times from environmental stochasticity and carrying capacity. *Conservation Biology* 8:124–137.

Forsman, E. D., S. DeStefano, M. G. Raphael, and R. J. Gutierrez, eds. 1996. Demography of the northern spotted owl. *Studies in Avian Biology* 17:1–122.

Gaillard, J. M., M. Festa-Bianchet, and N. G. Yoccoz. 1998. Population dynamics of large herbivores: Variable recruitment with constant adult survival. *Trends in Ecology and Evolution* 13:58–63.

Hamilton, S., and H. Moller. 1995. Can PVA models using computer packages offer useful conservation advice? Sooty shearwaters *Puffinus griseus* in New Zealand as a case study. *Biological Conservation* 73:107–117.

Knight, R. R., and L. L. Eberhardt. 1985. Population dynamics of Yellowstone grizzly bears. *Ecology* 66:323–334.

LaHaye, W., R. J. Gutierrez, and H. R. Akçakaya. 1994. Spotted owl metapopulation dynamics in southern California. *Journal of Animal Ecology* 63:775–778.

Lande, R. 1987. Extinction thresholds in demographic models of territorial populations. *American Naturalist* 130:624–635.

———. 1988. Demographic models of the northern spotted owl (*Strix occidentalis caurina*). *Oecologia* 75:601–607.

Lebreton, J. D., and J. Clobert. 1991. Bird population dynamics, management, and conservation: The role of mathematical modelling. Pages 105–124 in C. M. Perrins, J. D. Lebreton, and G. J. M. Hirons, eds., *Bird Population Studies: Their Relevance to Conservation and Management.* Oxford: Oxford University Press.

Lindenmayer, D. B., and H. P. Possingham. 1996. Ranking conservation and timber management options for Leadbeater's possum in southeastern Australia using population viability analysis. *Conservation Biology* 10:235–251.

Link, W. A., and J. D. Nichols. 1994. On the importance of sampling variation to investigations of temporal variation in animal population size. *Oikos* 69:539–544.

Ludwig, D. 1999. Is it meaningful to estimate a probability of extinction? *Ecology* 80:298–310.

Mace, G. M., and R. Lande. 1991. Assessing extinction threats: Toward a reevaluation of IUCN threatened species categories. *Conservation Biology* 5:148–157.

Mace, R. D., J. S. Waller, T. L. Manley, L. J. Lyon, and H. Zuuring. 1996. Relationships among grizzly bears, roads, and habitat in the Swan Mountains, Montana. *Journal of Applied Ecology* 33:1395–1404.

Manly, B. F. J., L. L. McDonald, and D. Thomas. 1993. *Resource Selection by Animals.* London: Chapman & Hall.

Marmontel, M., S. R. Humphrey, and T. J. O'Shea. 1997. Population viability analysis of the Florida manatee (*Trichechus manatus latirostris*), 1976–1991. *Conservation Biology* 11:467–481.

Meyer, J. S., and M. S. Boyce. 1994. Life historical consequences of pesticides and other insults to vital rates. Pages 349–363 in R. J. Kendall and T. E. Lacher, eds., *Wildlife Toxicology and Population Modeling: Integrated Studies of Agroecosystems.* Washington, D.C.: Lewis.

Meyer, J. S., L. L. Irwin, and M. S. Boyce. 1998. Influence of habitat abundance and fragmentation on northern spotted owls in western Oregon. *Wildlife Monographs* 139:1–51.

Mills, L. S., S. G. Hayes, C. Baldwin, M. J. Wisdom, J. Citta, D. J. Mattson, and K. Murphy. 1996. Factors leading to different viability predictions for a grizzly bear data set. *Conservation Biology* 10:863–373.

Mills, L. S., D. F. Doak, and M. J. Wisdom. 1999. Reliability of conservation actions based on elasticity analysis of matrix models. *Conservation Biology* 13:815–829.

Murphy, D. D., and B. R. Noon. 1992. Integrating scientific methods with habitat conservation planning: Reserve design for northern spotted owls. *Ecological Applications* 2:3–17.

National Marine Fisheries Service (NMFS). 1995. *Status Review of Steller Sea Lions (Eumetopias jubatus)*. Seattle: National Marine Mammal Laboratory, NOAA, Alaska Fisheries Science Center.

Nations, C., and M. S. Boyce. 1997. Stochastic demography for conservation biology. Pages 451–469 in S. Tuljupurkar and H. Caswell, eds., *Structured Population Models in Marine, Terrestrial, and Freshwater Systems*. New York: Chapman & Hall.

Noon, B. R., and K. S. McKelvey. 1996. Management of the spotted owl: A case history in conservation biology. *Annual Review of Ecology and Systematics* 27:135–162.

Nur, N., and W. J. Sydeman. 2000. Demographic processes and population dynamic models of seabirds: Implications for conservation and restoration. *Current Ornithology* 15:149–188.

Romme, W. H., M. G. Turner, L. L. Wallace, and J. S. Walker. 1995. Aspen, elk, and fire in northern Yellowstone National Park. *Ecology* 76:2097–2106.

Royama, T. 1992. *Analytical Population Dynamics*. New York: Chapman & Hall.

Schullery, P. 1992. *The Bears of Yellowstone*. Worland, Wyo.: High Plains.

Shackleton, D. M. 1997. *Wild Sheep and Goats and Their Relatives: Status Survey and Conservation Action Plan for Caprinae*. Gland, Switzerland: IUCN.

Shaffer, M. 1981. Minimum population sizes for species conservation. *BioScience* 31: 131–134.

Stacey, P. B., and M. Taper. 1992. Environmental variation and the persistence of small populations. *Ecological Applications* 2:18–29.

Stenseth, N. C., O. N. Bjørnstad, and W. Falck. 1996. Is spacing behaviour coupled with predation causing the microtine density cycle? A synthesis of current process-oriented and pattern-oriented studies. *Proceedings of the Royal Society* B263:1423–1435.

Taylor, B. L. 1995. The reliability of using population viability analysis for risk classification of species. *Conservation Biology* 9:551–558.

Thomas, J. W., et al. 1990. *A Conservation Strategy for the Northern Spotted Owl: A Report of the Interagency Scientific Committee to Address the Conservation of the Northern Spotted Owl*. Portland, Ore.: U.S. Department of Agriculture, Forest Service, U.S. Department of Interior, Bureau of Land Management, Fish and Wildlife Service, and National Park Service.

Tuljapurkar, S. D. 1989. An uncertain life: Demography in random environments. *Theoretical Population Biology* 35:227–294.

Tuljapurkar, S. D., and S. H. Orzack. 1980. Population dynamics in variable environments. I: Long-run growth rates and extinction. *Theoretical Population Biology* 18:314–342.

Walters, C. J. 1986. *Adaptive Management of Renewable Resources.* New York: Macmillan.

————. 1997. Challenges in adaptive management of riparian and coastal ecosystems. *Conservation Ecology* 1(2):1–19. [www.consecol.org/vol1/iss2/art1]

Watkinson, A. R., and W. J. Sutherland. 1995. Sources, sinks, and pseudo-sinks. *Journal of Animal Ecology* 64:126–130.

White, G. C. 2000. Population viability analysis. In L. Boitani and T. Fuller, eds., *Research Techniques in Animal Ecology: Controversies and Consequences.* New York: Columbia University Press.

Wiegand, T., J. Naves, T. Stephan, and A. Fernandez. 1998. Assessing the risk of extinction for the brown bear (*Ursus arctos*) in the Cordillera Cantabrica, Spain. *Ecological Monographs* 68:539–570.

York, A. E., R. L. Merrick, and T. R. Loughlin. 1996. An analysis of the Steller sea lion metapopulation in Alaska. Pages 259–292 in D. R. McCullough, ed., *Metapopulations and Wildlife Conservation.* Washington, D.C., and Covelo, Calif.: Island Press.

Chapter 9

....

Modeling Wildlife Resource Selection: Can We Do Better?

Lyman L. McDonald and Bryan F. J. Manly

In this chapter we discuss modeling in the context of resource selection by animals. Following some general remarks on modeling, we review the theory behind the use of resource selection functions and outline the critical issues for modeling with these functions. Based on our experience, we then propose four rules that promote useful modeling of resource selection by animals and explain how they can be applied in practice.

Two types of models are used in science (Cox 1990; Lehmann 1990): *substantive models,* which are based on specific assumptions about cause-and-effect relationships, and *empirical models,* which are derived from relationships observed in the data (without there necessarily being any underlying theory to justify the equations that are used). With empirical modeling it is useful to remember three principles that have been highlighted by McCullagh and Nelder (1983), among others. These are:

- All models are wrong, but some are more useful than others.
- Modeling in science is at least partly an art rather than a completely objective process.
- It is not a good idea to fall in love with one model to the exclusion of alternatives.

Heeding these principles will go a long way toward ensuring useful modeling. Most scientists are aware of these principles, of course, although it is sometimes difficult to accept that a carefully chosen model is wrong. It may be easier to admit that the model is not absolutely correct but may still be useful. Model building is an art because two independent scientists with the same data and objectives and similar training may produce two quite different models. Both may be useful, but not necessarily.

The third principle—not to fall in love with one model—is particularly important. It is not unusual, particularly in the courtroom, to have two scientists quarreling with each other's predictions when the basis for their disagreement is two models that are in fact only approximations of reality. The two models may or may not be useful, but the combatants adore their models and would defend them to the death rather than admit that the alternative model may have merits.

There is a fourth principle as well. This is:

• Do not overfit the data.

With empirical modeling there is often an equation to describe the data values (Y), with many variables $(X_1, X_2, \ldots, X_p)$ that may or may not be included in the equation to account for the variation in Y. Overfitting occurs when the equation finally chosen for use accounts for too much of the observed variation. In other words, some of the variation in the data that is in fact random is apparently accounted for by the X variables. Overfitting the data is a common problem in modeling. Almost all model-fitting algorithms end up with at least four models that fit the data reasonably well but will not necessarily pass the test of time. Even a model that is a good approximation of reality is unlikely to be as good as it seems based on the data that were used to develop it.

Given these four principles, it seems impossible to define *valid modeling* of resource selection precisely. How can we define valid modeling if all models are partly the result of art and indeed in the end are wrong, even if they are useful? After reviewing the current procedures for modeling resource selection, sample designs for field studies, and an example, we then give four rules for *useful modeling* of resource selection.

CURRENT PROCEDURES

Most modeling of wildlife resource selection has been empirical rather than substantive because of the inherent complexity of the selection process. This is certainly the approach we use. We view the problem as one of predicting the probability (or more often the relative probability) of the use of different types of resources based on equations that seem reasonable for the data

at hand but are not based on assumptions about cause-and-effect relationships.

Suppose there is a large set of available resource units: individual items
of food (with food selection), for example, or blocks of land (with habitat
selection). Each resource unit is characterized by the values it possesses for
certain variables $X_1, X_2, \ldots, X_p$, representing things like size and color
(with food selection) or distance from water and habitat type (with habitat
selection). Our formulation of the problem in terms of modeling resource
selection involves three mathematical functions (Manly et al. 1993). These
functions can be illustrated via a simple hypothetical example with one X
variable as in Figure 9.1.

The first function is the probability distribution function of X for the
set of available units. For our hypothetical example this is a normal distribution with mean $\mu = 20$ and variance $\sigma^2 = 2.5$. The second function is
the probability distribution function for those units that are used by the animal. Hypothetically, this is a normal distribution with mean $\mu = 22$ and
variance $\sigma^2 = 1.9$. The third function is the resource selection function. This
is the function that shows how units must be selected from the available set

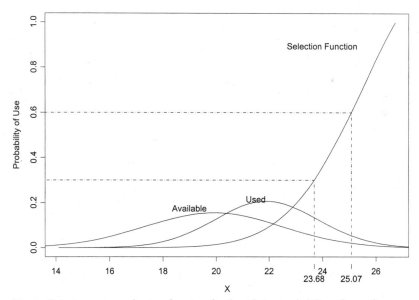

Figure 9.1. A resource selection function for the relative probability of use of
resource units with a single variable X. The available curve is for the normal distribution with mean 20 and variance 2.5; the used curve is for the normal distribution
with mean 22 and variance 1.9. These two distributions determine the resource selection function.

in order to produce the distribution for the used set. More precisely: if a sample is taken from the available units in such a way that the probability of selecting a unit with $X = x$ is proportional to the resource selection function, then this will produce the distribution of X that is shown for the used units. In Figure 9.1, for instance, we can see that to change the available distribution into the used distribution, units with $X = 25.07$ must be selected with about twice the probability of units with $X = 23.68$.

A resource selection function gives a complete summary of the selection process. We contend that the estimation of this function should be the goal of most resource selection studies. Our example uses normal distributions to illustrate the distributions of X for the available and the used units. For this case, the resource selection function is uniquely determined by a formula that is given by Manly (1985:61). In reality, however, normal distributions seldom occur for resource units, and the estimation of the resource selection function requires the use of logistic regression, log-linear models, and other special statistical methods. Moreover, there is usually more than one X variable, so that the resource selection function is multivariate. These matters are discussed in detail by Manly et al. (1993).

Preference has been defined as the likelihood that a resource unit will be selected if offered on an equal basis with others—that is, if resource units of different types are equally available (Johnson 1980). Some controlled laboratory studies do measure preference directly in this sense—for example, equal abundances of different types of food pellets can be offered to a caged animal, with pellets being replaced as they are eaten. Although it is rarely possible to estimate preference functions directly in wildlife field studies, the resource selection function does this indirectly. That is, if all types of available units were equally abundant, the resource selection function gives the distribution of used units that would result.

The definition of available resource units is critical in estimating a resource selection function because it determines the available probability distribution function (Figure 9.1). If the distribution of X variables changes for available units, the resource selection function must change as well to generate the same distribution for used units. Used units are easier to define in most studies, however, because evidence of use (tracks, browsing, the presence of animals) is observed.

There is another critical aspect: the variables $X_1, X_2, \ldots, X_p$ that are used to characterize the sample units must include the appropriate ones for quantifying the probability of use. Few scientists would be bold enough to say that exactly the right set of variables has been measured in a field study. The best we can hope for is an approximate model with measures of bias and precision that are applicable to the animal population under study at the time and location when it was sampled.

SAMPLE DESIGNS

Thomas and Taylor (1990) and Manly et al. (1993) discuss three designs for resource selection studies. With Design I, the available and used resource units are defined for the whole population of animals. With Design II, the available units are assumed to be the same for all the animals in the population, but the used units are identified for individual animals. With Design III, both the available and used units are identified for individual animals. Moreover, various sampling protocols are defined for obtaining data. With one of the sampling protocols, for example, all available resource units and a random sample of used units are measured. Most resource selection studies fit into one of the combinations of sampling designs and protocols, and separate resource selection functions are defined and estimated for different times and places if necessary. Recently, new methods have been developed for analyzing data where the available resource units are changing rapidly (Arthur et al. 1996).

Consider a situation where the use of a resource selection function has not been developed: researchers measure variables X_1 to X_p at a point where an animal is seen and then at another point located a certain distance and direction from the used point. The second point is then regarded as being "available" in the sense that presumably it could have been used by the animal. Given a sample of these pairs of points, the data clearly convey information on selection, but it is not clear how we can bring in the concept of a resource selection function.

AN EXAMPLE

To get a better idea of the process used to estimate a resource selection function in a particular situation, suppose that a random sample of available resource units has been collected and also a random sample of used resource units. Assume also that the variables X_1 to X_p have been measured on all the sampled resource units in order to characterize them. It must then be assumed that:

1. Every available resource unit has the same probability of being included in the random sample of available units.
2. Every used resource unit has the same probability of being included in the random sample of used units.
3. The total number of available resource units is very large.
4. The sampling fractions are small for both available and used units.

There is a standard practice that we recommend in this case. Assume that the resource selection function is well approximated by a function of the form

$$w(X_1, X_2, \ldots, X_p) = \exp(\beta_0 + \beta_1 X_1 + \beta_2 X_2 + \ldots + \beta_p X_p)$$

The coefficients in the X variables in the equation can then be estimated using logistic regression, as described by Manly et al. (1993: 126), and the estimators of the coefficients will be approximately normally distributed for large data sets (say, with 100 or more resource units in each sample). Whether or not this is useful modeling depends on the quality of the data being analyzed and the applicability of the assumptions.

In practice, there are likely to be several of the X variables that are not really related to the selection of resources. Some sort of model selection procedure will therefore be applied—perhaps using Akaike's Information Criterion (AIC) or one of its modifications. If there are several competing models that have roughly the same value of the criterion, estimates of the resource selection function may be based on model averaging (Burnham and Anderson 1998). Again, whether or not this is useful modeling depends on the circumstances.

FOUR RULES FOR USEFUL MODELING

As we have seen, a critical aspect of resource selection studies concerns the definition of the set of available resource units. Arguments may arise due to different definitions of available units. In a study of the northern spotted owl (*Strix occidentalis caurina*), for example, one scientist might define the available resource units to be the 1-hectare plots contained within a 2-kilometer circle surrounding a nest. Another scientist might define the available units to be the 1-hectare plots within the home range as determined by a standard method. As a result, the selection functions that the scientists estimate will differ to an extent that may be of biological importance.

The definition of what units are available also determines the scale at which selection is being studied. It is possible, for example, to estimate a resource selection function for the use by pronghorn antelope (*Antilocapra americana*) of land within the state of Wyoming, for the selection of home ranges by buck antelope in the Red Desert of Wyoming, or for the selection of feeding sites within the home range of a given buck antelope. All this is useful modeling so long as the procedures are correct in each case. The results will, of course, be very different because of the different assumptions. This example suggests our first rule for useful modeling of resource selection:

> Rule I: Clearly state the assumptions being made, the scale at which selection is being studied, the animals to which inferences are to be drawn, the time period under consideration, and the study area.

Fortunately, in many studies, resource selection functions are reasonably robust with respect to the definition of available units. Units that are rarely used (such as clear-cuts in the northern spotted owl illustration) have little effect on the resource selection function because the function will assign approximately zero as the probability of use to such units. If the distribution of available units is changed substantially for units that have moderate or high use, however, the corresponding resource selection functions may differ dramatically.

One of the first applications of resource selection functions was with a study of prey selection by tree swallows (*Tachycineta bicolor*) in Wyoming (McDonald et al. 1990). In one part of the study it was assumed that the length of the insects available for selection (the resource units) had a normal distribution and that the length of the insects selected as food for chicks also followed a normal distribution. The resource selection function was then estimated by using the appropriate equation based on these assumptions (Manly 1985: 61), yielding a selection function similar in shape to that of Figure 9.1. With hindsight this example does not necessarily seem to be useful modeling. Insects were trapped in the study area using standard procedures and assumed to give a random sample of the insects available to the tree swallows. Insects fed to chicks were collected from chicks in a sample of nests and assumed to give a random sample of those used as food items for chicks. Neither assumption is particularly easy to justify, but there was no strong evidence of bias. The biggest problem is with the assumption of a normal distribution for the length of insects selected as food for chicks—in fact, the distribution of length for the insects selected as food items is slightly skewed to the left (toward small insects). At the time of the analysis, the assumption of a normal distribution was necessary, as methods for analysis with other distributions were not developed. Nowadays logistic regression would be used to estimate the resource selection function because it applies with normal or nonnormal data (Manly et al. 1993).

The example of selection by the tree swallows helps justify our second and third rules for useful modeling in resource selection studies:

> Rule II: Critically evaluate the assumptions used with data collection—including the adequacy of the sampling protocols, the likelihood that the variables measured are related to the probability of units being selected for use, and possible bias in the measurement procedures.

> Rule III: Use models that are justified by the sampling design or flexible regression models. Avoid assumptions about specific distributions for the data.

Our final rule for useful modeling in resource selection studies is a comment generally applicable to modeling in scientific studies:

Rule IV: Assume responsibility for predictions based on the resource selection function.

This rule means that useful modeling requires all team members to assume responsibility for the final product and predictions based on the model. This is more than just signing the report. The project statistician should assume responsibility for biological predictions in the specific case, not just for correctness of the computations during the model-fitting process. The principal investigator and the rest of the team should assume responsibility for the model selected and predictions based on the model, not just for collecting the data and interpreting results that come from a black box. Without mutual understanding of every aspect of the modeling process—from data collection to model fitting to results and conclusions—useful modeling is unlikely to occur.

RECOMMENDATIONS

We conclude with a summary of our recommendations concerning useful modeling with resource selection studies:

- Understand what is being modeled. This is the relative frequency of use of resources in comparison to availability—which is not necessarily the same as the importance to the animals.
- Define available and used resource units carefully. The resource selection function, if properly estimated, shows how units must be selected from those available in order to produce the distribution of those used.
- Give careful thought to which variables can be measured on resource units and should also be related to the probability of use. Continuous, discrete, and categorical variables can generally be accommodated in the models.
- Consider the assumptions (explicit and implicit) that are required in the protocol for sampling resource units of different types, and ensure that they are met as far as possible.
- Produce descriptive statistics for the samples of resource units taken (available, used, unused), and compare the samples using standard statistical methods.
- Choose variables for the resource selection function by using objective methods such as AIC.
- Summarize the resource selection function in terms of the units that, based on the fitted model, are most likely to be selected.

- Make predictions from the model about the future, other study areas, and other populations—based on professional judgment, the assumptions made, the background literature, and the model's track record in other times and places.

REFERENCES

Arthur, S. M., B. F. J. Manly, L. L. McDonald, and G. W. Garner. 1996. Assessing habitat selection when availability changes. *Ecology* 77:215–227.

Burnham, K. P., and D. R. Anderson. 1998. *Model Selection and Inference: A Practical Information-Theoretic Approach.* New York: Springer-Verlag.

Cox, D. R. 1990. Role of models in statistical analysis. *Statistical Science* 5:169–174.

Johnson, D. H. 1980. The comparison of usage and availability measurements for evaluating resource preference. *Ecology* 61:65–71.

Lehmann, E. L. 1990. Model specification: The views of Fisher and Neyman, and later developments. *Statistical Science* 5:160–168.

Manly, B. F. J. 1985. *The Statistics of Natural Selection.* London: Chapman & Hall.

Manly, B. F. J., L. L. McDonald, and D. L. Thomas. 1993. *Resource Selection by Animals: Statistical Design and Analysis for Field Studies.* London: Chapman & Hall.

McCullagh, P., and J. A. Nelder. 1983. *Generalized Linear Models.* London: Chapman & Hall.

McDonald, L. L., B. F. J. Manly, and C. M. Raley. 1990. Analyzing foraging and habitat use through selection functions. In M. L. Morrison, C. J. Ralph, J. Verner, and J. R. Jehl Jr., eds., *Avian Foraging: Theory, Methodology, and Applications.* Studies in Avian Biology 13. Los Angeles: Cooper Ornithological Society.

Thomas, D. L., and E. J. Taylor. 1990. Study designs and tests for comparing resource use and availability. *Journal of Wildlife Management* 54:322–330.

Chapter 10

···················

Using Models to
Facilitate Complex Decisions

William L. Kendall

Managing wildlife and their habitats is a very complex task. The decision process often involves more than one person and indeed could involve more than one organization, including various governmental and non-governmental organizations, each with its own constituency and interests. Even when operational management decisions are made by one person, such as a refuge or park manager, the problem is frequently complex. Perhaps decisions must be made at various spatial and temporal scales. Landscape management decisions might be made every 10 years; harvest or predator control decisions might be made yearly. A management decision might be required for an individual patch of forest, a breeding area, or an entire region. Finally, as with any biological system, the dynamics of animal populations and communities—and the impacts of management decisions thereon—are only partially understood. This problem is exacerbated in the case of migratory species, where there is great spatial separation between breeding and wintering areas and distinct breeding populations often intermix on wintering grounds.

In this chapter I discuss how models can be used to manage in the face of uncertainty while allowing for reduction in that uncertainty in the process. I focus on *adaptive resource management* (Holling 1978; Walters 1986) as a paradigm for achieving this end. Under this paradigm the elements of a decision process, including a model or set of models of the dynamics of the system of interest, are considered separately and then reassembled to arrive at an optimal, or nearly optimal, decision. I hope managers will see in this discussion a conceptual framework by which they can bring science to bear directly, instead of obliquely, on their management problems. For researchers, this chapter may suggest how they can approach the design and execution of their research to maximize its usefulness to managers.

PROBLEMS IN WILDLIFE MANAGEMENT

The problems that commonly occur in wildlife management can be classified into either confusion or disagreement over objectives, or uncertainty about the biology of the animal or the ecology of the system and the impacts of decisions thereon.

Sometimes objectives are not clearly defined. A refuge manager might be directed to manage for black ducks (*Anas rubripes*), for instance, but does that mean managing for nesting cover for breeding ducks or managing for food and loafing areas for wintering ducks? When decisions involve multiple parties with different interests (stakeholders), objectives are often difficult to agree upon and may be viewed in various ways. In managing a section of a forest where a particular amphibian community exists, for instance, the objective might be to maximize wood production while maintaining a minimum level of amphibian diversity. Conversely, the objective might be to maximize amphibian diversity while maintaining a minimum level of wood production. The management decision is likely to differ for these two objectives, each favoring different stakeholders.

Management must be conducted in the face of several sources of uncertainty. (See Williams 1982; Walters 1986; Nichols et al. 1995; Williams and Johnson 1995; Williams et al. 1996.) *Structural* (or *ecological*) *uncertainty* results from competing hypotheses about the nature of the dynamics of the population, community, or landscape of interest. *Environmental variation* occurs even when the system's structure is agreed upon: it is manifested in residual variation (or noise) due to factors that are unaccounted for. Then there is *partial controllability* when a management decision must be applied indirectly to a system, thereby creating variation in the impact. If a decision is made to remove 50 percent of the predators from an area, for example, you set the number of traps expected to be required for the task. But instead of exactly 50 percent being removed, perhaps 45 percent are removed in one instance and 55 percent in another. And, finally, *partial observability* of natural systems is the norm because our assessment must almost always rely on sampling a subset of the target population, community, habitat, and so forth. This sampling has a spatial component—only certain areas are assessed—and often there is measurement error because some subjects associated with a sampled area are not detected, whether it is the number of animals of a species, the number of species present, or the number of young produced per nest. These four sources of uncertainty make it more difficult to manage. In most cases, therefore, reducing any of these sources should improve the management process.

THE DECISION PROCESS

Establishing clear objectives (perhaps based on a consensus of multiple stakeholders)—and then managing for these objectives in the face of multiple sources of uncertainty—can be a daunting task. Both the ecological system to be managed and the decision process itself are complex. Modeling is an excellent tool for contending with all this complexity. The term *model* has been defined consistently in this book as a simplified abstraction of a real-world system (see Chapter 2). The decision process itself can be modeled as well by decomposing it into simpler parts. Informed decision making consists of several elements: objectives, management options, an understanding of the structure of the ecological system to be managed, and, in the common case where decisions are made periodically, a program for monitoring the results of management that informs the next management decision.

In weighing various management options, managers must predict the outcome of each decision in order to choose the best option. Even if this assessment is conducted subjectively, it must nevertheless be based on a "simplified abstraction," or model of the system, that the manager holds in his or her head. Thus modeling is not just a useful tool: it is inseparable from the decision process. The question, then, is not whether or not to model but whether formal conceptual or mathematical modeling would provide an advantage over intuitive modeling. Although effective, even optimal, decisions can be based on subjective assessment by an expert, this becomes more difficult to achieve as the complexity of the system or the objectives increases. In these cases modeling and formal decision-analytic approaches can, at the very least, structure the problem and its sources of uncertainty—thus increasing everyone's understanding of both the system and the decision process. To illustrate how models can assist the wildlife management process, I will be focusing on the situation where these formal approaches are most useful: where the decision process includes multiple stakeholders and there is uncertainty about the structure of the ecological system.

Figure 10.1 illustrates four possible management scenarios, with respect

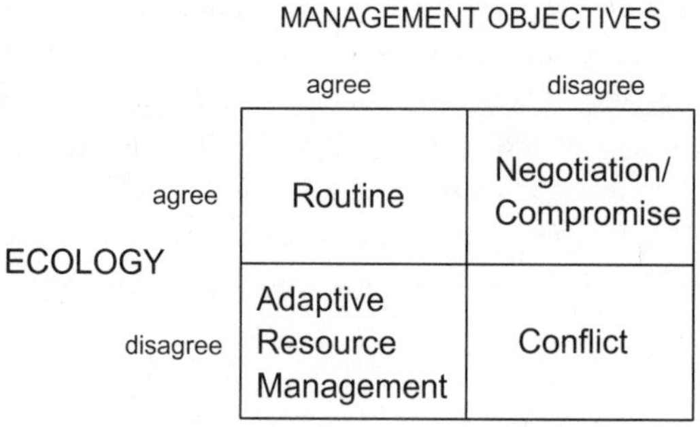

MANAGEMENT OBJECTIVES

	agree	disagree
agree	Routine	Negotiation/ Compromise
disagree	Adaptive Resource Management	Conflict

ECOLOGY (label at left, with agree/disagree rows)

Figure 10.1. Matrix of approaches to making management decisions dependent on agreement/disagreement over objectives and ecology (from Lee 1993:106).

to objectives and ecological knowledge, and possible solutions to these problems. Each of these scenarios assumes there are multiple stakeholders giving input to the management process. The right-hand side of the figure reinforces the need to agree on objectives and state them clearly—otherwise there is no basis for optimizing management decisions. Given that objectives are spelled out and agreed upon, there are two possible scenarios. In the first, there is agreement on how the system will react to management actions. Thus one predictive model is accepted by all. In the second, there are competing hypotheses about how the system will react. In this case optimal decisions must be made in the face of structural uncertainty, taking into account the predictions of multiple models. By monitoring the system's reaction to management and comparing the result against the predictions of each of the competing models, we can discern over the long run which of the candidate models produces better predictions and then favor that model in future decisions. This is the essence of adaptive resource management (ARM; Walters 1986). The term *adaptive* derives from the learning aspect. ARM does not offer a panacea that avoids the difficulties inherent in a complex decision process. Rather, it offers a framework for addressing these complexities and managing in the face of uncertainty.

ADAPTIVE RESOURCE MANAGEMENT

Several papers (Johnson et al. 1993; Nichols et al. 1995; Williams and Johnson 1995; Williams 1996; Williams et al. 1996) have discussed the application of the principles of ARM to waterfowl harvest. Indeed, Johnson et al. (1997) actually applied it—a good example for illustrating the principles of ARM. Briefly, the United States is divided into four administrative flyways—Atlantic, Mississippi, Central, and Pacific—based on the migration pattern of waterfowl populations (USFWS 1975). Harvest regulations for each flyway are promulgated annually by the U.S. Fish and Wildlife Service (USFWS) and Canadian Wildlife Service (CWS) in consultation with the states and provinces through the flyway councils and commentary from nongovernmental organizations and the general public. Much of the USFWS's decision making occurs in July and August, based primarily on aerial surveys of ducks and habitat conducted in May and July (Caithamer and Dubovsky 1997). Given this information, decision makers must anticipate how fall and winter hunting will affect the size of the population that returns to breed in the spring. Since 1995, annual recommendations sent to the director of the USFWS have been based on adaptive resource management (Johnson et al. 1999).

ARM is based on two premises: the first is that uncertainty exists in the system to be managed and reduction of that uncertainty would improve the management process; the second is that, despite the uncertainty, decisions must be made periodically. ARM consists of the following components: a statement of objectives; a set of management options; a set of models of system dynamics along with an associated measure of a model's relative credibility; and a monitoring program. From a set of options a management action is selected for evaluation. Each model predicts the impact of that action on the system, which will result in some expected return in terms of the objective (say, a change in a diversity index). This expected return is averaged with the returns predicted by the other candidate models, weighted by the relative credibility values associated with each model, to arrive at an overall expected return for that action. The other management options are evaluated in the same way. Finally, the action that produces the optimal total expected return over the time frame of interest is chosen. With this process in mind, we turn to the four basic components of ARM.

Statement of Objectives

Effective management requires well-defined objectives. A few simple examples: maximize the population size of species A; minimize the population size of parasite species B; maximize the diversity of passerine species in a patch of forest; maximize the combined reproductive rates of species C and D in their common breeding area. Often constraints on an objective may be appropriate. For instance, the main objective may be to maximize wood production in a patch, but conditional on the persistence of a certain bird species. Ideally we should be able, through compromise and negotiation, to construct a mathematical *objective function* (or utility function) and an accompanying set of constraints that balances the concerns of all stake-holders. To the extent that the construction of this function is not possible, the objectives of management remain obscure.

In the case of midcontinent mallard duck (*Anas platyrhynchos*) harvest regulation, the objective function balances the competing objectives of maximizing long-term harvest and maintaining 8.1 million mallards in the breeding population—the goal of the North American Waterfowl Management Plan (NAWMP) (Johnson et al. 1997). The objective is to choose the management option that maximizes the following function:

$$\sum_{\tau=t}^{T} u_\tau H_\tau \qquad\qquad\qquad [10.1]$$

where τ indexes time from the present year t to the end of the time frame of interest T, in this case infinity. H_τ is the total harvest of mallards in year τ. Therefore, part of the objective is to maximize the total harvest over all future time. This obviously tends to benefit hunters, but it also protects the resource because ducks cannot be harvested in the distant future if they do not exist in the distant future. Therefore, this option provides for sustainable harvest. The other factor in the function, u_τ, is a linear penalty function that devalues the expected harvest if the expected resultant population size for the following spring ($N_{\tau+1}$) is less than the NAWMP goal of 8.1 million mallards (Figure 10.2). The result of this penalty is stricter regulation based on a balance between the value of H_τ and u_τ. In this case, as the expected value of $N_{\tau+1}$ ($E[N_{\tau+1}]$) resulting from a given management option decreases further from the goal, the value of harvest continually declines—thus placing more emphasis on population growth. If $E(N_{\tau+1}) < 4.0$ million, harvest has no value, thereby eliminating that option. Although the function in Figure 10.2 is linear, it could have been any function. A step function that dropped to zero where $E(N_{\tau+1}) < 8.1$ million would preclude any option expected to result in a population below the NAWMP goal. Other smooth functions would inflict either a more severe (concave upward) or gradual (concave downward) initial penalty than the linear function.

The objective functions presented here are simple in form: a simple objective (maximize harvest) with a relatively simple constraint (satisfy the NAWMP goal for breeding mallards). There is great potential for more complex objective functions when we want to optimize on more than one variable. A necessary condition for this endeavor is to find common currency (units) for all variables in the objective. For instance, if the competing objectives are conservation of northern spotted owls (*Strix occidentalis caurina*) and harvest of old-growth timber (economic considerations), we

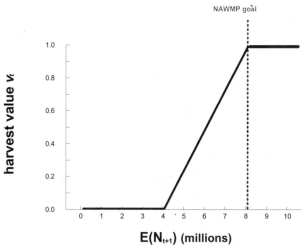

Figure 10.2. Adjustment to value of harvest of midcontinent mallards as a function of expected size of the following year's population and the NAWMP goal (Johnson et al. 1997).

must be able to put a monetary value on the conservation of northern spotted owls. The only way to avoid the need for common units is to optimize on only one variable and incorporate all the others through constraints, as in the mallard example. In the spotted owl example this could entail maximizing the harvest of timber such that a minimum specified number of breeding owls is sustained. Conversely, it could entail minimizing the probability of extirpation such that a minimum amount of timber production is maintained.

The development of an objective function is itself a modeling exercise. It is a process of abstracting the objectives of stakeholders as a group (that is, balancing competing objectives) into one mathematical expression and set of constraints. As with any model, the final form of the function is an approximation of these objectives, but it should be a very close approximation. Although it may be more complex and difficult than modeling the ecological system, it is just as crucial to the decision process. Because of this complexity, decision-analytical methods can be very useful even when the ecological system is well understood (only one model of system dynamics). In some cases we might even discover that constraints are so restrictive that none of the management options is viable.

Especially in the case of a complex system, it is natural to want to consider the implications of various objectives for the resulting choice of management actions. There is a danger, however, that this practice may devolve into altering the objective function until it calls for a desired management option that has been chosen beforehand—a case of the tail wagging the dog. To avoid, to the extent possible, the danger of corrupting the process, an objective function should be established independent of the other elements of the decision analysis.

Management Options

There might be a myriad of options for managing a population or community. In some cases direct management actions can be expressed in terms of a continuous variable—such as setting the water level in an impoundment to a specific depth. In many other cases the decision variable is either qualitative or discrete and limited in range. In harvesting timber, for instance, the choice might be to clear-cut, selectively cut, or not cut at all. Each option, however, must produce a measurably different return with respect to the objective function. If two management options yield the same return (say, number of trees to be cut) for each state of the system, then choosing between them is a meaningless exercise. For this reason, and to keep the effect of management options tractable—and in many cases to keep formal optimization practical—the number of options should be limited.

The history of mallard harvest management has included many different combinations of bag limits and season lengths as well as other customized features such as split seasons, zones, and point systems. In implementing ARM for mallard harvest in 1995, three regulatory packages were chosen. These options were based on historical periods of "restrictive," "moderate," and "liberal" regulations (Figure 10.3; Johnson et al. 1997). The intent was to have meaningfully distinct options based on historical regula-

		ATL	MIS	CEN	PAC
hours		1/2 hr before sunrise - sunset			
dates			Oct 1 - Jan 20		
days	R	30	30	39	59
	M	40	40	51	79
	L	50	50	60	93
basic bag	R	3	3	3	4
	M	4	4	4	5
	L	5	5	5	6

Figure 10.3.
Set of management options (R = restrictive, M = moderate, L = liberal) for the harvest of mallards in the Atlantic (ATL), Mississippi (MIS), Central (CEN), and Pacific (PAC) Flyways of the United States in 1995 (Johnson et al. 1997).

tions so that a valid (see Chapter 7 in this volume) model of their impact on the system could be developed.

When management options are not expressed in terms that are meaningful with respect to the ecological system, they must be translated. The effect of harvest on the population dynamics of midcontinent mallards, for example, cannot be expressed in terms of bag limits and season lengths. But it can be expressed in terms of harvest rate, which is an element of mortality rate. Moreover, the relationship between a regulations package and harvest rate is not deterministic—due to temporal variability in weather, bird behavior, hunter numbers, and the like. Johnson et al. (1997) translated the three regulations packages into harvest rate distributions using band recovery data (estimated recovery rates were adjusted by a reporting rate taken from the literature to produce a harvest rate estimate) for each of the sets of years when those packages had been applied (Figure 10.4). These three distributions are fairly distinct but still overlap considerably.

Sometimes managers want to consider management options for which little or no historical experience is directly available. In the mallard harvest case, the regulations packages were revised and a "very restrictive" package was added for the 1997 hunting season (Johnson et al. 1999). As a result, the expected distributions for harvest rates were more distinct. Because there was no direct historical experience with the revised set of management options, trends in hunter numbers from harvest surveys were used to adjust the predicted harvest rates from the original set of packages. This approach required more assumptions about hunter behavior (Johnson et al. 1999). Using ancillary information in this way is a viable option for relating the set of management options to the ecological system. But it must be done cautiously, and the results should be monitored to validate these predictions. Because of the availability of data from mallard bandings, information from

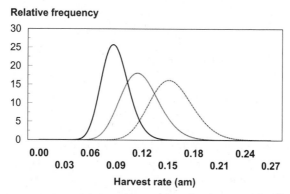

Figure 10.4. Historic distribution of harvest rates for three sets of mallard harvest regulations defined in Figure 10.3 (Johnson et al. 1997).

years when these new packages are implemented can be used to evaluate and further adjust these predictions. To achieve this, however, stakeholders would have to refrain from further revising the set of management options for multiple iterations of the decision process.

Models of System Dynamics

Details of developing individual models are found throughout this volume. I will touch on this briefly, using mallard harvest as an example. My focus will be on the elements of model building as they relate to management, incorporating intuitive models, and considering multiple models simultaneously.

Model Development. Given explicit objectives, a set of management options, and the state of the system x_t at time t, the manager must predict the value v_t with respect to the objectives for each option. If the objective is simply to maximize the total mallard harvest over all future time, for example, then v_t is the number of mallards harvested in year t. If the decision process involves more than one time step—or if v_t is a function of the state of the system in the next time step, x_{t+1} (such as sustainable harvest or persistence of a population)—the manager must also predict x_{t+1}. Equation (10.1) provides a good example. In this case $v_t = u_t H_t$, where u_t devalues expected harvest based on the predicted population size for the following year (Figure 10.3). This prediction is a function of the management action (decision d_t) and any other pertinent factors z_t, including environmental variables and human-induced factors that are not under the control of this decision maker. This prediction, as noted, requires a model (m_i) of the system dynamics—either informal (and based on expert opinion and data) or explicit and mathematical (and based on expert opinion and data). This model of system dynamics can be simplistically represented by

$$x_{i,t+1} = x_t + f_i(x_t, d_t, z_t) \tag{10.2}$$

where the function f_i is defined by the model used. Each of these variables is in boldface type to denote that any of them could be multidimensional. If the problem were to harvest timber while conserving a bird species, for example, the state of the system might be two-dimensional, including the amount of available timber and the size of the bird population. The decision might be two-dimensional, consisting of a quota for timber harvest and the number of nesting boxes to install. Environmental variables z_t in this case might include multiple climatic variables that would predict the probability of forest fire. The value of the decision d_t can be expressed as a different function of the same variables:

$$v_{i,t} = g_i(x_t, x_{i,t+1}, d_t, z_t')$$ [10.3]

The variables included in the array z_t' might not be identical to those in Equation (10.2). For instance, z_t' might include economic variables such as the market price for timber. Based on the model notation introduced here, the objective function in Equation (10.1) could be generalized to optimize:

$$\sum_{\tau=t}^{T} v_\tau$$ [10.4]

The state variables have certain key features: they must be pertinent to the system dynamics or the objective, and they must be estimable at the time the decision is made and at the appropriate scale. In the mallard harvest case (Johnson et al. 1997), x_t consisted of the size of the midcontinent population, N_t, and the number of ponds in the prairie-pothole region of Canada, P_t. These values are estimated from the annual May aerial survey conducted by the USFWS, CWS, and state and provincial personnel (Caithamer and Dubovsky 1997).

If the system is well understood—all stakeholders agree there is no structural uncertainty—only one model need be considered. If there are competing hypotheses, then multiple models can be considered, each a mathematical representation of a competing hypothesis. When the set consists of more than one model, there should be two basic characteristics (Johnson et al. 1993; Williams and Johnson 1995). First, different models must call for different management actions over at least part of the range of the state of the system. Otherwise the question of which model best approximates reality might be of academic interest but would be irrelevant for management purposes. Second, different models must predict different changes in the system state for at least one of the management options d_t. If each model predicts exactly the same result, no matter what decision is made, then comparing the models cannot be achieved through management.

Other chapters in this volume address the construction of models for various purposes. Model formulation involves both theoretical (Chapter 4) and empirical (Chapter 3) considerations. The proper approach to model formulation depends on the model's purpose (Chapters 2 and 7). As indicated in Equations (10.2) and (10.3), management-oriented models predict the system's response to various management actions. In this case a model should include the key components of the system that are affected by the decision d_t or affect the return to the objective, v_t. How complex does a model need to be in this case? No more than is necessary—which will partly depend on the complexity of the decision and the objectives. Again, for management purposes the interest is not in how the system operates per se but in simply being able to predict the effect of management actions.

The model's components should also be empirically based to the extent possible—which may limit its complexity if there are few data to estimate model parameters (Chapters 3, 6, and 8). Suppose there are 5 years of data on the proportion of patches occupied by species A, and you model this proportion as a function of four predictor variables. The resulting model would fit the data perfectly, but it would probably have little predictive power. Thus there is a danger of severe prediction bias (Neter and Wasserman 1974) when complex models are fit to few data. If there are crucial parameters that cannot be estimated directly, they should be included cautiously—perhaps by estimating them indirectly (using published estimates from another system, for example)—and the sensitivity of the system dynamics to their value should be analyzed. Sensitivity analysis is a valuable tool for building models in any case. Varying a parameter's value to examine its impact on system dynamics highlights the parameters where estimation effort should be focused. If there are few data for that parameter, it indicates a direction for future research efforts.

Whether the model is complex or simple, it must describe the system's dynamics system from time t to $t + 1$ as expressed in Equation (10.2). All sources of uncertainty must be either modeled explicitly or treated as uncontrollable noise. In many cases there might be such a paucity of data that there is little hope for a reasonable formal model. In this case it is perhaps best to rely on an intuitive prediction based on a mental model by someone who is familiar with the system. Such a model should be included in any case to acknowledge that formal modeling is not necessarily superior to a manager's intuition. Nevertheless, the prediction should be specific: a point prediction with a confidence interval around it. In this way the manager can discipline his or her own thinking and revise this intuition based on a comparison of prediction and results. If there is such a paucity of data that there is no reasonable intuition, the problem may be intractable. This is often the case where no effort has been made to study the system.

Example: Mallard Harvest. We can illustrate this modeling process by using the mallard harvest example of Johnson et al. (1997). The population and habitat dynamics were modeled for each model m_i as

$$N_{i,t+1,s} = N_{t,s}\,\phi_{i,t,s} + \gamma_{i,t,s}\,\phi'_{i,t,s} \qquad\qquad [10.5]$$

$$\phi_{i,t,s} = \alpha_s \beta_{i,t,s}\,\gamma$$

$$\phi'_{i,t,s} = \beta_{i,t,s}\,\gamma$$

$$\gamma_{i,t,s} = A_{i,t}\,\alpha_\varphi N_t/2.2$$

where $N_{t,s}$ is the number of mallards of sex s in May; annual adult survival rates $\phi_{i,t,s}$ are decomposed into the probability of surviving the summer α_s, the hunting season $\beta_{i,t,s}$, and the winter γ; $\phi'_{i,t,s}$ is the probability that a young bird survives the hunting season $\beta'_{i,t,s}$ and winter; $\gamma_{i,t,s}$ is the number of young of sex s in the fall population; and $A_{i,t}$ is the ratio of young females to adult females in the fall population.

The subscripts i indicate that survival of the hunting season and recruitment are model-dependent. Johnson et al. (1997) constructed two competing models for recruitment into the fall population: either weakly or strongly density-dependent, where N_t was used as density and P_t was added as another covariate (Figure 10.5). Although the young are actually hatched in the summer, the researchers had data on age ratios in the fall from parts collection surveys, which they adjusted for relative vulnerability to harvest. In this way they estimated the product of production rate and summer survival rate of the young, which are confounded parameters. This is an example of adapting the details of the modeling approach to the available data.

For survival during the hunting season, the researchers accounted for a long-standing debate over compensatory versus additive mortality (Anderson and Burnham 1976; Burnham et al. 1984; Smith and Reynolds 1992) by incorporating both types in the model set (Figure 10.6). A completely

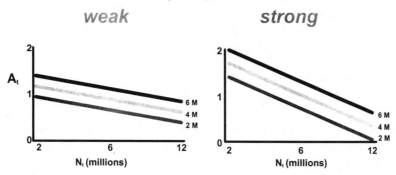

Figure 10.5. Age ratio of female mallards in the fall population (A_t) as a function of breeding population size for three levels of spring pond numbers (in millions): 2, 4, 6 (Johnson et al. 1997).

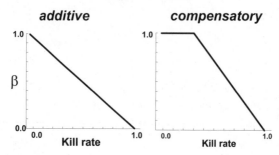

Figure 10.6. Survival of the hunting season (β) as a function of kill rate (Johnson et al. 1997).

additive effect of harvest results in lower survival. Complete compensation, by contrast, means that, up to a threshold kill rate, hunters have no effect on overall survival. These two survival submodels frame the question of compensation by allowing for either extreme. Johnson et al. (1993) point out that a more mechanistic model (one that incorporates density dependence) is likely to be more robust, but the appropriate predictor variables must be found and the model calibrated before it can be useful. This is an example where more complexity is appealing, but there are not yet enough data to support it. Of the other parameters in Equation (10.5), Johnson et al. (1997) estimated γ from previous studies and then used an analysis of band recoveries to derive α_s. The constant 2.2 came from an assumed sex ratio of 1:1 for young of the year, and an adult sex ratio in May of 1.2 males per female, derived from the literature.

The effect of a management action is included in the model through the kill rate in Figure 10.6. To arrive at kill rate, Johnson et al. (1997) adjusted the harvest rates indicated in Figure 10.4 for assumed crippling loss (taken from the literature). Partial controllability was introduced to the model by making the value of harvest rate a random variable based on the gamma distributions in Figure 10.4.

The transition of the other state variable, May ponds, is described by

$$P_{t+1} = -3,835,087.53 + 0.45P_t + 13,695.47r_t \qquad [10.6]$$

where r_t is total annual precipitation. This part of the model was calibrated with pond data from the May aerial survey and precipitation data from weather stations in the surveyed area. The researchers modeled r_t as a normal random variable, thus introducing environmental variation.

Two recruitment models, combined with two survival models, produce a set of four complete models of midcontinent mallard population dynamics, incorporating structural uncertainty. Environmental variation is incorporated through stochastic rainfall; partial controllability is incorporated by making harvest rate a stochastic process. Given the appropriate data, both recruitment and survival models could be improved—perhaps by including more appropriate measures of density. Moreover, these models ignore spatial variation within the population and consider the midcontinent population in isolation, disregarding other populations and species that share the areas where harvest occurs. Nevertheless, they reflect the current state of knowledge and uncertainty about a system that must be managed yearly, in the face of whatever uncertainty exists, using monitoring programs that are limited (due to practicality) to a coarse scale. The idea is that through this management there will be an opportunity to learn which model reflects reality more closely, and in turn improve management. In addition to the role research plays in developing the initial model set, it has a continuing important role in developing improved models to include in the model set. Efforts to improve the model set for waterfowl by incorporating multiple stocks and species, as well as spatial variation, are ongoing (Johnson et al. 1999).

The Role of Experts. The purpose of ARM—or any decision modeling, for that matter—is to optimize decisions, which could mean improving management over the status quo. This premise should be evaluated by including the model on which the status quo is based as one of the models in the set. Suppose management is currently based on an expert's intuitive model of the effect of various actions on the system. This model should be included—even if the expert's knowledge was used to construct all of the other formalized models in the set. This practice benefits the process in at least two ways. First, if this historic approach to making decisions is truly better than those based on other competing models, this should become apparent, as the expert's model will predict the dynamics of the system more accurately. The performance of the expert's model provides a benchmark for the mathematical models. Second, if one of the mathematical models is based completely on this expert's intuitive model, it will be validated against that intuition through this process. If the performance of the mathematical model matches that of the expert's model over the entire state space (the range of values a state variable can take), then that person's expertise will have been successfully extracted for this management problem. If the expert's predictions perform better than the mathematical model, then either some key factor(s) that the expert considers in his or her "black box" was omitted from the mathematical model, or the form of the relationship was not correctly translated (perhaps a linear model was used when an exponential one should have been used). In either case, additional work with a modeler might produce an improved model. Even when no models can be developed that are superior to an expert's predictions, this modeling exercise is still important because experts might move on to other areas of endeavor.

Whether the system to be managed is relatively simple or complex, whether the experts for that system are one person or more, modeling should be done collaboratively (Aber 1997; Chapter 12 in this volume). Involving a diversity of people not only enhances the product but is likely to yield insights, expertise, and synergisms that are impossible when only a few individuals are involved.

Measures of Relative Model Credibility. When more than one model of system dynamics is considered, management will be based on an average of the dynamics predicted by each of the M competing models. This averaging process requires some weighting factor or measure of relative model credibility $p_{i,t}$ for each model $m_i(\sum_{i=1}^{M} p_{i,t} = 1)$. If the decision is based on just one model, then $p_{i,t}$ equals 1 for that model and 0 for the others. By updating these model weights based on how well each model predicts the impact of an implemented decision on the system, these model weights provide a metric for learning which model has the best predictive ability as the decision process iterates. If the model set consists of at least one reasonably valid model, knowledge of the system will increase. This increasing knowledge will, in turn, facilitate better decisions in the future. Bayes' theorem (Walters 1986:165; Williams 1996) provides the mechanism for updating these model weights through time:

$$p_{i,t+1} = \frac{p_{i,t} P_i(\hat{x}_{t+1})}{\sum_{j=1}^{M} p_{j,t} P_j(\hat{x}_{t+1})} \qquad [10.7]$$

where $P_i(\hat{x}_{t+1})$ is the probability of the observed state of the system at time $t + 1$ predicted by model m_i. The learning rate—that is, the rate of change in the value of $p_{i,t}$—will depend not only on the distance between the predicted and actual observed values, $\hat{x}_{i,t+1} - \hat{x}_{t+1}$, but on the variance (amount of uncertainty) of the prediction.

A key consideration in this process is the appropriate initial distribution of these model weights. We could use historical data to retrospectively update weights to the current period, but this method would not be valid if the same data had been used to parameterize any of the candidate models. Walters (1986:166) has advocated using *flat priors*—that is, equal weights for each model—when there is disagreement among stakeholders. If one model in the set is clearly superior to the others, that model will gain credibility (weight) in the updating process. The speed at which this will occur is the question—and this depends on the amount of noise in the system and on our ability to monitor it. In the mallard example, the process was started with equal weights on each model. In the ensuing years weight has increased for the models that include additive hunting mortality (Johnson et al. 1999).

Summary of Model Sets. To assess the adequacy of a model set, a few questions should be asked. First: have all the hypotheses put forward by stakeholders been fairly represented in at least one of the models, including a model that reflects management predictions to date? Second: do the prediction intervals from each model in the set fully reflect the uncertainty associated with stochastic variation or sampling error? If linear regression is used in a model, for example, the mean square error (a measure of the residual variation after the model is fit) is included in the prediction interval under a chosen model. The prediction interval of the model set is a weighted function of the prediction intervals under each model, weighted by the model weights discussed earlier. Third: have all the parameter values of the model been estimated in an unbiased fashion? Potential bias could result from naive statistical methods or, when models are constructed subjectively, from the prejudice of a stakeholder or expert. If you suspect bias, what are the implications? To answer this question, you must consider whether the model is likely to be biased in a particular direction and assess the sensitivity of the model's predictions to the value of this parameter.

Monitoring Program

A monitoring program serves three crucial roles in the decision-making process. First, it should provide information about the current state of the system and allow for an informed management decision based on predictions from the models under consideration. Second, it should provide information about the new state of the system after the decision is implemented. By comparing this information against the system change predicted by the candidate models, we can increase knowledge about which model is more correct. Third, empirical predictive models are often based on historical monitoring data. Therefore, the initial set of models might be based heavily on monitoring information. Future information from monitoring can continue to be used, in conjunction with data from research projects, to develop new candidates for the model set in the future. Given these roles, variables measured in the monitoring program must be relevant to the objective function and appear as components of the models in the model set. Finally, the smaller the measurement error in the monitoring program (that is, the more exact our knowledge of the current system state), the less uncertainty we have to face in the decision process and the faster our learning rate. The more effort we put into monitoring, therefore, the better.

In the mallard example, several ongoing monitoring programs have been exploited: May and July aerial surveys to count waterfowl; preseason banding programs; and harvest and parts collection surveys. The continual development of geographic information systems (GIS) permits even greater exploitation of habitat information.

Choosing an Optimal Policy

ARM involves both a management component and, if there is more than one element in the model set, a learning component. Given that the elements of ARM are in place, the objective function will determine the relative focus on these two components. Figure 10.7 indicates that if the objective focuses exclusively on learning, then ARM calls for *classic experimentation,* or probing (Walters 1986). The idea is to focus on science initially in order to identify the best model quickly and then base our management on that model. The other extreme is *passively adaptive management* (Walters 1986:232; Johnson et al. 1997), where the objective emphasizes other management objectives exclusively. Monitoring programs would still permit the comparison of predicted and observed dynamics, however, so that learning could still occur. Thus science is conducted under passively adaptive management, but as a by-product of management. A compromise between these two extremes is *actively adaptive management* (Walters 1986: 232; Walters and Holling 1990; Johnson et al. 1993; Williams 1996), where the objectives consist of both management and learning.

The objective function used by Johnson et al. (1997) in the mallard example was to maximize

$$\sum_{\tau=t}^{T} \sum_{i=1}^{M} P_{i,\tau} v_{i,\tau} \qquad [10.8]$$

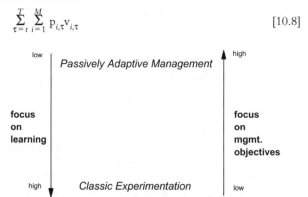

Figure 10.7. Relative positions of passively adaptive management and classic experimentation on two continua: focus on learning and focus on management objectives.

Both information (through $p_{i,\tau}$) and harvest (through $v_{i,\tau}$) are included in this function.

The derivation of an optimal strategy—once the elements of ARM are all fully assembled—can be done mathematically, at least in theory, as a Markov decision process (Puterman 1994:2). It is Markovian because the system dynamics and the rewards or costs of a selected action in Equations (10.2) and (10.3) depend only on the current state of the system and the current action. (Previous states and actions are ignored.) The elements as I have described them include decisions being made at discrete points in time, a discrete number of alternatives in the set of management options, and a discrete number of models in the model set. If the state space is also discretized, it is possible to derive an optimal policy using discrete stochastic dynamic optimization (Bellman 1957; Anderson 1975; Williams 1982; Puterman 1994). Although there are algorithms and software (Lubow 1994, 1995; Williams 1996) to find the optimal policy, complex processes (many states, management options, models, and so on) can cause dimensionality problems and make optimization impractical with current computer technology (Lubow 1995; Williams 1996; Chapter 6 in this volume).

The mallard harvest decision problem (Johnson et al. 1997) was kept sufficiently small so that stochastic dynamic programming via Program SDP (Lubow 1995) could be used to derive an optimal policy. This solution was based on passively adaptive optimization even though learning is part of the objective function in Equation (10.8). A key feature of an algorithm for actively adaptive optimization is the ability to anticipate the change in the model weights resulting from a management action and then to carry these weights as an *information state* throughout the optimization process (Williams 1996). The version of SDP used at that time did not have this capability.

Apart from problems of high dimension, a purely mathematical approach to finding the optimal policy is often impractical because a modeling team cannot sufficiently formalize one or more elements of ARM. Sometimes the problem is sufficiently framed that simulation can be used to find a solution that, although not optimal, represents a big improvement over the status quo (see Chapter 6 in this volume). Moore et al. (n.d.) used a genetic algorithm (a guided simulation approach) to closely replicate the results of Johnson et al. (1997) for the mallard harvest problem. Even when this approach does not work well, modeling the decision process forces stakeholders and scientists to clarify and communicate their objectives and biological opinions—thereby improving the decision process. Walters (1986) has devoted much attention to this point.

In summation, it is worth repeating Walters' (1986:145) recommendation that the ARM process should be developed collaboratively. He advocated that a decision modeling team should include:

- Modelers with experience in math and simulation
- Research scientists
- Resource managers with a knowledge of management options and the history of the system
- Policy analysts with responsibility for defining management objectives

Although each person has his or her own expertise, the more each knows about the specialty of the others, the smoother the communication and collaboration. In the case of mallard harvest, the technical development of ARM is guided by a working group composed of biologists, biometricians, modelers, and administrators from state wildlife agencies, the USFWS, CWS, USGS, and nongovernmental organizations (Johnson et al. 1999).

THE ADVANTAGES OF ARM

All informed wildlife management is based on predictive models—even when the prediction comes strictly from a manager's intuition. In this chapter we have examined a model of the decision process epitomized by adaptive resource management. ARM incorporates predictive models of the system to be managed as well as their relationship to the set of management options and the objective function. There is no need for the tools outlined here if a manager or decision-making body is completely satisfied with the status quo with respect to every element of the decision process (that is: objectives are specific, clear, and accepted by all stakeholders; management options are agreed upon and their impact on the ecological system and the objectives is sufficiently understood; and an adequate monitoring program is in place to confirm this). But if either of the common problems mentioned at the beginning of the chapter exists—confusion or disagreement over specific objectives or disagreement about the pertinent structure of the system to be managed—the question becomes whether (or to what extent) to use the tools presented here. My suggestion is to try to use them as fully as possible. Try to write down a mathematical expression that captures the objectives. Try to develop a complete, though simple, model for the system dynamics that captures the essential features for management purposes. Try to incorporate any disagreements into a set of competing models. Try to encapsulate the management options into a set that is limited enough that the results are tractable. There are three potential outcomes to this process:

- You might succeed in simplifying the process and limiting the number of pertinent state variables, management options, and models enough that adaptive optimization (Williams 1996) can be used to recommend an optimal policy.

- You might succeed in formulating the problem but find the dimensionality so great that today's software and hardware cannot handle it. In this case, simulation may prove useful (see Chapter 6 in this volume).
- The formulation process might encounter obstacles. Perhaps the stakeholders cannot agree on an objective function and constraints. If this is the only problem, several optimal strategies could be derived—one for each of the objective functions favored by individual stakeholders. If these strategies do not differ, there is no problem. If they do, stakeholders have no choice but to continue to strive for a consensus (unless one has veto power). Until this issue is resolved, management will be conducted without direction.

Another obstacle to fully formulating the problem is dissatisfaction with the potential for any model to improve on intuitive predictions. This is not a problem if an expert's subjective assessment is included as one of the models in the set used for adaptive management—even if the expert participated in constructing other models in the set. Including an expert's intuitive predictions benefits the management process by incorporating all reasonable means for predicting the effect of management. It would confer benefits from a modeling perspective by validating a mathematical model derived from the expert's input against his or her intuitive predictions (see Chapter 7 in this volume).

The model of decision making considered here has been confined mostly to discretized elements. This need not be the case, however. Williams (1996) has discussed continuous state variables. He also discusses the case where the model set consists of a continuum of models defined by the values of one or more parameters. In this case, structural uncertainty is reflected in the distribution of each parameter, defined by a set of hyperparameters (Williams 1996).

The theme of this chapter has been *management science*—that is, mathematics and science used to build a model to improve management. With ARM, however, where scientific uncertainty is formally acknowledged by including competing models, science and management shift from a somewhat commensal to a more mutualistic relationship. This approach is consistent with Popper's (1979) paradigm of a "natural selection of hypotheses," Chamberlin's (1897) multiple-model approach to science, and a Bayesian approach to statistical inference. Chapter 2 in this volume expounds on this topic, including the case where management is not part of the objective.

Vigilance should be exercised in constructing a model set—especially when there is a paucity of data. Candidate models should make biological sense. Moreover, a "safeguard" model should be considered and be given a nonnegligible initial weight. Such a model should be biologically reasonable and include pessimistic predictions about certain management actions. Its role is to keep management actions conservative until enough iterations of the management process (and updating of model weights) are completed to validate more optimistic models. Future studies and monitoring information should also be used to evaluate the set of models and modify or add to the set periodically.

Incorporating models in the process of management—epitomized by ARM—is not a panacea. In the end it might be determined that the use of formal mathematical models is not practical or even necessary in some cases. Nevertheless, considering the management problem in this context assists in structuring a complex decision-making process, focuses discussion on its elements, and forces participants to clarify their thinking and put their cards on the table. Even without reaching the step of writing out mathematical expressions, the exercise often yields insights that might never have been discovered without putting the problem in this framework. ARM leads to a management process that uses current information optimally, accounts for competing scientific views, and concurrently produces scientific information.

ACKNOWLEDGMENTS

The thoughts presented here are an outgrowth of my participation in the application of adaptive resource management to waterfowl harvest regulation. I have benefited from many discussions with other participants in that process, including F. A. Johnson, J. A. Dubovsky, J. D. Nichols, B. K. Williams, C. T. Moore, G. W. Smith, D. F. Caithamer, and J. R. Kelley Jr. I thank J. A. Dubovsky, R. Bennetts, and an anonymous reviewer for helpful reviews of the manuscript and am grateful to the editors for their review and guidance. I also thank J. A. Dubovsky for assistance with graphics.

REFERENCES

Aber, J. D. 1997. Why don't we believe the models? *Bulletin of the Ecological Society of America* 78:232–233.

Anderson, D. R. 1975. Optimal exploitation strategies for an animal population in a Markovian environment: A theory and an example. *Ecology* 56:1281–1297.

Anderson, D. R., and K. P. Burnham. 1976. Population ecology of the mallard. VI: The effect of exploitation on survival. Resource Publication 128. Washington, D.C.: U.S. Fish and Wildlife Service.

Bellman, R. 1957. *Dynamic Programming*. Princeton: Princeton University Press.

Burnham, K. P., G. C. White, and D. R. Anderson. 1984. Estimating the effect of hunting on annual survival rates of adult mallards. *Journal of Wildlife Management* 48:350–361.

Caithamer, D. F., and J. A. Dubovsky. 1997. Waterfowl population status, 1997. Administrative Report. Washington, D.C.: Office of Migratory Bird Management, U.S. Fish and Wildlife Service.

Chamberlin, T. C. 1897. The method of multiple working hypotheses. *Journal of Geology* 5:837–848.

Holling, C. S., ed. 1978. *Adaptive Environmental Assessment and Management.* London: Wiley.

Johnson, F. A., B. K. Williams, J. D. Nichols, J. E. Hines, W. L. Kendall, G. W. Smith, and D. F. Caithamer. 1993. Developing an adaptive management strategy for harvesting waterfowl in North America. *Transactions of the North American Wildlife and Natural Resources Conference* 58:565–583.

Johnson, F. A., C. T. Moore, W. L. Kendall, J. A. Dubovsky, D. F. Caithamer, J. R. Kelley Jr., and B. K. Williams. 1997. Uncertainty and the management of mallard harvests. *Journal of Wildlife Management* 61:202–216.

Johnson, F. A., J. A. Dubovsky, J. R. Kelley Jr., W. L. Kendall, M. T. Moore, M. C. Runge, and S. E. Sheaffer. 1999. Adaptive harvest management: Considerations for the 1999 duck hunting season. Administrative Report. Washington, D.C.: Office of Migratory Bird Management, U.S. Fish and Wildlife Service.

Lee, K. N. 1993. *Compass and Gyroscope: Integrating Science and Politics for the Environment.* Washington, D.C., and Covelo, Calif.: Island Press.

Lubow, B. C. 1994. Stochastic dynamic programming (SDP) user's guide. Version 1.06. Fort Collins: Cooperative Fish and Wildlife Research Unit, Colorado State University.

———. 1995. SDP: Generalized software for solving stochastic dynamic optimization problems. *Wildlife Society Bulletin* 23:738–742.

Moore, C. T., M. J. Conroy, K. Boston, and W. D. Potter. N.d. A genetic algorithm for dynamic optimal control of wildlife harvests. *Ecological Modelling.* In review.

Neter, J., and W. Wasserman. 1974. *Applied Linear Statistical Models.* Homewood, Ill.: Irwin.

Nichols, J. D., F. A. Johnson, and B. K. Williams. 1995. Managing North American waterfowl in the face of uncertainty. *Annual Review of Ecology and Systematics* 26:177–199.

Popper, K. P. 1979. *Objective Knowledge: An Evolutionary Approach.* Oxford: Oxford University Press.

Puterman, M. L. 1994. *Markov Decision Processes.* New York: Wiley.

Smith, G. W., and R. E. Reynolds. 1992. Effect of hunting on mallard survival, 1979–88. *Journal of Wildlife Management* 56:306–316.

U.S. Fish and Wildlife Service (USFWS). 1975. *Final Environmental Statement for the Issuance of Annual Regulations Permitting the Sport Hunting of Migratory Birds.* Washington, D.C.: USFWS.

Walters, C. J. 1986. *Adaptive Management of Renewable Resources.* New York: Macmillan.

Walters, C. J., and C. S. Holling. 1990. Large-scale management experiments and learning by doing. *Ecology* 71:2060–2068.

Williams, B. K. 1982. Optimal stochastic control in natural resource management: Framework and examples. *Ecological Modelling* 16:275–297.

———. 1996. Adaptive optimization and the harvest of biological populations. *Mathematical Biosciences* 136:1–20.

Williams, B. K., and F. A. Johnson. 1995. Adaptive management and the regulation of waterfowl harvests. *Wildlife Society Bulletin* 23:430–436.

Williams, B. K., F. A. Johnson, and K. Wilkins. 1996. Uncertainty and the adaptive management of waterfowl harvests. *Journal of Wildlife Management* 60:223–232.

Individual-Based Models: Tracking Variability Among Individuals

Donald L. DeAngelis, Wolf M. Mooij,
M. Philip Nott, and Robert E. Bennetts

The classic models of population and community ecology—the Lotka-Volterra equations and their numerous elaborations—are based on the same assumptions as models of chemical reaction kinetics: species populations can be treated as if all individuals within a population are the same and in large enough numbers that statistical fluctuations can be ignored. But unlike the case for physico-chemical systems, these assumptions are generally not satisfied for ecological populations—often not even approximately so. Although these models are seldom strictly justified, they have been valuable in providing insights into how ecological systems behave. Many key concepts of population and community behavior (limit-cycle oscillations, competitive exclusion, keystone predation) can be described in terms of simple classical models.

There may be problems applying such simple models to management problems, however, because the variation that exists among individuals in ecological populations leads to differences in their success in survival and reproduction. Difference in age is an obvious and inevitable type of variation. There are other differences as well, resulting from the unique genetics of individuals and from the vagaries of life experiences among individuals. In this chapter we show that in many cases individual variations matter to the total population and should not be ignored. We also describe a modeling approach—individual-based modeling—that deals directly with the variability in various characteristics within a population. We illustrate the approach through some examples.

WHY VARIATION WITHIN POPULATIONS MATTERS

Variation within populations arises from a few basic sources. The most obvious source of variation is ontogenetic changes in organisms, or changes during their life cycle. Every organism grows in age and size, and its physiological and behavioral characteristics change as well. A second source of variation is genetic. In sexually reproducing organisms, individuals vary genetically from each other. This is important not only on evolutionary but also on ecological time scales for organisms living in spatially and temporally varying environments, as slight differences in physiological and behavioral characteristics may fit organisms better or worse to various conditions (Williams 1975). The third source of variation is more complex. This source has to do with the experiences an organism undergoes in its environment, which differ from those of every other individual in the population. Except under extremely artificial circumstances—such as microorganisms in a controlled environment—every organism is subject to its own unique local interactions with the environment that affect its growth, exposure to mortality, parasite load, finding of mates, and so forth. This is true for plants, each of which exists on a site with its own slope, aspect, microclimate, soil characteristics, neighbors, and so forth, and for animals, each of which has its own unique trajectory through the environment.

Several general types of variation result from these sources. *Physiological variation* may include health, condition, strength, and agility as well as less obvious physiological differences such as resistance to various diseases and parasites. *Behavioral variation* may be complex in higher animals, and there may be variations within a population in traits like aggressiveness, curiosity, knowledge, and intelligence. *Social variation* is another trait associated with animals and may include such things as caste membership in social insects, position in a dominance hierarchy in certain vertebrates, association in flocks, and presence of a mate or offspring. The *spatial location* of an individual in its environment is yet another individual characteristic exhibiting variation. While the range of environmental conditions available to a population may be considered a characteristic of the environment, the location of an individual at a particular place in the spectrum of conditions is a property of the individual. Location is most crucial to plants and sessile animals, which are fixed in a given location and at the mercy of the environmental conditions and proximity of other nearby organisms. But it is important to mobile animals as well, which may occupy fairly localized territories or home ranges.

Given that characteristics vary within a population, does this matter to describing and making predictions concerning the population? At a straightforward level, there are many practical questions for which we want to know not just the numerical size of a population but how individual characteristics vary within the population—whether or not they are crucial to the overall dynamics of the population. A wildlife ecologist or commercial user of the population may need to know, for example, the age structure of a population, its spatial distribution, or what percentage of the population is healthy, mature, or larger than a certain size. Such variation may not always affect the dynamics of the total population, but sometimes it will.

An obvious case of variation that may affect population dynamics is age structure. Because of age structure there is a lag in a population's numerical response to environmental conditions. This leads to the possibility of periodicities—such as the baby boom and subsequent baby boomlet in the population of the Western world following World War II—and large oscillations in many animal and plant populations. Similar instabilities may affect the size structure of populations. Initially small size variations in cohorts of plants and animals such as fish may amplify through time and ultimately affect the number of survivors in the population (Huston and DeAngelis 1987; Claessen et al. 2000). Size variations may also affect interactions between different species. Temperature-controlled minor differences in size of larval prey fish species may play a decisive role in the vulnerability of the prey to predatory fish species that spawned a few weeks earlier (Mooij 1996). An enormous literature exists in the field of age and size structure, and there are a host of models, such as Leslie matrix models (Caswell 1989) and McKendrick–von Foerster partial differential equations (Metz and Diekmann 1986), to study the phenomena associated with age and size structure.

Other types of variation in a population are also important. Uchmanski (2000) used an individual-based model to describe a population that tends to overexploit its resources and crash. When all individuals in the model were parameterized to behave identically, the population oscillated and eventually went extinct. When the individuals varied in their resource assimilation rates, however, the model population survived for longer time periods that increased with increasing variation. Variation in assimilation rate led to gradual rather than sharp crashes, increasing the probability that there would be survivors. This model demonstrated that variation among individuals may be important, or even essential, to population stability.

Or suppose that individuals within a certain population vary in susceptibility to a particular stress, such as a potentially lethal change in temperature. This difference in susceptibility may be due to genetic differences among organisms, to differences in the amount of lipids that animals have stored, or to differences in the specific microhabitats in which plants or animals are located, which can moderate the effect of cold. Assume that over a period of time the population is subjected to cold shocks of various intensities. If variation in susceptibility to cold shock can be predicted, then we can predict the numbers of individuals that suffer mortality with each cold shock and ultimately the effect of the sequence of cold shocks on the whole population. Perfect knowledge of the variation in susceptibility to cold shock within the population is not possible, of course, but given some information on this variation we can make predictions. How precise these predictions are depends on the quality of the information. Modeling may be indispensable in using the information to make predictions.

INDIVIDUAL-BASED MODELING

Mathematical or computer models can be helpful in investigating the complex ways in which variation affects population-level dynamics. The individual-based modeling approach, in particular, can accommodate numerous types of variation within a population when information is available. This approach has been used in ecology for at least 30 years (Huston et al. 1988; DeAngelis et al. 1994), but individual-based models (IBMs) are far less well known than the classic state-variable or aggregated-variable models of ecology such as the logistic and Lotka-Volterra models. A state-variable population model, in its simplest form, has a single variable, say N, representing the size of the population and a single equation that describes the dynamics of N. The IBM, on the other hand, is a computer simulation that can be thought of as an extension of a model for a single organism to a whole population of individuals modeled simultaneously. In this approach, variables are attached to each discrete individual. An IBM for deer, for example, may contain variables such as age, weight, current location in space, and so forth for each deer in the population.

It is useful at this point to distinguish what we are calling IBMs from such population models as the Leslie matrix model and the McKendrick–von Foerster partial differential equation model. These models are used to describe the age, stage, and size structures of populations. They are sometimes referred to as IBMs—a convention that is followed in DeAngelis and Gross (1994). Models of the Leslie matrix and McKendrick–von

Foerster type do not follow individual organisms, however, but describe distribution functions for such characteristics as age, stage, or size. IBMs differ fundamentally from such in that variables are attached to individual organisms in the population rather than aggregating over individuals. Therefore, the number of variables in an IBM is proportional to the number of organisms in the population. An IBM of a deer population in which four individual characteristics (age, weight, sex, and location) are considered has $4 \times N$ variables, where N is the current number of individuals in the population. The number of individuals changes with both births and deaths. Another key property of IBMs is that they are almost always Monte Carlo simulations. This means that individual events—such as finding food or mates, dispersing successfully, or surviving through time—have some stochastic component. A single-population simulation using an individual-based modeling approach produces only one realization for that population. Replicate simulations must be performed to produce means and variances.

Apart from the various characteristics attached to individuals in IBMs, there may also be equations or rules describing changes in these characteristics. The equation for age is simple: an organism ages each time step in the model by the size of that time step (minute, day, year). The equation for weight is more complex: growth is a function of what the organism assimilates minus its metabolic costs. Activities such as mating and having offspring, being attached to a group, having a territory, or having a certain social status are usually described by rules, which may be probabilistic.

Spatially explicit IBMs are those that incorporate the spatial locations of individuals on some landscape. In these models, we need a description of the landscape as well as the details of individual differences within the population. Not all IBMs are spatially explicit. The model of Uchmanski (2000) or the model of first-year fish (to be described), for example, do not follow the spatial location of individuals. In these cases, it is assumed the cohort is well mixed: all individuals are exposed to the same environment.

An example of a spatially explicit IBM is one developed by Wolff (1994) for a colonially nesting wading bird colony. These birds nest together at a fixed site and forage over a large area surrounding the nesting site. The spatial pattern of prey availability may shift from one area to another as a function of water levels, the exploitation of prey, and prey population dynamics (Fleming et al. 1994). Each wading bird follows its own path on the landscape in searching for food, though sometimes joining a flock for periods of time. The reproductive output of the colony taken as a whole depends on foraging and other decisions, time and energy budgets, and chance factors at the individual level. As with wading birds, most populations are confronted with a highly dynamic, spatially varying environment. The individual-based modeling approach to determining how well the population will do is to model individuals, equipped with physiological and behavioral repertoires and learning behavior, and allow them to respond over time to a realistically simulated landscape.

From the foregoing considerations, then, we can say that the IBM approach may be useful for addressing problems in ecology in which variability among individuals of a population is important. A key feature of individual-based models is that they can represent simultaneously many types of variation within a population. A related motive for using an individual-based approach is that many populations or subpopulations of interest are very small. In such cases, not only are the effects of individual variability more significant than in large populations but demographic stochasticity may also be a crucial factor. IBMs represent this stochasticity in a realistic way (Nichols et al. 1980; Smies 1983).

SPECIFIC MODELS

The concepts and applications of IBMs are best illustrated through examples. Three examples, chosen from many available, are presented here in some detail. Each is designed for application to real systems. To show the motivation for the model and some key characteristics of the population, a brief introduction is given. We then sketch a conceptual model to convey the ecological content. In describing how the model is implemented, we include more of the specifics and a few results. These examples represent three ways in which variation within a population can affect its dynamics. The model of first-year fish illustrates the importance of detailed size distribution in the early life history of fish: a slight variation in this distribution, coupled with size-dependent predation ability, can affect recruitment substantially. The model of the Cape Sable seaside sparrow indicates how fine-scale details of individual locations on the landscape affect reproductive success. The model of a snail kite population allows for individual movement patterns of kites, which can affect yearly survival and reproduction.

The Dynamics of First-Year Fish

Many fish species produce large numbers of offspring, few of which survive to recruit into the adult population. Survival probability through the first year of life may be especially low as individuals are subjected to many types of mortality. The growing-season dynamics of these first-year (age-0) fish are complex, including size-dependent competition and sometimes cannibalism. The few age-0 fish that survive their first year tend to be ones with the capability or luck to grow faster than most of their cohort and pass quickly through the bottleneck of food limitation and high mortality.

The outcome of such age-0 within-cohort interactions is difficult to predict. Above all, divergent behavior of the cohort is possible, leading to various outcomes. There are two extremes of these alternatives: (1) small size variations among the fish at the larval stage may amplify through the growing season, such that a few fish grow much faster and dominate the food sources, and smaller fish will tend to be suppressed in growth and die from factors related to their small size; (2) no fish are able to monopolize resources so that all fish in the cohort grow at nearly the same rate, which is slow because the resources are divided among many fish. In the first extreme, only a few fish may recruit to the population, but they will be large and healthy. In the second extreme, many age-0 fish may survive the growing season, but all of them will be stunted and might not survive their first winter. Thus the dynamics of the entire population is ultimately affected by the dynamics of age-0 recruits.

Small variation among some members of a population (the age-0 cohort) may have a large impact on the dynamics of the population as a whole. The problem posed here is whether predictions can be made concerning the number of survivors through the first year—given knowledge of the number of eggs that hatch, the available food for age-0 fish, background sources of mortality, and other relevant factors.

Conceptual Model. Several models have addressed the problem of age-0 recruitment by describing the size-structure dynamics using IBMs. They model a cohort of individual age-0 fish that grow and interact with each other in a small lake. (See DeAngelis et al. 1979, 1991, 1993a, 1993b; Adams and DeAngelis 1986; Rose and Cowan 1993; Scheffer et al. 1995.) The main conceptual features of this IBM model are:

- A temporal pattern of production of hatchlings during spawning season is simulated. As soon as these hatchlings reach the swim-up stage, they are modeled as individuals.
- The model simulates foraging of individual fish. The densities, turnover rates, and exploitation of prey of various size classes are modeled, with encounters between larval fish and prey occurring stochastically. Prey that are encountered and of capturable size are consumed. As the individual fish grow in size, the size of the area they can search and their maximum feeding rates increase accordingly.
- The amount of food ingested per day is converted bioenergetically to weight gain of the individual fish. From the weight gain, the increase in

length of each fish is calculated. Under periods of insufficient food inges-
tion to maintain growth, fish length remains fixed, but body weight and
condition decline due to metabolic demands of the fish. An individual
fish starves when its weight falls below a critical threshold for a given
length.
• In addition to the possibility of starvation, fish are subjected to both size-
dependent and size-independent background mortality.

Thus the model simulates the cohort of year-0 fish as individuals—each
having its own interactions with the prey and its own growth and survival
through time. Density dependence is manifested through reduction of prey
densities. A reduced prey density has a feedback effect on the age-0 fish,
resulting in lower than optimal growth rates and higher mortality rates. In
this conceptual model all individuals of the population are simulated. At the
end of 1 year, the number of fish that remain alive in the simulation constitutes the survivors or recruits to the next age class. Because the model has
stochastic elements, no two simulations would produce the same outcome.

Implementation. A model using this conceptual scheme was formulated for
the smallmouth bass (*Micropterus dolomieu*) population in a bay of Lake Ope-
ongo, Ontario. The data on smallmouth bass and prey availability came from
a number of sources that are discussed in DeAngelis et al. (1991, 1993b).

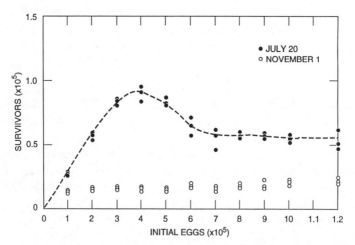

Figure 11.1. Output from an individual-based model of an age-0 smallmouth bass
cohort. The surviving numbers of model age-0 smallmouth bass, as a function of the
initial density of viable eggs, are shown at two points in time during the simulation:
20 July and 1 November (from DeAngelis et al. 1993b).

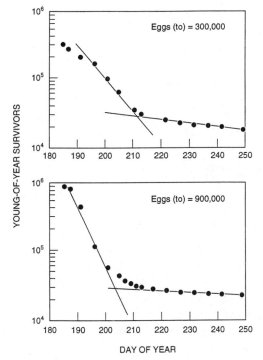

Figure 11.2. Output from an individual-based model of an age-0 smallmouth bass cohort. The predicted number of survivors is a function of the day of the year for two different initial egg densities. Note that there are two characteristic mortality rates: a high mortality, governed by starvation early in the year, and a much slower rate of mortality later in the year (from DeAngelis et al. 1993b).

The model was formulated as an IBM. But rather than every single individual year-0 fish in the bay, a representative sample of several thousand age-0 fish was simulated. The variation inherent in the growth of each fish contributed to increasing variance in size distribution through time—especially at the time when some smallmouth bass reached the size at which they could start feeding on fish and other large prey.

Model simulations were performed to investigate the relationship between the initial number of fertilized eggs in a spawning area and the survival and size distribution of age-0 fish through a growing season. To accomplish this, DeAngelis et al. (1993b) performed a sequence of simulations in which they successively increased the number of viable eggs produced during the spawning season (Figure 11.1). Here the surviving numbers of age-0 smallmouth bass as a function of the initial numbers of fertilized eggs are shown on 20 July and 1 November. Note that the model predicts a hump-shaped relationship in July, but by November the number of survivors is relatively uniform.

The temporal dynamics predicted by the IBM show some general patterns. For example, an initial period of rapid exponential mortality lasted for a few weeks early in the year. This was followed by a period of much lower mortality during the rest of the growing season (Figure 11.2). These and other details produced by the IBM allow us to unravel some of the intricacies of age-class dynamics of a fish population.

Cape Sable Seaside Sparrow

The Cape Sable seaside sparrow (*Ammodramus maritima mirabilis*) is an ecologically isolated subspecies of the seaside sparrow (Beecher 1955). Recent surveys estimate its population size at fewer than 3000 individuals and its range as restricted to the extreme southern portion of the Florida peninsula (Werner 1975; Bass and Kushlan 1982). The sparrow breeds in marl prairies typified by dense stands of grass species usually below 1 meter in height and naturally inundated by fresh water part of the year. As water levels recede during the dry season in late winter and spring, the sparrows establish territories and start nesting in the grass. Pairs may produce up to three broods if their nesting sites remain dry. If water levels do not recede early enough in spring, nesting may be delayed; if reflooding occurs during the nesting season, eggs or nestlings may be lost.

Recent declines have occurred in the sparrow population, probably due to higher water levels in recent years (Pimm et al. 1995). Because the sparrow's current range is limited to a few hundred square kilometers subject to flooding and fires, the population is highly vulnerable. Changes to the hydrology of the southern Everglades, planned as part of a restoration project (U.S. Army Corps of Engineers 1999), will change hydrology in the sparrow's range. It is essential to predict the effects of these changes on the sparrow.

Conceptual Model. The purpose of the model is to predict future population size of the Cape Sable seaside sparrow under the different prospective hydrological regimes. Several factors argue in favor of using a spatially explicit IBM to predict the future dynamics of the population. First, merely modeling total population levels would not provide the detailed information needed to make specific management recommendations. It is essential to simulate the spatial distribution of the population as some parts of its spatial domain may be more vulnerable to inopportune flooding than others. Second, a detailed representation of the sparrow's environment is possible with spatial GIS data and a spatial hydrological model. Water levels in the sparrow's range can be predicted at fine temporal and spatial resolutions as a function of rainfall regime and water management protocols. And third, the sparrow's preference for breeding habitat, its behavior during reproduction, and the influence of water levels on its reproductive behavior are known from previous studies.

For these reasons, a predictive model relating landscape hydrology to sparrow population dynamics is possible. Conceptually, the model is designed as follows:

- The sparrow's landscape is modeled explicitly as a set of 500 × 500-meter spatial cells—resolution fine enough to represent areas of similar vegetation, topography, and hydrology.
- Each sparrow in the population is modeled during a breeding period. In particular, the model tracks the sex, age, and breeding status of each model individual from egg to the end of its life. For mature males, the model tracks its search for an available territory, its finding a mate, nest initiation, and the status of eggs and nestlings on a daily basis. Females search for single males with territories.
- The relationship of sparrow breeding activity to water depth is modeled. Water depth in spatial cells is recorded daily through a hydrological model. A spatial cell is not available for nesting until the water level in that cell falls below about 5 centimeters. Any rise in the water level above 10 centimeters in a spatial cell during the nesting season is assumed to cause sparrows that have nests in the cell to abandon them. The main variation incorporated in this model is that of the specific spatial locations of sparrows' nests in different spatial cells and thus the elevation of individual nests. This elevation relative to the water stage determines the length of the effective reproductive season for the pair of sparrows and the nest's vulnerability to flooding. This source of variation in the model was essential to forecasting the sensitivity of sparrow reproduction to hydrology.
- The sparrows are not modeled in detail during the nonbreeding season. Age-specific mortalities are assigned to individuals during that period probabilistically based on empirical data. The following spring, when the next breeding season begins, older males search for nesting territories as close as possible to the site they used the previous year, if it was successful, while new adult males begin their search close to their natal site.

Implementation. The conceptual model was implemented as a Monte Carlo simulation (Nott 1998) and applied to a major subpopulation of the Cape Sable seaside sparrows in the Everglades. The size of this subpopulation has reached as high as 3000 sparrows, and the model was capable of tracking

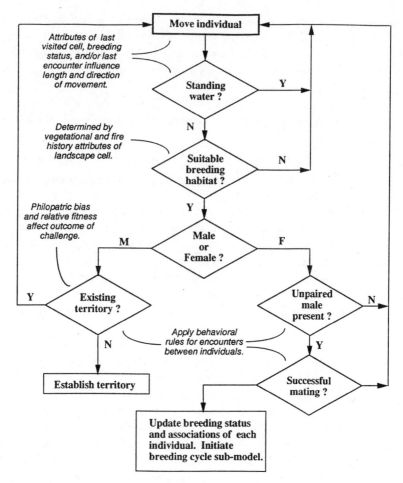

Figure 11.3. Flowchart showing the way the individual-based model of the Cape Sable seaside sparrow describes the occupation of nesting territories and reproduction.

the locations and breeding status of all these birds during the breeding season. The model increased the age of an individual each day and updated its status according to movement and behavior rules. The core of the model was a simple flow of decisions and actions that affect individuals in relation to abiotic factors and other individuals (Figure 11.3). At each step the model updated the breeding status and tracked associations between individuals.

Because the model is a Monte Carlo simulation, the movement rules were probabilistic and the finding of a territory and mate had stochastic components. Moreover, there was some probability for mortality each day.

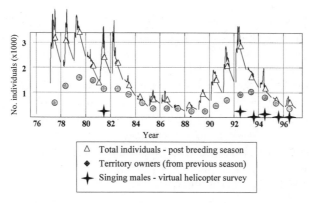

Figure 11.4. IBM simulation run of Cape Sable seaside sparrow numbers. This run depicts a single Monte Carlo replicate for a 20-year period (1977–1996). The model keeps track of total individuals in the population and territory owners. The starting value of population size in 1997 was chosen to calibrate the model to empirical estimates of sparrow numbers in 1981. Moreover, the model simulates the numbers of individuals expected to be counted by the helicopter survey. These model values are shown for 1981 and for 1993–1997, years for which comparisons with empirical data could be made. The low model values predicted for 1993–1996 correspond closely to empirical values for these years.

Information on the sparrow's life history and the results of field observations provided the ecological parameters for the model: survival and fecundity rates, egg incubation period, nestling period, mean dispersal distances, and so forth (Werner 1975; Lockwood et al. 1997; Curnutt et al. 1998).

Using the historical hydrology from 1976 to 1996, the model predicted a population number sequence of one of the sparrow subpopulations from 1976 to 1996 (Figure 11.4). Seven population estimates are available—1981 and 1992–1997—and these are shown on the graph of model output. Nott (1998) chose the initial population size for 1977 such that the 1981 model prediction agreed reasonably well with the population estimates for the subpopulation. The model predicted rapid growth during the late 1970s, a relatively dry period. The middle 1980s were relatively wet and the population declined, but it climbed again in the late 1980s and early 1990s. Aside from 1981, there were no field data to check the model against until 1992. Starting with that date, the model correctly predicted the rapid decline in population during the relatively wet years from 1992 to 1996.

Snail Kite

The snail kite (*Rostrhamus sociabilis plumbeus* Ridgway) is a wetland hawk whose distribution in the United States is limited to the freshwater marshes of southern and central Florida (Bennetts et al. 1994). It is listed as an endangered species in the United States. Because the snail kite feeds almost exclusively on the apple snail (*Pomacea paludosa*), it is an example of an extreme prey specialist and would be expected to be at high risk from environmental variations that affect apple snail dynamics. Apple snails occur in areas of extended inundation, and their availability to kites is greatly reduced during droughts. Snail kites typically nest in areas where water depths are in the range of 15 to 100 centimeters. Moreover, the snail kites need woody vegetation in which to build their nests and nearby areas of relatively open wet prairie for effective foraging. Long-term changes in hydrology could affect such habitats and make an area unsuitable for snail kites.

The snail kite's high degree of vulnerability to both long-term and short-term changes in the environment is partly offset by two characteristics of the bird. First, the snail kite matures early and is capable of rapid population growth under favorable conditions. Second, it is nomadic and therefore able to move large distances from temporarily poor habitats in search of adequate habitat areas (Sykes 1979; Takekawa and Beissinger 1989). Movements of radio-tagged adult snail kites were recorded between discrete wetland areas in southern and central Florida during their summer dispersal season (Figure 11.5; Bennetts and Kitchens 1997). Because climatic conditions usually vary spatially within the bird's range in southern and central Florida, snail kites forced to abandon a nest in an area where

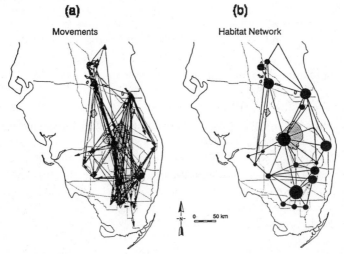

Figure 11.5. Depiction of the range of snail kites in central and southern Florida showing (**a**) the movement patterns of adult radio-tagged snail kites over a 1-year period from April 1992 to April 1993 and (**b**) the network of habitats utilized by the snail kite. (From Bennetts and Kitchens 1997.)

drought has reduced the availability of apple snails may be able to reach more favorable areas of wetland where they can renest or at least survive.

How viable is the snail kite population of central and southern Florida over the long term? To a large extent this is a question of the degree to which the spatial extent and climatic variability of the kite's range is great enough to reduce the effects of drought conditions when they occur in the region. This depends not only on the existence of enough wetland areas across its range but also on the snail kite's ability to reach alternative areas. This ability is partly a function of the knowledge that individual kites accumulate over their lifetime, which they may learn through exploratory flights (Bennetts and Kitchens 1997).

Conceptual Model. The ability of individual snail kites to move quickly over long distances from poor to good habitat sites is an important adaptation. To understand how this attribute can affect the snail kite population's survival under changing environmental conditions, we model the population in a spatially explicit manner over its entire range and also include in the model the spatially and temporally varying hydrologic conditions in this region. Some of the key characteristics of the conceptual, spatially explicit IBM are the following:

- Each snail kite is individually modeled. Attached to each individual are state variables representing age, sex, spatial location, and reproductive status.
- The model snail kites nest across an array of wetlands of southern and central Florida (assumed, on the basis of studies, to consist of 14 disjunct areas), with mean water depth in each provided by hydrological models. The habitat quality within each of these areas is assumed to be relatively uniform. There is also one aggregated peripheral habitat representing areas of inferior quality that snail kites may use to survive, though not for nesting.
- Each of the 14 individual wetlands is allowed to undergo changes in average water level, which affects food availability for the snail kites. The sites are somewhat independent of each other, as the annual rainfall that drives water levels is spatially correlated for the sites only partially. Moreover, the water levels can be regulated for the individual wetlands by canals and dikes. Drying—or severely low water levels in a wetland— often causes the kites to move away and, for those that stay, results in a reduced reproductive rate and increased mortality rate.
- The kites' movement patterns are stochastic, but there is a general tendency to move to nearby wetlands rather than distant ones and a seasonal tendency to move south in the winter and north in the summer. The

effects of an individual kite's experience on movement may be important, too, although this factor is not yet included in the model.

Implementation. The snail kite IBM, as currently implemented (Mooij et al.,
n.d.), incorporates four biological processes for each kite—aging, reproduction, movement, and mortality—and runs on a time step of a month.
The model can read in historical hydrological data on mean water levels in
the 14 wetlands, can use output from hydrological models, or can use hypothetical data. The snail kite's ability to move between wetlands is a key feature of the model. According to a hypothesis of Bennetts and Kitchens
(1997), a systemwide drought is likely to result in increased mortality,
whereas the birds can respond to a local drying out of a wetland by moving to wetlands unaffected by the drought.

The model was used with 30 years of hydrological data to produce good
agreement with the trends seen in data from an annual quasi-systematic
count of snail kites from 1969 to 1994 (Sykes 1979; Rodgers et al. 1988;
Bennetts et al. 1994). The quality of these field data is questionable because
of changes in observers during that period, so these results must be regarded
as preliminary until better methods of population estimation (Dreitz et al.,
in press) allow more rigorous testing. Theoretical use of the model has provided useful insights, however. Hypothetical, plausible time sequences of
water levels were used in the model to explore the effects of different levels of spatial correlation of droughts (that is, how synchronous the drought
conditions were among the different wetlands). The results of five different
levels of spatial correlation, from 0.0 to 1.0, were compared (Figure 11.6).
Within each of the spatial correlation treatments are seven different mean
time intervals between droughts for each of the 14 wetlands in the model.
The y axis plots the mean number of snail kites in the population over a
25-year period. Note that mean snail kite numbers tend to increase with
increasing time interval between droughts. For each drought return interval, the mean number of kites is highest when the spatial correlation for
droughts is zero. The effect of spatial correlation, however, is much smaller
than the effect of time intervals between droughts.

In addition to these three examples, many other models have illustrated
how types of variation influence the dynamics of populations or communities. Plant-competition models, for example, showed how slight variations
in initial size in an even-aged cohort can amplify through time to create
major changes in population structure (Diggle 1976; Gates 1978; Ford and
Diggle 1981; McMurtrie 1981). In a model of herbivore/plant interactions,
variations in patchiness of the plants affected the feeding rate of the herbivores (Cain 1985; Hyman et al. 1991; Turner et al. 1993, 1994; Mooij and

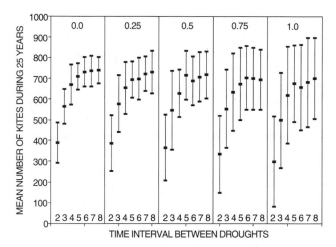

Figure 11.6. Results of the snail kite model comparing the effects of spatial correlation of droughts across the range of the snail kite on mean snail kite numbers in a 25-year simulation. Five different values for spatial correlation are used—ranging from 0.0, which means the occurrence of drought in each of the 15 modeled wetlands is independent of that in others, to 1.0, which means droughts are spatially correlated across all of the wetlands. For each degree of spatial correlation, seven different mean return time intervals for droughts in individual wetlands were assumed. The mean number of snail kites observed in the simulations over 25 years was plotted against these two treatments (Mooij et al., n.d.).

DeAngelis 1999). Results of an epizootic model for rabies illustrated how the behavior of just a few hosts, through long-distance movement, can dramatically alter the spread of the disease (David et al. 1982). This list could be greatly expanded.

THE ADVANTAGES OF IBM

This chapter has reviewed some of the types of variation that can occur within a population and the ways in which this variation can affect the dynamics of the population. We have also considered the utility of the individual-based modeling approach in exploring the consequences of these dynamics. Several questions might be asked with regard to this issue. First, given that IBMs are relatively complex, could simpler models be just as effective for management purposes? Second, how do we reconcile the considerable data needs of IBMs with the usual scarcity of data for ecological systems? Third, how do we evaluate the reliability of IBMs? Finally, would the majority of ecologists find it practical to use such models?

You might ask if analytic approaches—such as the Leslie matrix, Mc–

Kendrick–von Foerster models, or other modeling approaches—would be just as suitable as IBMs in modeling the variability in populations considered in our three main examples. We believe that IBMs are probably the best approach for these cases. Consider the model of age-0 fish population dynamics. A McKendrick–von Foerster model describing the age and size structure as a partial differential equation, coupled with differential equations from prey biomasses, could be applied to this problem. Analytic solutions would be impossible, however, and even a numerical evaluation would be difficult. More important, the key factor of stochasticity of individual growth, known to have population-level effects (DeAngelis et al. 1993a), would be lost. Consider next the model of the Cape Sable seaside sparrow population. The IBM for this species was able to simulate the complex spatial pattern of habitats used by the sparrows, as well as the daily changes in water levels in each 500×500-meter spatial cell. These spatial details are important in management applications where decisions must be made at a fine spatial scale in altering the timing and spatial distribution of water levels in the sparrow's habitat. An analytic model that tried to simplify the situation by averaging spatially over habitat type and water levels would miss the subtle effects of variation within the sparrow's habitat that determine how many adults will nest successfully. The same comments hold for modeling the snail kite. This population makes use of 14 major wetland sites, each with its own hydrological pattern through time. Because the snail kites move between sites frequently, a metapopulation approach (Hanski 1999) is not appropriate. Data on individual movement patterns of snail kites are available and can be conveniently incorporated in a spatially explicit IBM. The model could easily be extended to allow kites to have different movement capabilities based on experience, which has been hypothesized to be important (Bennetts and Kitchens 1997).

Apart from analytic models, another method of predicting population responses to environmental conditions is an empirical, correlative approach. In the correlative approach, data on population size are collected over many years along with concurrent data on environmental conditions. Given these two sets of time-series data, we can correlate population change with environmental conditions and derive a predictive statistical model. In developing a statistical model for population dynamics of snail kites in central and southern Florida, for example, Beissinger (1995) determined the relationship between the annual change in estimated snail kite abundance with low, high, or average rainfall from 1975 to 1986. In this correlative model, we do not need to know anything about the mechanistic details of such population processes as reproduction. If a year has low rainfall, for example, a statistically derived coefficient relevant to the low-rainfall-year type is multiplied by the current population to predict the population for the next year. The correlative approach is problematic, however, in that it requires a long time series of high-quality data, which may not be available. In the case of the snail kite, the 1969–1994 count data are available, and Beissinger was able to fit a simple correlation model to 17 years of these data. The quality of these data has been questioned (Bennetts and Kitchens 1997), however, and Beissinger's model cannot predict the effects of drought or other impacts that affect only some of the wetlands in the kite's range.

The possibility of developing a useful IBM requires, of course, that sufficient information on individual behavior and physiology be available. Certainly such data are not available for all species, but they may be available for many high-profile species of conservation interest. Behavioral and physiological ecology are active fields of study that are continuing to produce vast amounts of data at the individual level. Few population ecologists have used these data, however, because the traditional models, variations on the Lotka-Volterra equations or matrix and partial differential equations, are not designed to accommodate such data. IBMs, by contrast, can use almost all relevant physiological and behavioral data produced by field and laboratory studies.

Modeling the whole life cycle of organisms may run into the problem, of course, that key data are missing. But often what is required for management is not a complete life-cycle model but a model of selected parts of the life cycle such as reproduction or survival through a season. For many bird species, a great deal is known about nesting behavior and the associated foraging. Thus an IBM might be feasible for the breeding season of a bird population but perhaps not for the times when the birds are less conspicuous to observers and when the behavior of individuals is less well known. Although a model of the breeding season alone would not be sufficient to model the long-term population dynamics of the bird population, it still may be extremely useful. In the Everglades, one of the key questions concerning wading birds is why breeding success in the southern Everglades has declined in recent years—prompting Wolff's (1994) individual-based model of a wood stork breeding colony. Models such as Wolff's for wading birds or those for the Cape Sable seaside sparrow and age-0 fish described earlier—aimed at limited components of a life cycle or limited spatial or temporal scales—are frequently referred to as tactical models. Tactical models are distinguished from strategic models in that they deal with limited aspects of a problem. A strategic model might be used to describe the population dynamics of the whole population over many years; tactical models, by contrast, look at a small part of the population dynamics. By focusing on limited but essential aspects of a problem, IBMs often require only a few key traits of the organisms in a population (in addition to GIS information on the environment when the model is spatially explicit). The

Cape Sable seaside sparrow model, for example, is composed of a few simple rules at the individual level requiring fewer than 30 parameters. At the heart of the model are simple natural-history observations of the sparrows: the territory size that a nesting pair needs (which determines the spacing of nests) and their nesting behavior in response to time of year and water level. These data are relatively easy to collect. Even so, there are uncertainties in some of the data used. Search patterns for nesting sites, used in the model, are not well known. Assumptions based on the best available knowledge of experts have to be used, and the model must be subjected to careful uncertainty analysis for such parameters.

Our descriptions of specific IBMs did not consider difficulties of model validation and interpretation of the results. Such issues must be addressed, however, for models that are used in providing information for management decisions. As Bart (1995:412) has noted: "Models should not be used to make or defend management decisions until they have been thoroughly evaluated and the results of the evaluation have been subjected to peer review." Bart has classified the aspects of evaluation into four major categories: objectives of the model, description of the model, analyses of the model's reliability, and synthesis.

The need for clearly defining the objectives is particularly important for IBMs. The ultimate object of most IBMs is predicting population change, but this objective is pursued by modeling individuals. Many expect the results of a simulation, or realization, of the model to yield accurate predictions concerning individuals. This is a false expectation. Although simulated individuals should behave realistically, they are probabilistic entities and only their aggregated properties are reliably predictable.

A model should be described in terms that allow anyone to understand its basic features. In describing the three conceptual models discussed earlier, we did so in the briefest of outline forms, but the full descriptions of these models come with complete documentation. Bart (1995), citing Schamberger and O'Neil (1986), recognizes four facets that must be considered in analyzing a model's reliability: structure, parameter values, secondary predictions, and primary predictions. Structure refers to the model's components and how they are joined. In the Cape Sable seaside sparrow model, detailed simulation of potential nest flooding was included, but not modeling of predation. This neglect of predation could be a weakness of the model if water regulation affects predation rates. The sources for the parameter values for each process in the model must be identified along with the uncertainty in the estimate, and sensitivity analyses should be performed on all parameters. This may be difficult for large IBMs, but it is essential.

Secondary predictions are not the primary focus of the model but are generated in the course of the simulations. IBMs are particularly rich in secondary predictions. In addition to the primary predictions of reproductive success for a particular season, for example, the Cape Sable seaside sparrow model makes predictions concerning both the spatial and temporal patterns of nests in the species' habitat. These data are routinely collected and have contributed to validating the sparrow model. Finally, Bart (1995) advises that the model's results should be synthesized to provide an overall picture of the model's reliability. At a minimum, comparisons of best-case and worst-case scenarios can be included. For the Cape Sable seaside sparrow and snail kite models, hydrological conditions for 30 years were available and predictions of reproduction under a range of hydrological conditions could be produced. Since IBMs simulate demographic stochasticity, the component of variation due to this source can also be reported.

Individual-based models vary in their complexity and ease of implementation. They range from simple models such as those of Scheffer et al. (1995) for an age-0 fish population—which require less than a half-dozen parameters and can be used to perform thousands of replicate simulations on a PC—to much more complex ones, such as Wolff's (1994) wading bird model, that include over a hundred behavioral rules and equations for individuals.

Object-oriented modeling languages, such as C++, lend themselves to individual-based modeling. But because they require careful bookkeeping, even the simplest models may be difficult to develop as computer programs from scratch. For this reason, there is a trend toward using modeling platforms developed explicitly for IBMs. For example, the snail kite IBM was built on a modeling program, OSIRIS (Mooij and Boersma 1996), that handles all of the input/output and internal bookkeeping. The part of the code dealing with the snail kite IBM required only about 50 additional lines. Other IBM platforms are Gecko—developed by Schmitz and Booth (1997), based on the SWARM software of the Santa Fe Institute—and HADES (Donalson and Nisbet 1999). General modeling packages such as MatLab also provide a convenient format for IBMs. The Cape Sable seaside sparrow model (Nott 1998) was developed on MatLab. The chief disadvantage of a general package such as MatLab is the slow speed with which IBMs execute. Prospective IBM modelers with limited modeling ability should perhaps look into some of these alternatives or others that have come along.

Despite the potential complexity of IBMs, there is no doubt that continuing software developments will make their use easier. For some time to come, computer capabilities will continue to outstrip empirical data for developing models. For the latter, though, there is reason to hope that technological advances in radio tracking and other means of field observations will eventually enable a great deal of relevant individual-based data to be collected.

ACKNOWLEDGMENTS

Support for this work was provided by the Environmental Protection Agency and the U.S. Army Corps of Engineers. M. P. Nott was supported through Cooperative Agreement 1445-CA09-95-0094 between the U.S. Geological Survey and the University of Tennessee; W. M. Mooij was supported through Cooperative Agreement 1445-CA09-0111 between the U.S. Geological Survey and the University of Miami; R. E. Bennetts was supported through Unit Cooperative Agreement 14-45-0009-1544 between the U.S. Geological Survey and the University of Florida; and D. L. De Angelis was supported by the Department of the Interior's Critical Ecosystems Studies Initiative and the Florida Caribbean Science Center.

REFERENCES

Adams, S. M., and D. L. DeAngelis. 1986. Indirect effects of early bass-shad interactions on predator population structure and food web dynamics. Pages 103–117 in W. C. Kerfoot and A. Sih, eds., *Predation in Aquatic Ecosystems.* Hanover, N.H.: University Press of New England.

Bart, J. 1995. Acceptance criteria for using individual-based models to make management decisions. *Ecological Applications* 5:411–420.

Bass, O. L., Jr., and J. A. Kushlan. 1982. *Status of the Cape Sable Sparrow.* Report T-672. Homestead, Fla.: South Florida Research Center, Everglades National Park.

Beecher, W. J. 1955. Late-Pleistocene isolation in salt-marsh sparrows. *Ecology* 36:23–28.

Beissinger, S. R. 1995. Modeling extinction in periodic environments: Everglades water levels and snail kite population viability. *Ecological Applications* 5:618–631.

Bennetts, R. E., and W. M. Kitchens. 1997. *The Demography and Movements of Snail Kites in Florida.* Technical Report 56. Washington, D.C.: U.S. Geological Survey, Biological Resources Division.

Bennetts, R. E., M. W. Collopy, and J. A. Rodgers Jr. 1994. The snail kite in the Florida Everglades: A food specialist in a changing environment. Pages 507–532 in S. M. Davis and J. C. Ogden, eds., *Everglades: The Ecosystem and Its Restoration.* Delray Beach, Fla.: St. Lucie Press.

Cain, M. L. 1985. Random search by herbivorous insects: A simulation model. *Ecology* 66:876–888.

Caswell, H. 1989. *Matrix Population Models: Construction, Analysis, and Interpretation.* Sunderland, Mass.: Sinauer.

Claessen, D., A. M. de Roos, and L. Persson. 2000. Dwarfs and giants: Cannibalism and competition in size-structured populations. *American Naturalist* 155:219–237.

Curnutt, J. L., A. L. Mayer, T. M. Brooks, L. Manne, O. L. Bass Sr., D. M. Fleming, M. P. Nott, and S. L. Pimm. 1998. Population dynamics of the endangered Cape Sable seaside sparrow. *Animal Conservation* 1:11–22.

David, J. M., L. Andral, and M. Artois. 1982. Computer simulation of the epienzootic disease of vulpine rabies. *Ecological Modelling* 15:107–125.

DeAngelis, D. L., and L. J. Gross, eds. 1994. *Individual-Based Models and Approaches in Ecology.* New York: Chapman & Hall.

DeAngelis, D. L., D. C. Cox, and C. C. Coutant. 1979. Cannibalism and size dispersal in young-of-the-year largemouth bass: Experiments and model. *Ecological Modelling* 8:133–148.

DeAngelis, D. L., L. Godbout, and B. J. Shuter. 1991. An individual-based approach to predicting density-dependent dynamics in smallmouth bass populations. *Ecological Modelling* 57:91–115.

DeAngelis, D. L., K. A. Rose, L. B. Crowder, E. A. Marschall, and D. Lika. 1993a. Fish cohort dynamics: Application of complementary modeling approaches. *American Naturalist* 142:604–622.

DeAngelis, D. L., B. J. Shuter, M. S. Ridgway, and M. Scheffer. 1993b. Modeling growth and survival in an age-0 fish cohort. *Transactions of the American Fisheries Society* 122:927–941.

DeAngelis, D. L., K. A. Rose, and M. A. Huston. 1994. Individual-oriented approaches to modeling ecological populations and communities. Pages 390–410 in S. A. Levin, ed., *Frontiers of Mathematical Biology.* Berlin: Springer-Verlag.

Diggle, P. J. 1976. A spatial stochastic model of interplant competition. *Journal of Applied Probability* 13:662–671.

Donalson, D. D., and R. M. Nisbet. 1999. Population dynamics and spation scale: Effects of system size on population persistence. *Ecology* 80:2492–2507.

Dreitz, V. J., J. D. Nichols, J. E. Hines, R. E. Bennetts, W. M. Kitchens, and D. L. DeAngelis. The use of resighting data to estimate the rate of population growth of the snail kite in Florida. *Journal of Applied Statistics* (in press).

Fleming, D. M., W. F. Wolff, and D. L. DeAngelis. 1994. Importance of landscape heterogeneity to wood storks in the Florida Everglades. *Environmental Management* 18:743–757.

Ford, E. D., and P. J. Diggle. 1981. Competition for light in a plant monoculture modelled as a spatial stochastic process. *Annals of Botany* 48:481–500.

Gates, D. J. 1978. Bimodality in even-aged plant monocultures. *Journal of Theoretical Biology* 71:525–540.

Hanski, I. 1999. *Metapopulation Ecology.* Oxford: Oxford University Press.

Huston, M. A., and D. L. DeAngelis. 1987. Size bimodality in monospecific populations: A critical review of potential mechanisms. *American Naturalist* 129:678–707.

Huston, M. A., D. L. DeAngelis, and W. M. Post. 1988. New computer models unify ecological theory. *BioScience* 38:682–691.

Hyman, J. B., J. B. McAninch, and D. L. DeAngelis. 1991. An individual-based simulation model of herbivory in a heterogeneous landscape. Pages 443–475 in M. G. Turner and R. H. Gardner, eds., *Quantitative Methods in Landscape Ecology.* Ecological Studies 82. New York: Springer-Verlag.

Lockwood, J. L., K. H. Fenn, J. L. Curnutt, D. Rosenthal, K. L. Balent, and A. L. Mayer. 1997. Life history of the endangered Cape Sable seaside sparrow. *Wilson Bulletin* 109(4):720–731.

McMurtrie, R. 1981. Suppression and dominance of trees with overlapping crowns. *Journal of Theoretical Biology* 89:151–174.

Metz, J. A. J., and O. Diekmann, eds. 1986. *The Dynamics of Physiologically Structured Populations*. Lecture Notes in Biomathematics 68. Berlin: Springer-Verlag.

Mooij, W. M. 1996. Variation in abundance and survival of fish larvae in shallow eutrophic Lake Tjeukemeer. *Environmental Biology of Fishes* 46:265–279.

Mooij, W. M., and M. Boersma. 1996. An object-oriented simulation framework for individual-based simulations (OSIRIS): *Daphnia* population dynamics as an example. *Ecological Modelling* 93:139–153.

Mooij, W. M., and D. L. DeAngelis. 1999. Individual-based modelling as an integrative approach in theoretical and applied population dynamics and food web studies. Pages 551–575 in H. Olff, V. K. Brown, and R. H. Drent, eds., *Herbivores: Between Plants and Predators*. Oxford: Blackwell.

Mooij, W. M., R. E. Bennetts, D. L. DeAngelis, and W. Kitchens. N.d. An exploratory spatially explicit individual-based model of the Florida snail kite (*Rostrhamus sociabilis*): Interplay between habitat quality dynamics and snail kite behavioral population dynamics responses. Unpublished manuscript.

Nichols, J. D., G. L. Hensler, and P. W. Sykes Jr. 1980. Demography of the Everglades kite: Implications for population management. *Ecological Modelling* 9:215–232.

Nott, M. P. 1998. Effects of abiotic factors on population dynamics of the Cape Sable seaside sparrow and continental patterns of herpetological species richness: An appropriately scaled landscape approach. Ph.D. dissertation, University of Tennessee, Knoxville.

Pimm, S. L., K. Balent, T. Brooks, J. L Cornutt, J. L. Lockwood, L. Manne, A. Mayer, M. P. Nott, and G. Russell. 1995. *Cape Sable Sparrow Annual Report*. Homestead, Fla.: National Biological Service/National Park Service, Everglades National Park.

Rodgers, J. A., S. T. Schwikert, and A. S. Wenner. 1988. Status of the snail kite in Florida: 1981–1985. *American Birds* 42:30–35.

Rose, K. A., and J. H. Cowan. 1993. Individual-based model of young-of-the-year striped bass dynamics. I: Model description and baseline simulations. *Transactions of the American Fisheries Society* 122:415–438.

Schamberger, M. L., and L. J. O'Neil. 1986. Concepts and constraints in habitat-model testing. Pages 5–10 in J. Verner, M. L. Morrison, and C. J. Ralph, eds., *Wildlife 2000*. Madison: University of Wisconsin Press.

Scheffer, M., J. M. Baveco, D. L. DeAngelis, E. H. R. R. Lammens, and B. J. Shuter. 1995. Stunted growth and stepwise die-off in animal cohorts. *American Naturalist* 145:376–388.

Schmitz, O. J., and G. Booth. 1997. Modeling food web complexity: The consequence of individual-based spatially explicit behavioral ecology on trophic interactions. *Evolutionary Ecology* 11:379–398.

Smies, M. 1983. Simulation of small bird populations. I: Development of a stochastic model. *Ecological Modelling* 20:259–277.

Sykes, P. W., Jr. 1979. Status of the Everglades kite in Florida: 1968–1978. *Wilson Bulletin* 91:495–511.

Takekawa, J. E., and S. R. Beissinger. 1989. Cyclic drought, dispersal, and conservation of the snail kite in Florida: Lessons in critical habitat. *Conservation Biology* 3:302–311.

Turner, M. G., Y. Wu, W. H. Romme, and L. L. Wallace. 1993. A landscape simulation model of winter foraging by large ungulates. *Ecological Modelling* 69:163–184.

Turner, M. G., Y. Wu, W. H. Romme, L. L. Wallace, and A. Brenkert. 1994. Simulating winter interactions among ungulates, vegetation, and fire in northern Yellowstone Park. *Ecological Applications* 4:472–496.

Uchmanski, J. 2000. Individual variability and the regulation of populations: An individual-based approach. *Oikos* 90:539–548.

U.S. Army Corps of Engineers. 1999. *Central and Southern Florida Project Comprehensive Review Study: Final Integrated Feasibility Report and Programmatic Environmental Impact Statement.* Jacksonville: U.S. Army Corps of Engineers, Jacksonville District, and South Florida Water Management District.

Werner, H. W. 1975. *The Biology of the Cape Sable Sparrow.* Homestead, Fla.: Report to U.S. Fish and Wildlife Service, Frank M. Chapman Memorial Fund, International Council for Bird Preservation, and U.S. National Park Service.

Williams, G. C. 1975. *Sex and Evolution.* Monographs in Population Ecology. Princeton: Princeton University Press.

Wolff, W. F. 1994. An individual-oriented model of a wading bird nesting colony. *Ecological Modelling* 72:75–114.

Chapter 12

When Modelers and Field Biologists Interact: Progress in Resource Science

William R. Clark and Richard A. Schmitz

Skepticism about the application of modeling to wildlife management is still prevalent among both modelers and field biologists. This situation surprises us. Most wildlife biologists and researchers would agree that they use conceptual models every day in the process of making decisions. But it is natural for questions to arise when wildlife scientists extend the conceptual framework into the realm of statistical and simulation modeling. Other chapters in this book outline accepted practices of valid modeling and offer examples of the application of modeling to a variety of problems in wildlife research and management. We want to emphasize that field biologists and modelers can collaborate effectively if they share a common interest in the underlying ecological concepts, communicate about the field data, and recognize the limits of their knowledge.

The title of this chapter might lead readers to conclude that biologists and modelers cannot solve problems without each other—or at least that progress will be more rapid when they cooperate. Although the mutual benefits of cooperation seem obvious, they are not always recognized. We have all seen cases where modelers build models without reasonable data support or without regard to application in the field. And despite many examples of successful applications of models, wildlife biologists still make many decisions without a conceptual framework and quantification. In our experience, cooperation is enhanced by recognizing the importance of *goals* in directing research and management and emphasizing the key points of interaction during the problem-solving sequence. After discussing the role of modeling in wildlife ecology and management, we present an example of how we connected field biology and modeling to investigate landscape fragmentation effects in the Midwest.

THE ROLE OF MODELING

Wildlife ecology and management are historically rooted in natural science and observation. As we read Paul Errington's famous treatise on muskrat populations (Errington 1963), for example, we were impressed with the excruciating detail of the observations. Ultimately he developed a conceptual model of the compensatory nature of the interactions among causes of mortality in natural populations that forms the basis for the management of many species (Clark 1990). Although Errington's observations are a good example of how a biologist starts with the observational process, he failed to uncover some of the inconsistencies in his understanding of the population processes (Taylor 1984) because he did not quantify the conceptual framework. Recent concepts about the compensatory and additive mechanisms in populations and how they influence management (Nichols et al. 1984; Williams 1997) are substantially more quantitative than Errington's original ideas. Quantification of the conceptual model not only offers a means for checking the details but also provides a framework for generality.

Although observational data collection has become more sophisticated with the advent of advanced technology such as radiotelemetry, automatic data loggers, and remote sensing devices, science and management still start with observation (Williams 1997). With new observing tools including satellite imagery and geographic information systems (GIS), we now are able to visualize management problems over large regions (Koeln et al. 1988). The increase in scale from the individual animal in a population to the level of the landscape or even continents has begun to influence how we approach problems and solutions (Walters and Green 1997). The convergence of new "observational technology," advances in computing (White and Clark 1994), and a theoretical framework for landscape ecology (Hansson et al. 1995) have led to recognition of the importance of spatial variation in populations and landscape-level habitat relationships. Only by combining large-scale field data collection and a quantitative modeling framework can wildlife biologists hope to understand management at regional and continental scales.

Most wildlife biologists are trained to think in terms of classic replicated experiments. Science is viewed as a sequential process with a repeated sequence of the "hypothesis and test" paradigm. The process has been viewed as analogous to a spiral staircase that comes back around to the same point but moves the depth and breadth of knowledge "up a flight" (Burge 1967). An appealing feature of this paradigm is that it prescribes that systems under investigation must be simplified to small functional units and then studied by holding constant the variable influences not germane to the research objective (Kuhn 1970). In the context of complex natural systems, this approach promotes the isolated, sequential study of ecosystem components and leads to the conclusion that there is closure and advancement as the neatly packaged experiments are completed (Platt 1964). Research and management so structured could be viewed as reductionist because it does not pretend to comprehend natural resource systems in their totality but rather confronts problems as they emerge—frequently according to their socioeconomic importance (Busch and Lacy 1983). Furthermore, this approach does not always recognize that there may be several reasonable outcomes to a natural resource management problem. Such thoughts are leading wildlife scientists to rethink how classic paradigms and research designs can be viewed in the context of the information needs of wildlife ecology and management and to recognize that the management of complex natural systems is not going to be subject to complete testing. At the very least, it is clear that controlled experimentation with replication is difficult when we are trying to explore questions that involve responses of large populations at landscape scales (Hargrove and Pickering 1992).

Eberhardt and Thomas (1991) have nicely summarized the issues and paradigms involved in designing and executing environmental field studies. Even with careful planning, most field studies should be considered observational if events are not controlled. Eberhardt and Thomas describe a variety of powerful design approaches that may be less familiar to most biologists—including intervention analysis, analytic and descriptive sampling, and sampling for modeling. In many field studies the emphasis is on estimation, a perspective that has received some attention in this book (see Chapters 3 and 5), or decision making rather than classic hypothesis testing (Walters and Green 1997).

Here we focus our attention on simulation models as opposed to statistical models (see Chapter 3 in this volume). The distinction between these broad classes of models has long been debated (Eberhardt 1977), and we could frame the discussion in terms of either perspective. Instead we want to emphasize the reassurances involved in valid modeling by illustrating points of contact between the field biologist and the simulation modeler during the process. Starfield and Bleloch (1991) and Starfield (1997) have taken a similar approach in discussing modeling of natural resource systems.

First it is useful to distinguish the goal of forecasting from that of projection (Caswell 1989). Forecasting attempts to predict an exact state of nature at some time in the future. Such a goal is philosophically related to the sequential testing paradigm that converges on a specific conclusion. Projection, by contrast, tries to describe what would happen given a set of hypotheses and assumptions. Projection modeling leads to "what if" experiments, and we view it as philosophically aligned with the "multiple outcomes" viewpoint expressed earlier. Although the distinction between forecasting and projection has been recognized since the earliest applications of models (Pearl and Reed 1920), there is still considerable misunderstanding about the utility of projection. To some extent this is because field biologists and managers must deal with specific states of nature when making decisions, whereas modelers often find it useful to consider a variety of scenarios. Our example of modeling the effects of various agricultural policies in Iowa on pheasant populations falls into the category of projecting multiple outcomes. The results of our projections are best evaluated relative to specific goals such as target population levels or expected economic costs.

An Example: Modeling Pheasant Populations

Field biologists and managers were asking why fragments of apparently effectively managed perennial habitat in a matrix of agricultural land were not adequate to support large pheasant populations. This was the question that motivated the pheasant modeling. With the establishment of the Conservation Reserve Program (CRP) in the late 1980s, biologists hoped that the large blocks of perennial grassland cover would substantially increase pheasant populations. At the same time, agricultural policymakers immediately recognized that economic tradeoffs would influence the balance between agricultural production and environmental benefits such as wildlife (Hurley et al. 1996). We recognized that the most useful approach to the question would start by having field biologists, modelers, and policymakers define objectives (Clark 1995). This initial communication about objectives was a key part of reassurance for all groups.

To be effective, the modeler needs not only clearly stated objectives but also a well-defined theoretical structure for the model. In this case, it was clear that we needed a population model that could link the behavior of individuals in small habitat fragments to population phenomena aggregated to much larger scales. The concepts expressed by Caswell and John (1992) offer a theoretical and practical framework for linking the state of individuals in the population to the state of the entire population. We aggregated the components of location and movement, survival probability, and reproductive status of each individual in the population to model the state of the population. By using this kind of conceptual framework for a spatially explicit, individually based model (see Chapter 11 in this volume) at the earliest stages of research, we were able to outline "what if" projections in biological and practical management terms and organize our data collection approaches.

At this point, biologists and modelers both recognized the complexity of such a large-scale problem. Biologists focused on the difficulties of collecting the necessary data. Modelers thought about the underlying modeling structure and checking the validity of a model while using it to evaluate alternatives. An obvious point to start was for field biologists, statisticians, and modelers to collaborate on designing data collection to link individual characteristics to population-level responses. We recognized that current approaches—including hazard analyses (Conroy et al. 1996; Riley et al. 1998) and logistic regression (Rotella and Ratti 1992; Jeske et al. 1994)—are powerful statistical tools to infer population parameters from data on individuals (Caswell and John 1992). We designed sampling protocols for estimating survival and reproduction from radiotelemetry data on individual pheasants (Schmitz and Clark 1999). The field biologists envisioned the behavior of the pheasants—thereby contributing to effective collection of telemetry data while learning the value of sampling design for precise estimation of parameters. The statisticians imagined various techniques for analyzing the spatial and survival data while appreciating the difficulties in collecting uncontrolled observational data.

The collaboration on sampling design and the shared goal of deriving statistical models that effectively quantified the observations led to many components of our simulation model. For example, we derived a hazard function that relates survival of hen pheasants in spring to measures of the amount of edge in fragmented agricultural landscapes in Iowa (Schmitz and Clark 1999). Our radiotelemetry observations of habitat selection by hens during the prenesting period could be split into two distinct groups that were ultimately distinguished in terms of survival as well. One group selected large blocks of perennial grasslands, so that their home ranges comprised a high average percentage of grassland and low amounts of edge between cropland and perennial habitat. Another group selected areas surrounding isolated patches or along linear habitats where grassland composition was low and the amount of edge was more variable among individuals (Figure 12.1; Schmitz and Clark 1999). The model quantified the observations in a way that made sense to the biologists.

For another part of our simulation model we developed a logistic regres-

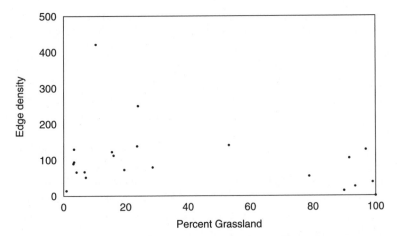

Figure 12.1. Edge density (m/ha), a measure of landscape fragmentation, and percentage of grassland, a measure of landscape composition, within the home range of 22 hen pheasants tracked during the prenesting period in Kossuth County, Iowa (1992–1993).

sion function (Kleinbaum 1994) for nest site selection probability as a function of landscape variables. As the biologists expected, the predicted probability of selection of nest sites was greatest in the centers of large patches of grassland and somewhat lower around the edges of patches and in linear habitats along roads and fence lines (Clark et al. 1999). Then we developed a logistic regression function that yields the predicted probability of nest success at a given location based on land use and the context of the surrounding landscape (Clark et al. 1999). In Figure 12.2, for example, nests in darker gray shades have the greatest predicted probability of success, whereas those in areas with lighter shades are predicted to have a lower probability. Such figures have value to both the field biologist and the modeler and often stimulate further discussion about the system. Above all, we want to emphasize that the simulation model is built slowly from successive analyses of such data-driven functions, so that the complex computer code we call the model becomes mostly a matter of bookkeeping. We do not mean to trivialize the problem of aggregation in complex, discontinuous systems, however, which is a serious problem itself (O'Neill and Rust 1979; Caswell and John 1992).

Validation and Confirmation

Biologists and modelers alike are concerned with a model's validity, and validation is another point of interaction between the two groups. There is an entire literature on verification and validation (Caswell 1976; Chapter 7 in

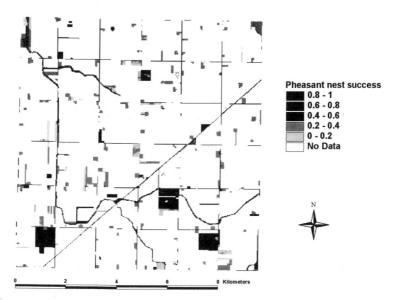

Figure 12.2. Predicted probability of nest success calculated from a logistic regression equation that is a function of percent grassland and mean core area index within the home range of hen pheasants and the cover type of the patch in which the nest is located. Data were collected in agricultural landscapes in Kossuth County, Iowa (1992–1993).

this volume), and the terms are not always used consistently. Essentially, verification is used to imply correspondence to absolute truth, which is obviously not accessible (Oreskes et al. 1994). Validation, by contrast, implies legitimacy of assumptions about system structure, defensible parameter estimation, and utility of results (Oreskes et al. 1994; Starfield 1997). It is useful to think about the philosophical difference between projection (examining the logical consequences of the model) and accurate forecasting. The most common form of validation is *confirmation*—that is, comparison of the model's output with independent observations not used to estimate the model's parameters (Oreskes et al. 1994). We assessed our logistic regression function of nest success, for example, by using concordance/discordance analysis that is similar to a rank correlation goodness-of-fit statistic. Functions with higher values have better predictive ability than functions with lower values. After validating or confirming individual functions that made up our simulation model, we also confirmed the aggregated model by comparing output with observations—for example, we compared simulated movements and home range estimates with observed radiotelemetry data. Ultimately, biologists and modelers alike should agree that the model is based on underlying biological principles, statistical rigor, and usefulness for the objectives specified (Mankin et al. 1977; Starfield 1997).

The pheasant landscape modeling effort led us to important ecological insights, including quantification of the influence of variability in survival and reproduction as a result of local conditions and the spatial arrangement of landscape elements. Quantifying the ecological influences on the variability is essential because the variability is simultaneously a fundamental property of the natural systems we manage and also a limitation to our ability to understand the natural system. Our field data and modeling show that pheasant populations are periodically reduced by poor survival during snowy winters (Perkins et al. 1997) or cool, wet springs (Riley et al. 1998; Clark et al. 1999). In fragmented agricultural landscapes, population levels do not increase quickly because of poor reproduction and survival; in landscapes with aggregated blocks of undisturbed habitat, however, populations respond quickly after such declines.

Further Collaboration

Although this ecological insight is valuable, agricultural and environmental policy often is driven, not by the science of wildlife ecologists and managers, but rather by politics and economics. (See Busch and Lacy 1983; Costanza 1996; CARD 1997.) Recognizing this fact led us to further collaboration with natural resource economists. When we, as biologists and ecological modelers, began to interact with economists, we had to go through the same steps of assurance we outlined earlier. Our research group had to decide which policy alternatives should be compared and whether our pheasant/landscape model would be useful in evaluating them. We are still trying to account for the influences of scale: although we model pheasants in areas the size of townships, agricultural policies may be set at the state and national levels. We also had to consider a value system for the marginal gains in wildlife benefits or marginal losses in economic return when we know that agricultural policymakers, landowners deciding to participate in farm programs, and wildlife biologists do not necessarily view them from the same perspective.

As we have proceeded, we have succumbed to the natural tendency to counteract these difficulties with the same reductionist approaches we criticized earlier. But by focusing on a specific question—"What are the pheasant demographic consequences and economic tradeoffs when we compare (1) losing all CRP grassland authorized under the 1985 farm legislation, (2) maintaining all CRP grassland as originally authorized, or (3) converting large blocks of CRP grassland to buffers along streams and waterways?"—we could reasonably resolve some of the issues of complexity, scale, and value. You can visualize our approach and potential results by examining Figure 12.2. If all CRP grassland were maintained, the landscape would have most of the grassland cover in blocks like the three quarter-sections in

Figure 12.2. But if you confine cover on the entire landscape to strips of cover like the grassed waterways and streams on the map, you can visualize the buffer initiative. Simulations of pheasants under these two landscape scenarios produce average population levels that are an order of magnitude less under the buffer initiative.

A similar approach was taken by Hurley et al. (1996), who showed that the amount and distribution of CRP grassland in North and South Dakota would depend on whether they used the policy of targeting CRP by erodibility index or by modeled potential density of waterfowl breeding pairs. Although we are confident that our pheasant model is useful for comparing different scenarios biologically, we have not yet reached the point of modeling the time-dynamic tradeoffs in the policy system. Ultimately, the most dynamic modeling and experimentation will be done by directly involving stakeholders (farmers, land managers, sportsmen) in the process of understanding sustainable ecosystem management (Costanza 1996; Walters and Green 1997).

RECOMMENDATIONS

Many of the issues that stimulated this book have been topics of debate ever since models were first applied in biology and ecology. Effective problem solving begins with clearly stated objectives; modeling helped us put boundaries on objectives and possible solutions to problems; modeling can be used to determine when we have achieved objectives; modeling is useful in directing data collection in a cost-effective manner; modeling should focus on estimation and testing of parameters, model revision, and variable selection in relation to field data collection; inferential statements apply to characteristics of the models—such conclusions, and the implications for the real world, have been stated before many times (Hilborn and Mangel 1997; Starfield 1997).

Ideas about the ways in which wildlife biologists, ecological modelers, and policymakers can interact to make inferences about the effect of management are currently receiving a good deal of attention in the literature, including this book (see Chapter 6 of this volume). Adaptive management (Walters and Holling 1990) has been described as the science of integration of parts, designed to identify gaps in knowledge, in order to evaluate consequences of actions against manipulative or unplanned interventions. Wildlife biologists, ecological modelers, and policymakers must assess the relative risks of inaction versus management based on imperfect information, including field data and models. The analysis of uncertainty and the evaluation of alternative experimental management have become topics themselves (Walters and Green 1997).

One reason that we do not see field biologists and modelers as separate groups is because each of us is trained in both. We think that modern curricula in wildlife ecology and management should include both aspects so that students and practitioners will learn to use the insights and tools of both perspectives. When collaboration starts between people with very different backgrounds, we have found it useful to read some simple papers that illustrate the typical approaches taken by each group. Collaboration should start at the beginning of a project, when objectives are developed and data collection is designed. Biologists and managers have a key role in conveying the mechanistic understanding of the natural resource systems based on components that can be clearly identified, quantified, and manipulated. Biologists and stakeholders who will be affected by management decisions must be involved in setting the objectives of large-scale experimentation and modeling. Modelers should be involved in defining the quantitative, conceptual framework that links natural processes with management systems and in estimating the relative importance of components in the behavior of complex, large-scale processes. Modelers must be careful not to "take the data and produce a model" without interacting with biologists. Biologists must recognize that quantitative solutions, as opposed to general statements about ecological consequences, are most effective at influencing policy. Field biologists and ecological modelers alike must get used to working with socioeconomic modelers in order to evaluate policy alternatives. We hope biologists and modelers will adapt to new approaches and not insist on perfect models or all-encompassing data. We cannot expect complete closure to a wildlife management problem. Natural and human systems are dynamic, and we will have to reevaluate the solutions continually. If biologists and modelers learn to question each other's approaches while keeping an open mind, they will be practicing the sort of interaction that is essential to progress in management of wildlife resource systems.

ACKNOWLEDGMENTS

This research was funded in part by the Iowa Department of Natural Resources (Project W-115-R); Todd R. Bogenschutz was the project collaborator. This is Journal Paper J-18798 of the Iowa Agriculture and Home Economics Experiment Station, Ames, Iowa; Project 3299.

REFERENCES

Burge, M. 1967. *Scientific Research I: The Search for System.* New York: Springer-Verlag.
Busch, L., and W. B. Lacy. 1983. *Science, Agriculture, and the Politics of Research.* Boulder: Westview.

Caswell, H. 1976. The validation problem. Pages 313–325 in B. C. Patten, ed., *Systems Analysis and Simulation in Ecology.* New York: Academic Press.

———. 1989. *Matrix Population Models.* Sunderland, Mass.: Sinauer.

Caswell, H., and A. M. John. 1992. From the individual to the population in demographic models. Pages 36–61 in D. L. DeAngelis and L. J. Gross, eds., *Individual-Based Models and Approaches in Ecology.* New York: Chapman & Hall.

Center for Agriculture and Rural Development (CARD). 1997. *Resource Analysis Policy System 1997: Agricultural and Environmental Outlook.* Ames: Iowa State University.

Clark, W. R. 1990. Compensation in furbearer populations: Current data compared with a review of concepts. *Transactions of the North American Wildlife and Natural Resources Conference* 55:491–500.

———. 1995. Modeling wildlife populations in complex landscapes: A discussion of critical issues. Pages 428–431 in J. Bissonette and P. Krausman, eds., *Proceedings of the International Wildlife Management Congress.* Bethesda: Wildlife Society.

Clark, W. R., R. A. Schmitz, and T. R. Bogenschutz. 1999. Site selection and nest success of ring-necked pheasants as a function of location in Iowa landscapes. *Journal of Wildlife Management* 63:976–989.

Conroy, M. J., J. E. Anderson, S. L. Rathbun, and D. G. Krementz. 1996. Statistical inference on patch-specific survival and movement rates from marked animals. *Environmental and Ecological Statistics* 3:99–118.

Costanza, R. 1996. Ecological economics: Reintegrating the study of humans and nature. *Ecological Applications* 6:978–990.

Eberhardt, L. L. 1977. Applied systems ecology: Models, data, and statistical methods. *Simulation Councils Proceedings Series* 5:43–55.

Eberhardt, L. L., and J. M. Thomas. 1991. Designing environmental field studies. *Ecological Monographs* 61:53–73.

Errington, P. L. 1963. *Muskrat populations.* Ames: Iowa State University Press.

Hansson, L., L. Fahrig, and G. Merriam, eds. 1995. *Mosaic Landscapes and Ecological Processes.* London: Chapman & Hall.

Hargrove, W. W., and J. Pickering. 1992. Pseudoreplication: A sine qua non for regional ecology. *Landscape Ecology* 6:251–258.

Hilborn, R., and M. Mangel. 1997. *The Ecological Detective: Confronting Models with Data.* Princeton: Princeton University Press.

Hurley, T. M., B. A. Babcock, R. E. Reynolds, and C. R. Loesch. 1996. Waterfowl populations and the Conservation Reserve Program in the prairie pothole region of North and South Dakota. Center for Agriculture and Rural Development Working Paper 96-WP 165. Ames: Iowa State University.

Jeske, C. W., M. R. Szymczak, D. R. Anderson, J. K. Ringelman, and J. A. Armstrong. 1994. Relationship of body condition to survival of mallards in San Luis Valley, Colorado. *Journal of Wildlife Management* 58:787–793.

Kleinbaum, D. G. 1994. *Logistic Regression: A Self-Learning Text.* New York: Springer-Verlag.

Koeln, G. T., J. E. Jacobson, D. E. Wesley, and R. S. Remple. 1988. Wetland inventories derived from Landsat data for waterfowl management planning. *Transactions of the North American Wildlife and Natural Resources Conference* 53:303–310.

Kuhn, T. S. 1970. *The Structure of Scientific Revolution.* Chicago: University of Chicago Press.

Mankin, J. B., R. V. O'Neill, H. H. Shugart, and B. W. Rust. 1977. The importance of validation in ecosystems analysis. *Simulation Councils Proceedings Series* 5:63–71.

Nichols, J. D., M. J. Conroy, D. R. Anderson, and K. P. Burnham. 1984. Compensatory mortality in waterfowl populations: A review of evidence and implications for research and management. *Transactions of the North American Wildlife and Natural Resources Conference* 49:535–554.

O'Neill. R. V., and B. Rust. 1979. Aggregation error in ecological models. *Ecological Modelling* 7:91–105.

Oreskes, N., K. Shrader-Frechette, and K. Belitz. 1994. Verification, validation, and confirmation of numerical models in the earth sciences. *Science* 263:641–646.

Pearl, R., and L. J. Reed. 1920. On the rate of growth of the population of the United States since 1790 and its mathematical representation. *Proceedings of the National Academy of Sciences* 6:275–288.

Perkins, A. L., W. R. Clark, P. A. Vohs, and T. Z. Riley. 1997. Effects of landscape and weather on winter survival of ring-necked pheasant hens. *Journal of Wildlife Management* 61:634–644.

Platt, J. R. 1964. Strong inference. *Science* 146:347–353.

Riley, T. Z., W. R. Clark, P. A. Vohs, and D. E. Ewing. 1998. Survival of pheasant chicks to age 4 weeks. *Journal of Wildlife Management* 62:36–44.

Rotella, J. J., and J. T. Ratti. 1992. Mallard brood survival and wetland habitat conditions in southwestern Manitoba. *Journal of Wildlife Management* 56:499–507.

Schmitz, R. A., and W. R. Clark. 1999. Survival of ring-necked pheasant hens during spring in relation to landscape features. *Journal of Wildlife Management* 63:147–154.

Starfield, A. M. 1997. A pragmatic approach to modeling for wildlife management. *Journal of Wildlife Management* 61:261–270.

Starfield, A. M., and A. L. Bleloch. 1991. *Building Models for Conservation and Wildlife Management.* Edina, Minn.: Burgess.

Taylor, R. J. 1984. *Predation.* New York: Chapman & Hall.

Walters, C. J., and R. Green. 1997. Valuation of experimental management options for ecological systems. *Journal of Wildlife Management* 61: 987–1006.

Walters, C. J., and C. S. Holling. 1990. Large-scale management experiments and learning by doing. *Ecology* 71:2060–2068.

White, G. C., and W. R. Clark. 1994. Microcomputer applications in wildlife management and research. Pages 75–95 in T. A. Bookhout, ed., *Research and Management Techniques for Wildlife and Habitats.* Bethesda: Wildlife Society.

Williams, B. K. 1997. Logic and science in wildlife biology. *Journal of Wildlife Management* 61:1007–1015.

Contributors

DAVID R. ANDERSON
Colorado Cooperative Fish & Wildlife Research Unit
Department of Fishery and Wildlife Biology
Colorado State University
Fort Collins, CO 80523
USA

ROBERT E. BENNETTS
Station Biologique de la Tour du Valat
Le Sambuc
Arles 13200
France

MARK S. BOYCE
University of Alberta
Department of Biological Sciences
Edmonton, AB T6G 2E9
Canada

KENNETH P. BURNHAM
Colorado Cooperative Fish & Wildlife Research Unit
Department of Fishery and Wildlife Biology
Colorado State University
Fort Collins, CO 80523
USA

WILLIAM R. CLARK
Department of Animal Ecology
Iowa State University
Ames, IA 50011
USA

MICHAEL J. CONROY
Georgia Cooperative Fish & Wildlife Research Unit
Warnell School of Forestry
University of Georgia
Athens, GA 30602
USA

DONALD L. DEANGELIS
U.S. Geological Survey—Biological Resources Division
Department of Biology
University of Miami
Coral Gables, FL 33124
USA

ØYVIND FIKSEN
Institutt for Fiskeri og Marinbiologi
Universitetet I Bergen
Høyteknologisenteret N-5020
Bergen
Norway

ALAN B. FRANKLIN
Colorado Cooperative Fish & Wildlife Research Unit
Department of Fishery and Wildlife Biology
Colorado State University
Fort Collins, CO 80523
USA

JARL GISKE
Institutt for Fiskeri og Marinbiologi
Universitetet I Bergen
Høyteknologisenteret N-5020
Bergen
Norway

DOUGLAS H. JOHNSON
Northern Prairie Wildlife Research Center
U.S. Geological Survey—Biological Resources Division
Jamestown, ND 58401
USA

WILLIAM L. KENDALL
Patuxent Wildlife Research Center
U.S. Geological Survey—Biological Resources Division
11510 American Holly Drive
Laurel, MD 20708-4017
USA

MARC MANGEL
Department of Environmental Studies
Institute of Marine Studies
University of California
Santa Cruz, CA 95064
USA

BRYAN F. J. MANLY
Department of Mathematics and Statistics
University of Otago
Dunedin
New Zealand

LYMAN L. MCDONALD
Western Ecosystems Technology, Inc.
2003 Central Avenue
Cheyenne, WY 82001
USA

WOLF M. MOOIJ
Centre for Limnology
Netherlands Institute of Ecology
3631 AC Nieuwersluis
Netherlands

CLINTON T. MOORE
Georgia Cooperative Fish & Wildlife Research Unit
Warnell School of Forestry
University of Georgia
Athens, GA 30602
USA

JAMES D. NICHOLS
Patuxent Wildlife Research Center
U.S. Geological Survey—Biological Resources Division
11510 American Holly Drive
Laurel, MD 20708-4017
USA

M. PHILIP NOTT
Department of Ecology and Evolutionary Biology
University of Tennessee
Knoxville, TN 37996
USA

RICHARD A. SCHMITZ
Department of Animal Ecology
Iowa State University
Ames, IA 50011
USA

TANYA M. SHENK
Colorado Division of Wildlife
317 W. Prospect Road
Fort Collins, CO 80526
USA

GARY C. WHITE
Department of Fishery and Wildlife Biology
Colorado State University
Fort Collins, CO 80523
USA

Reviewers

DAVID R. ANDERSON
Colorado Cooperative Fish & Wildlife Research Unit
Colorado State University
Fort Collins, Colorado

MARK BAKEMAN
Ensight Technical Services
Longmont, Colorado

RICHARD BARKER
Department of Mathematics and Statistics
University of Otago
Dunedin, New Zealand

ROBERT E. BENNETTS
Station Biologique de la Tour du Valat
Arles, France

KEVIN BESTGEN
Larval Fish Laboratory
Colorado State University
Fort Collins, Colorado

WILLIAM BLOCK
Rocky Mountain Research Station
Flagstaff, Arizona

MARY M. CONNOR
Department of Fishery and Wildlife Biology
Colorado State University
Fort Collins, Colorado

CHARLES GOWAN
Department of Biology and Environmental Studies
Randolph-Macon College
Ashland, Virginia

R. J. GUTIÉRREZ
Department of Wildlife
Humboldt State University
Arcata, California

PATRICIA L. KENNEDY
Department of Fishery and Wildlife Biology
Colorado State University
Fort Collins, Colorado

BRUCE C. LUBOW
Department of Fishery and Wildlife Biology
Colorado State University
Fort Collins, Colorado

L. SCOTT MILLS
School of Forestry
University of Montana
Missoula, Montana

MICHAEL L. MORRISON
Department of Biological Sciences
California State University
Sacramento, California

KENNETH H. POLLOCK
Department of Statistics
North Carolina State University
Raleigh, North Carolina

ERIC A. REXSTAD
Institute of Arctic Biology
University of Alaska–Fairbanks
Fairbanks, Alaska

JAMES A. RICE
Department of Zoology
North Carolina State University
Raleigh, North Carolina

THOMAS R. RYON
PTI Environmental Services
Boulder, Colorado

DAVID G. SALTZ
Mitrani Department of Desert Ecology
Blaustein Institute for Desert Research
Ben-Gurion University
Sede Boqer, Israel

Index